DOMESTIC WORKERS OF THE WORLD UNITE!

D0913656

Domestic Workers of the World Unite!

A Global Movement for Dignity and Human Rights

Jennifer N. Fish

NEW YORK UNIVERSITY PRESS

New York

NEW YORK UNIVERSITY PRESS
New York
www.nyupress.org

© 2017 by New York University
All rights reserved

References to Internet websites (URLs) were accurate at the time of writing. Neither the author nor New York University Press is responsible for URLs that may have expired or changed since the manuscript was prepared.

ISBN: 978-1-4798-4867-6 (hardback)
ISBN: 978-1-4798-7793-5 (paperback)

For Library of Congress Cataloging-in-Publication data, please contact the Library of Congress.

New York University Press books are printed on acid-free paper, and their binding materials are chosen for strength and durability. We strive to use environmentally responsible suppliers and materials to the greatest extent possible in publishing our books.

Manufactured in the United States of America

10 9 8 7 6 5 4 3 2 1

Also available as an ebook

To the pioneer domestic workers who founded

this global movement,

and to the spirits of those who lit their way.

CONTENTS

ACKNOWLEDGMENTS

This book emerges from generous forms of good fortune, kindness, and trust in this project. Most of all, I thank the members of the International Domestic Workers Federation who shared with me their life journeys and their time, even amid the rigorous demands of their activism. These stories are the anchor of this book and the guiding force in its potential reach.

From my earliest inquiry on domestic work in South Africa, I thank Myrtle Witbooi and Hester Stephens for inviting me to share a ride with the union. During this time, pivotal mentors shaped my understanding of domestic labor as a global institution. I absorbed the profound serendipity to cross paths with Bette J. Dickerson, Gay Young, Mary Romero, Nancy Naples, and Bonnie Thornton Dill; these intersections will always be a cornerstone of my academic and personal life.

Many kindred scholars and activists have invested in the growth of this book through generous reviews and input. I am deeply thankful to Premilla Nadasen, Rae Blumberg, Mary Romero, Michele Berger, Eileen Boris, Mary Margaret Fonow, Sonya Michel, Darcy du Toit, Fairuz Mullagee, Nelson Lichtenstein, Mary Goldsmith, Jill Jensen, Lauren Eastwood, Ito Peng, Fiona Williams, Rianne Mahon, Rachel Silvey, Dirk Hoerder, Silke Neunsinger, Victoria Haskins, Lorena Poblete, Dorothy Sue Cobble, and Dorothea Hoehtker.

Within the global policy-activism arena, my deep appreciation extends to the allies who guided this project from complementary positions "on the street" and "in the library," as Jane Addams promoted. To Ai-jen Poo, Barbro Budin, Karin Pape, Celia Mather, Marty Chen, Dan Gallin, Chris Bonner, Claire Hobden, Martin Oelz, Nisha Varia, and Jill Shenker—this book took form through your every wise input.

This project comes to fruition as a result of generous institutional support. I thank WIEGO at Harvard University, the Centre for Global

Social Policy at the University of Toronto, and the College of Arts and Letters at Old Dominion University. In particular, I am grateful to Charles E. Wilson for supporting a sabbatical that allowed me to devote considerable time and energy to this work. The Department of Women's Studies at ODU has provided a most generous and enriching space for feminist research. I am deeply thankful to Yvette Pearson, Lee Ellen Knight, Vaughan Frederick, Cathleen Rhodes, Ruth Triplett, and Liz Groeneveld for their belief in this work, their munificence as colleagues and friends, and their shared interest in scholar-activism. My profound gratitude extends to Mona Danner for her abundant mentoring and sisterhood. Throughout this project, Anita Clair Fellman grounded my commitment to feminist inquiry and my aspirations as a teacher, scholar, and activist.

Several generous colleagues contributed to particular aspects of this book's realization. Sofia Trevino and Raquel Perez-Lopez provided eloquent translation of the Spanish content. Corie Hardy, Madeleine Slater, Laura Castro, and Rebekah Joyce brought copious energy to research considerations. Erika Frydenlund, Skylar Wynn, and Savannah Russo inspire my purpose in teaching, research, and activism. Stacey Parks and Terri Hughes supported the writing process through their exemplary commitment to education and intellectual dialogue. To Moriah Shumpert—thank you for devoting such compassion and care to each breath of this scholar-activist journey.

I am grateful to NYU Press for its collective efforts to ensure a space for engaged scholarship and activist research. To Ilene Kalish, thank you for supporting this book early on and guiding its entrée into the public sociology conversation. I am deeply grateful for the opportunity to work with you. Caelyn Cobb and Melissa Dobson helped ensure that the life stories and historical narrative herein were clearly and accurately conveyed.

Lastly, this book came to fruition with the aid of support networks modeling an obligation to document the sources of our deepest affinity. Thank you Eric C. Tammes, Eric Miller, Lee Slater, Vicki Nesper, Karin Dekker, Margaret Woermann, Kathy Williamson, Pumla Gobodo-Madikizela, and Sara Agah for inspiring in your being. To Jane and Bob DuComb, your vision for this book has buoyed me through its completion. Without the origins of love and support from James Leon Fish and Louise Decker, I could not realize this life project.

To Jennifer Rothchild, Didi and Sister, you are always my level best and kindred heart.

For Tim Seibles, your love of the Muse shapes each turn of the sun and calibrates my perennial return to hope.

LIST OF ABBREVIATIONS

ACTRAV: Bureau des Activités pour les Travailleurs (Bureau for Workers Activities), ILO

AFL-CIO: American Federation of Labor and Congress of Industrial Organizations

BRAC: Bangladesh Rural Advancement Committee

CONLACTRAHO: Confederación Latinoamericana y del Caribe Trabajadoras del Hogar (Latin American and Caribbean Confederation of Domestic Workers)

GEFONT: General Federation of Nepalese Trade Unions

IDWF: International Domestic Workers Federation

IDWN: International Domestic Workers Network

ILC: International Labour Conference

ILO: International Labour Organization

IRENE: International Restructuring Education Network Europe

ITUC: International Trade Union Confederation

IUF: International Union of Food, Agricultural, Hotel, Restaurant, Catering, Tobacco and Allied Workers' Association

MFA: Migrant Forum in Asia

NDWA: National Domestic Workers Alliance

NUDE: National Union of Domestic Employees

SEWA: Self-Employed Women's Association

TUCP: Trade Union Congress of the Philippines

UN: United Nations

WIEGO: Women in Informal Employment: Globalizing and Organizing

1

"Look Deep in Your Hearts"

Making a Global Domestic Workers' Movement

In the backroom of my employer, I started questioning myself: Why do we have to suffer like this?
—Myrtle Witbooi, president, International Domestic Workers Federation[1]

We must ask, are our dreams simply individual?
—Ebrahim Rasool, former South African ambassador to the United States[2]

Hester Stephens has spent 53 years of her life as a domestic worker—cleaning, cooking, and caring for white families in South Africa's elite communities.[3] Over the past 25 years with one employer, she has raised the family's only child, kept a six-bedroom Victorian household spotless and secure, cooked meals to order, and managed the bedside care of her male employer throughout his struggle with terminal cancer. After seeing to the needs of this family each day, she returns to her outside room "on the premises" of her employer's household, a 15-hour bus ride from her own family in the rural Eastern Cape. She earns approximately eight dollars per day. Her vacation time depends on the holiday schedule of her employer. If she needs health care, she must ask her employer for support. Any personal relationships must be conducted off-duty and outside her residence; visitors are overseen by her "madam." Should Hester seek other work, she may face an HIV/AIDS exam, if potential employers fear that she could transmit the virus that has infected nearly one-fifth of South Africa's population. At 67, Hester would like to retire, after being in domestic service since the age of 15, when she left school to find work that would buy bread for her family. Even after investing five decades of her life in this work, she is not eligible for retirement benefits or social security—leaving her future livelihood to the benevolence of her employer.

Hester moved to Cape Town in 1966, at the height of South Africa's apartheid governance. As she worked behind the walls of white residences, she soon recognized that her own situation mirrored that of black women throughout the divided country.[4] At the time, government policies named domestic work as one of the few sanctioned professions for black women, creating race-, class-, and gender-based migrant-labor pools to serve the white minority population. Under these circumstances, Hester left her own son to care for the newborn child of a family she did not know, perhaps the most tragic part of her life story: she recalled that, returning to her rural home after a year's work, her son did not recognize her, calling her "auntie." In the city, exchanging her teenage years for the promise of an income for her parents and son, Hester met other domestic workers who lived under these same defining conditions of servitude and systemic injustice. As she took her employer's son for neighborhood walks, shopped for the family's groceries, and passed her weekly Thursday-afternoon "Maid's Day" off in public parks, she witnessed the scale of exploitation domestic workers faced, and the magnitude of the losses they endured.

Rather than accepting these circumstances, however, Hester strove to change them. In 1985 she began to organize the workers on her street, and eventually those employed throughout Cape Town's elite neighborhoods—an act for which she could have been imprisoned under the apartheid regime. These clandestine gatherings were the origin of South Africa's national union of domestic workers. Under apartheid, this organization linked women's labor to a larger struggle for liberation, as part of the labor and women's resistance movements. After 31 years of organizing, Hester currently holds the presidency of the national union. In the aftermath of apartheid, she stood on the front lines to push for the first national policies that assured domestic workers regular working hours, a minimum wage, vacation time, maternity leave, unemployment insurance, access to dispute-resolution systems, and the right to organize. Her union's fight for basic labor and social protections carved out a space for domestic workers in the national dialogue, as South Africa built a new democracy based on human rights.

The Global Domestic-Work Picture

Hester's struggle is shared by millions of domestic workers worldwide. Her life investment in the care of a family not her own reflects the global economy's escalating dependence on migration and service labor. Like Hester, millions of household workers rely upon this work for their daily existence.[5] In 2013 the International Labour Organization (ILO) estimated that between 52 million and 100 million workers provide domestic service in homes throughout the world, a range that indicates the difficulty of an accurate accounting of this informal, often migrant sector.[6] Behind closed doors, domestic workers care for children and elders, cook, clean, do laundry, garden, and even chauffeur—daily tasks that free their employers from the constraints of reproductive labor, those activities that sustain the daily running of the household. While men serve as "house boys" and cooks in some parts of the world, women and girls comprise 83 percent of this quintessentially feminized work.[7] They leave their own homes for jobs with other families, in many cases before completing secondary school. This labor path not only puts domestic workers at great risk for exploitation, it also sets most on a highly constricted life course, given the extreme isolation and limited opportunities of the profession.

Of the global household-labor supply, 17 percent of workers migrate across national borders to seek employment outside their home countries.[8] They leave their own families behind, creating demands on other family members, grandmothers and aunts, for example, to step in in their absence. In many cases, national economies rely upon the salary remittance exchanges from domestic workers' relocation. The trade of domestic workers builds formalized bilateral relations that undergird larger geopolitical power systems—as evident, for example, in state-supported work-visa systems, training programs, and employment-agency networks. The Philippines, for example, encourages women to leave their own families to promote the noble values of Filipina motherhood worldwide. The salary remittances of these *bagong bayanis*, modern-day heroes, as they are known, accounts for $24 billion annually, the largest source of export revenue for the Philippines.[9]

In contrast to these coordinated state systems of care-labor exchange, for many transnational migrants, the private home provides a means of employment when citizenship rights are inaccessible. Without legal documentation, many domestic workers are under constant threat of deportation. As one migrant domestic worker in the United Kingdom expressed, "I hold my life in my hands like an egg."[10] Transnational care workers must negotiate their daily lives as anonymous noncitizens, outside the purview of state officials. In these instances, while domestic workers pick up the pervasive and growing global care demands, their own well-being is seriously compromised.

In this transnational industry of care work, intimacy becomes a commodity. Motherhood is globalized; love is borrowed across borders; and states are freed from the social contract to care for the basic needs of their populations. Here is what transnational care work looks like, in snapshots of real-life incidents across the world:

- In Holland, a prominent domestic worker leader seriously injured in a car accident tried to flee the scene, fearing that a visit to the emergency room would result in deportation.[11]
- In Kuwait, the relative of a Nepalese member of Parliament spent four years working in a high-rise apartment complex, never once being able to leave the apartment.[12]
- In Singapore, hundreds of women from Sri Lanka, Indonesia, and the Philippines have jumped to their death rather than endure the abuse and isolation they suffer as domestic workers in high-rise apartment buildings.[13]
- In the United States, domestic workers from Mexico and Central America mother their own children via FaceTime and daily text messaging, while their hands tend to the needs of privileged children in their immediate contexts.[14]
- In Senegal, young women from rural villages leave school to become "house girls" in their extended families in Dakar, living at the crossroads of family responsibility and indentured labor, beyond the scope of legal protections.
- In Lebanon, the *kefala* system of immigration law governs not only labor, but love, allowing employers to investigate domestic workers' private lives in order to report local romances—a violation that can result in deportation.[15]

Paid domestic labor thus accounts for some of the world's most egregious labor injustices. As a sector associated with human trafficking, domestic labor for women, in the worst conditions, can be said to comprise modern slavery.[16] For example, in many parts of the world, employment "agencies" promise rural families hotel salaries in exchange for their daughters' labor, which is ultimately put up for sale in underground venues where prospective employers can (literally) choose their household helper.[17] Domestic workers' pay is among the lowest in the world, while their protections depend on their employers' practice of fair labor, compliance with national standards, and, ultimately, compassion.

The cumulative impact of these circumstances of exploitation presents one of the largest human costs of globalization. Legal scholar Darcy du Toit contends that the transnational conditions of domestic work "represent a human rights failure of significant proportions whereby tens of millions of people are prevented from achieving their full potential as persons, workers and citizens."[18] The structures of inequality that comprise this international industry build fear, insecurity, and psychological hardship into the daily lives of workers in this precarious sector. These everyday traumas, set in the context of a synchronized global system of economic trade, pose serious questions about the state of human development. Where are we as a global community when the most foundational tenets of human existence—health care, education, family security, safety, and well-being—are violated pervasively at an individual level in the interests of an international industry built upon the value of *care*? This question extends from the most intimate household exchanges to the widest reach of international relations.

On the macroscale, domestic work is the persistent contrarian of human rights. Yet not every household-labor environment is exploitative. Indeed, under the best circumstances, domestic workers describe their profession as dignified, fair, and rewarding. Across the world, "good employers" provide clear working conditions, worthy compensation, and flexibility in home-work contexts and relationships. In the ideal scenarios, domestic workers find autonomy, flexibility, and a harmonious environment as an equitable exchange for their care contribution. As one South African union organizer put it, "I'd rather work in my employer's home than a factory."[19] Some employers have even become among the strongest advocates for domestic worker rights, as part of a larger commitment to ethical care standards around the world.[20]

Ultimately, employment conditions vary widely across the globe, with national systems, institutions, economies, and cultural practices playing a vital role in the extent to which domestic workers can realize "justice in the home."[21] Those countries with structural race hierarchies and deep-seated class/caste systems are less likely to establish legal protections and more prone to violations of domestic workers' basic rights. In Saudi Arabia, Kuwait, Qatar, Malaysia, Madagascar, and Lebanon, for example, domestic workers are not allowed to organize. In India, the caste system renders legal rights incongruent with persons seen as destined to deal with the dirt. Similarly, in many societies, systems of stratification play out through daily practices of servitude. As Peruvian domestic worker activist Ernestina Ochoa contended, "We are in the twenty-first century and even then, we domestic workers still live in a state of semislavery and of racial degradation. Our silverware is separated; our washrooms are separated. We can't sit with our employers to eat, we can't! Why?"[22] In many parts of the world, domestic workers receive substantive portions of their salaries in used clothing and food. These conditions mark domestic work as a neocolonial industry, where care, intimacy, and service labor are integrally connected to historical conditions of inequality.[23] As pioneer domestic work scholar Mary Romero contends, "Colonialism marks every aspect of the global care chain."[24] Yet these daily injustices have been normalized in many societies. Austria receives domestic workers from eastern Europe, who travel across national borders each month on transit systems designed to ensure the supply of care providers for an aging population. In the most exclusive US neighborhoods, as Tamara Mose Brown portrays in *Raising Brooklyn*,[25] undocumented nannies push the babies of privileged families through parks, while the wider public sanctions this reliance upon the global import of care labor. Across a wide range of national contexts, women with the fewest resources are working to fill a global care deficit, most often at the cost of their own well-being, livelihoods, and families.

Domestic Worker Activist Alignments

These conditions link Hester Stephens's struggle in South Africa to a global crisis of care labor that takes its greatest toll on domestic workers. Responding to this crisis, domestic worker activists have over the past ten years reached across their national landscapes to advocate for the global recognition, rights, and protections of their sisters worldwide. In 2006 Hester traveled to Amsterdam for an international meeting of domestic worker activists. Along with representatives from 41 other domestic labor organizations in Asia, Latin America, Europe, the Middle East, Africa, and North America, and 15 international organizations, she founded the International Domestic Workers Network (IDWN), the first transnational organization of domestic workers.[26] Its mission: to put domestic work "on the map" of the world's human rights struggles and establish the first set of international standards for paid work in private households. Its first stop: the United Nations' International Labour Organization, the world's largest global governance body dealing with labor issues. Here, for the first time, domestic workers took part in discussions that would determine how this heavily exploited transnational sector of the informal economy could finally gain international rights.[27] Domestic workers sought dignity, while the ILO spoke of its commitment to "decent work." Over the course of two years, a global network of domestic workers and their allies brought their aligned activism to the ILO in ways that altered this historic institution and allowed those formerly relegated to "the kitchen" and "the backyard" of private households to claim a public voice.

In this global forum, the IDWN set out to expose the daily and systemic injustices of this contemporary form of servitude by aligning stories like Hester's with those of domestic workers throughout the world. The network's *Platform of Demands* set forth a common identity:

> We are called "maids" or "servants," barely worthy of attention or to be ordered around or even abused. Added to this, many of us are from communities and regions that have been disadvantaged over history. Many are migrants, living isolated from our host community, and far away from our own families and even our own children.[28]

In an international arena gathering together 187 member governments, employers, and workers, the newly formed network mobilized around the demand for universal rights. Over the course of two International Labour Conferences, in 2010 and 2011,[29] domestic workers told their stories to representatives of governments, national unions, and employer organizations from around the world.

To an extent unprecedented in the history of the ILO, workers themselves participated in formulating global labor policy.[30] As a transnational activist network, the IDWN spoke for the millions of domestic
workers at the center of this policy consideration. Gender-labor policy
expert Sofia Trevino acknowledged the challenges of building a transnational movement, contending, "It took *years* of organizing to get to
this moment."[31] For domestic workers who had suffered a lifetime of
injustice and labor exploitation, their ability to take part in this global
dialogue symbolized a "dream come true." For Hester, the conference
symbolized the culmination of a long struggle, allowing domestic
worker activists to "[pick] the fruit from the tree that we planted over
the years."[32] The founding women of this movement offer an original
account of individual agency and the power of collective activism.

This book tells the story of domestic workers' transnational organizing, from small meetings in employers' garages to policy sessions in Geneva, Switzerland. As the pioneering international development scholar
Rae Blumberg described it, this is the global women's activist version
of "the little engine that could."[33] By drawing from the life narratives of
domestic workers throughout the world, I explore how workers at the
grassroots level used a formal UN system to codify an identity and secure
their labor rights. The preamble to Convention 189, the ILO convention
governing domestic work, acknowledges that this work is "undervalued
and invisible," underscoring the significance of this global policy victory.[34]
Throughout this book, the ILO serves as a microcosm of the larger global
arena, where employers defend capitalism, workers demand rights, and
state governments vacillate between profit and people. From a feminist
standpoint, domestic work makes visible the interconnected societal, state,
and international structures behind the proliferation of the global "maid
trade."[35] While the policy process centered this movement around the attainment of global rights "on paper," this book is also concerned with how
this policy victory translates to women's day-to-day lives. Luc Demaret—
one of the principal ILO leaders responsible for placing domestic worker
rights on the agenda—asserted that this policy victory would directly benefit domestic workers worldwide. "They will move from a world of exploitation to one of dignity. This isn't theory, it is a tool for real change."[36]
Likewise, I explore how the ILO process has affected domestic workers

themselves, in their continued search for respect, recognition, and justice in their daily work lives.

Pictures of Power: Documenting a Global Moment

As national borders become more permeable to the global labor market and its demands for migrant workers, women supply intimate care work, often at the expense of human rights and standard labor protections. As this system of globalization expands, however, its dependence on technology opens new avenues of interconnectedness serving global activist movements. No longer are domestic workers completely isolated in their employers' "backyards"; they are WhatsApp-ing solidarity messages to their sisters throughout the world, texting union announcements, and organizing across wide geographic divides. In this larger constellation of forces, women workers' organizations have engaged with international governance to demand global recognition and tangible protections. This model of transnational activism—in the face of the predominant social, political, and economic forces of globalization—stands as one of the most promising human rights victories of the 21st century.

The global domestic workers movement emerged through a cast of key characters—most revolutionaries in their own rights—with a shared set of values for solidarity, justice, and a collective responsibility to assure the protection of *all* workers under the shifting terms of the international economy. In one of the lead roles, global union leader Dan Gallin cared deeply about bringing domestic workers into the international labor movement 20 years prior to the ILO conversations. As the former general secretary of the Geneva-based International Union of Food, Agricultural, Hotel, Restaurant, Catering, Tobacco and Allied Workers' Association (IUF), he led the first effort to include domestic workers in a global union. When no other national or global trade unions were willing to consider the "unorganizable," Gallin lobbied for global unions' ethical responsibility to build solidarity with this massive and highly feminized sector of the informal economy. He helped to found the IDWN, and sat alongside domestic workers as they took their fight to the ILO. In reflecting on the meaning of the ILO's recognition of domestic work, Gallin described these policy discussions as a form of photography depicting pivotal moments in workers' larger struggle for recognition:

> It'll be an instant picture of what the relations of power are. You know, if the law says female and male wages should be the same for the same kind of work, that is photography of an instance in history where women workers—through the labor movement, through whatever means—have gotten to the point where they can exercise sufficient influence. And this, it becomes the law of the land. And before they had such power and influence, you're not going to get this law. Now, a convention is a little bit the same way. It reflects the power relationship and in that sense the triumph of the domestic workers isn't out of place, it's not misplaced. They did have something to crow about. And it's that they've reached this power relationship and they realize that.[37]

In Gallin's terms, the narrative presented in this book is a "photograph" of a moment when the "poorest of the poor"[38] met with heads of state as the culmination of a much longer struggle for justice, rights, and recognition, "just like any other worker."[39]

Movements matter.[40] Domestic workers' transnational activism is the most vibrant, enlivened expression of the global women's movement at this particular historic moment. With "one foot in the labor movement and one foot in the women's movement,"[41] its vision reenergizes historic class struggles, confronting the very contemporary expressions of injustice found in unregulated domestic work. As Ai-jen Poo, leader of the National Domestic Workers Alliance (NDWA) and acclaimed US activist, contended, "So much of the unfinished business of this women's movement is really about bringing respect and dignity to this work."[42] In support of this vision, the ILO served as a meeting ground, bringing national movements together around a common plight for global human rights. By putting their demands on the table in an organized form, activists cracked open the world's largest labor institution and brought their voices to the development of policy protections intended for their own profession. As IDWN president Myrtle Witbooi attested, "This is something that the ILO has *never* seen before."[43] In actively engaging each other, domestic worker activists and the ILO institution evolved, while the negotiation process became a symbol for larger social struggles worldwide.

"Nothing signals 'Third World' in the international arena," asserts scholar Cinzia Solari, "like the mass emigration of women to do domestic labor abroad."[44] As neoliberal market forces dominate the global landscape, a "regime of labor intimacy" spans the Global North/South divide through women's bodies at work.[45] In this context, globalization hinges on the labor of women of color. Yet in terms of rights and protections, domestic workers are globalization's exiles. To what extent are the world's least resourced paying for the shiny technology of so-called development? As IDWN's President Witbooi asked of the privileged global policymakers, "Where would *you* be if a domestic worker didn't iron your shirt?"[46] Within these everyday relations of power between "maids and madams"[47] rests an entire global system of power, where states build agreements around the outsourcing of care labor, domestic service salary remittances mediate an enormous economic disparity, and the export of women's household work restructures families throughout the world. As these forces expand, domestic workers' orchestrated movement becomes a "vanguard to reconsider vast portions of the global labor force."[48] The dialectic of transnational power and collective action extends beyond domestic work to the rights of anyone involved in precarious labor, as the shifting global landscape allows for activism's wider reach.

The ILO's focus on domestic work provides the first opportunity to examine how global governance institutions may be shaped by the activism of local and transnational organizations. The domestic worker movement's process of entering the ILO space, and then unfolding globally, provides for analyses across scales—from the household, to civil society organizations, to the state, and finally to the international structures of governance. As leading sociologists Nancy Naples and Manisha Desai contend, "Globalization must be understood as a process generated from the everyday activities and negotiations of diverse individuals, communities, government bodies, and transnational coalitions."[49] This particular moment when domestic workers joined ILO policymaking allows us to situate a transnational movement within the lived experiences of women who draw from the human rights consequences of global capitalism to negotiate innovative processes that change institutions, public dialogues, and social policies, from community to state to regional and global levels. The interwoven activisms available in this global movement will, it is hoped, alter the circumstances of injustice that compromise the livelihoods of care workers throughout the world.

This book places domestic workers in conversation with the symbolic seat of international power, looking at how the "most vulnerable" workers used high-level international-governance structures to reach a groundbreaking policy victory. As Shirley Pryce, president of the Jamaica Household Workers' Union, conveyed in a poem she wrote for the 2011 International Labour Conference, "I am a Domestic Worker, watch me grow, I can stand with you toe to toe."[50] This book is not just about domestic workers and women, but what this movement can teach us about how societies treat their child workers, migrant workers, and those "invisible" portions of the population. By looking at the global economy from the perspective of those "oiling the wheels,"[51] the domestic workers' movement calls for transnational labor standards in principle and practice, as a moral imperative. In the current context, where the movement of people across borders for better livelihoods takes form amid a massive refugee crisis, it is my hope that this book offers insights about how rights can transcend national boarders, how global citizenship can be reconsidered, and how collective organization can provide a cathartic venue for the world's suffering. As global structures reconfigure to meet evolving human needs, the story of domestic workers' activism archives the seemingly impossible. As historian activist Rebecca Solnit captured in *Hope in the Dark*, "Despair in one institution or one site can lead to the location of alternatives, to the quest for doors, or to their creation . . . In this way, despair and hope are linked."[52] In the story of domestic workers' global struggle, hope wins. In the end, it bears witness to Martin Luther King's assurance that "the arc of the moral universe is long, but it bends towards justice."[53]

The Research Journey

This book draws from six years of research on the global domestic workers' movement, from Cape Town to New York to Geneva to Amsterdam to Montevideo to Kathmandu. I began to document this global movement by following Myrtle Witbooi, general secretary of South Africa's national domestic workers union, along with her sister-comrade Hester Stephens, to the ILO in 2010. We planned to take a practice we had refined during ten years of prior work together in South Africa to this international arena. Activist, organizer, unionist, visionary leader, Witbooi speaks, no script, no notes. Advocate, writer, teacher, photographer, I scribble and snap photos. Her voice commands; I document the details. Together we conjure context. We cowrite policy talk this way, in hopes of gaining rights for domestic workers. Chained to the gates of Parliament, in front of the TV cameras, under the spotlight of human rights honorees, on the streets, behind the gates of private homes, and, finally, at the headquarters of the United Nations, I have accompanied Myrtle Witbooi, and the International Domestic Workers Federation (IDWF), across five continents to document how this movement took form, as those "in the backyard" of private households mobilized to see the possibility for a reconfiguration of one of the world's most deeply embedded systems of labor exploitation. As we drive together, she narrates complex theories of social struggle and change. Her tales capture the depth of human relations and the heart of this intimate work. What made Hester Stephens and Myrtle Witbooi gather under apartheid's deep shadow? And how did so many domestic worker organizers like them achieve a global movement beyond their own national circumstances? These overarching questions centered my conversations and observations of the domestic worker leaders profiled in this book.

To document the activism of the visionary women in this global movement, I draw from extensive personal interviews collected over the course of five years. In many cases, these conversations occurred across contexts—from the women's home countries to the ILO policy meetings in Geneva. Media coverage of domestic workers' participation in this historic policymaking process formed the backdrop. The conversations that inform this book focused on domestic workers as activists, delving into the distinct experiences that formed each respondent's emergence as a national leader and founder of the global movement. I held conversations with original members of the IDWN over the course of three pivotal moments—in the two years of negotiations at the ILO (2010 and 2011) and a follow-up gathering in Montevideo (2013). At times we extended interviews over several occasions, met into the late hours and between formal sessions, as participants engaged in a very demanding policymaking process. Thus the narratives in this book are deeply intertwined with the specific dynamics of movement building at particular times.

As Chris Bonner, policy expert, organizer, and longtime advocate for domestic workers' rights, proclaimed, "The thing about domestic work is that it touches people, it touches so many lives, you know. If you are doing a convention on an industry, it tends to be industry-specific, you know for *those* workers, those. This cuts across all."[54] Likewise, my approach to gathering the content for this book cut across all venues to explore domestic work from multiple vantage points. I spoke with domestic worker activists, employers, government officials, ILO experts, policy advisers, and human rights leaders from around the world throughout each day of the official meetings in Geneva. My former work with the domestic worker union in South Africa gained me access to the official ILO meetings—a "pass" to look closely at privilege and power systems. In a windowless meeting room on the ground floor of the UN buildings, as 187 governments, and their partner employer/worker delegates hammered out 170 amendments to the 23 articles of this proposed international policy, some of the most revealing commentaries on domestic work emerged, on the public floor and in the semiprivate conversations surrounding this grand gathering. These interactions provided the basis for an extensive collection of fieldnotes from the official and unofficial record of the proceedings.

As an embedded ethnographer in this largest gathering of domestic workers from around the world, I also documented and reported on the IDWN's daily work, in words, photos, and film, working in both English and French. To gather content from the Spanish-speaking leaders, I worked with an interpreter both during and following the ILO meetings to review narrative material. Throughout the ILO meetings, I attended every session of the policymaking process, interviewed leaders across the board, traveled from the Ferney-Voltaire border-city hotel accommodations in France to the United Nations Office in Geneva with domestic workers each day, took part in public demonstrations and discussions throughout the Swiss city, and observed almost all of the IDWN's related gatherings, walking the line of reporter, supporter, and *técnica* organizational advocate.[55] My visual documentation did not go without notice among domestic worker leaders. At the end of the 2011 meetings, one IDWN representative asked me, "You are making a film about us, right?" As an advocate for the movement, I took the footage I had gathered for this book and developed *C189: Conventional*

Figure 1.1. Hester Stephens and Myrtle Witbooi

Wisdom[56]—a documentary that both archived the convention process and served as a promotional film for the newly formed IDWN.

The global-activist movement around Convention 189 comprises a substantive portion of this book's analysis. My larger inquiry on domestic labor, however, extends from my first 2001 study in South Africa's new democracy to the most recent assessments of this movement's impact. In 2013 the IDWN set a world benchmark when it became the International Domestic Workers Federation—the only women-led union in the world. As a culmination of this story, I attended the IDWF's first congress in Montevideo and documented the transition from organizational network to global union—a moment that drew Uruguay's president José Mujica to join in celebration of this gathering "of domestic workers, who have been eternally neglected, eternally postponed by human kind."[57]

As a scholar-activist, my intention is to contribute in solidarity with the larger movement for domestic workers' recognition and rights. As kindred domestic work researchers Premilla Nadasen, Mary Goldsmith, and Harmony Goldberg attest,[58] our work is not our own. Rather, it reflects the voices and analyses of people engaged in building a global movement. Our main contribution is to compile and document these sources, situate this evidence in relevant frameworks, and ultimately to integrate this knowledge within wider conversations in an effort to alter the structural conditions shaping domestic workers' lives. My commitment emerges from work with formative mentors, namely sociologists Bette Dickerson and Mary Romero, who helped me instill continued reflexivity in any analysis of social research's potential contribution to communities and the relative worth of documentarian.[59] While my close alignment with domestic worker organizations scaffolds this project, I work as an "outsider within" this larger movement—in my roles as technical consultant, professor, researcher, sister, and comrade. Within these simultaneous, and at times conflicting, roles, I step back from organizational immersion to examine the larger systems and develop greater consciousness around my own standpoint. This book comprises my most expansive effort to walk this line, with passionate detachment and a committed bias of hope in resilience and a greater collective leaning toward human dignity.

2

"Dignity Overdue"

Tracing a Movement

All week she's cleaned
someone else's house,
stared down her own face
in the shine of copper-
bottomed pots, polished
wood, toilets she'd pull
the lid to—that look saying

Let's make a change, girl.
—Natasha Trethewey, "Domestic Work, 1937"[1]

Aida Moreno worked in Chile's domestic service industry for 60 years. At the age of 14, her mother and aunt encouraged her to leave the village for work in Santiago. Aida recalled the impact of that move on her perception of the world. "For me, it was very impressive to arrive at the capital, by microbus, arrive to the house where there was a beautiful chalet. In comparison to where I lived in a rural community, I had my own room, by myself, and I was very impressed." In her employers' assessment she was "very thin" and too young to perform many of the tasks in such a demanding household, so Aida started her domestic labor role by taking care of the animals and serving at table. She grew from teen to adult in this household, where the other "servant staff" became her surrogate parents. In the beginning, Aida struggled most with the "different food" that pronounced her far from home. In this formative job, over the course of eight years, she learned not only the skills of domestic service but how to conform to the expectations of the role, including working inconspicuously, like a silent fairy whisking away the day's debris.

Aida proved to be a quick study. While learning to seamlessly perform her household tasks, she was able to reflect on her life and place it within a larger social system. She thirsted for more education and a connection to other women in similar circumstances. In 1958, just as she completed her basic education, Aida received a flyer about a workers' group in her area. In aligning herself with this group, Aida connected to a larger domestic workers' movement throughout her country. As in Natasha Trethewey's poem "Domestic Work, 1937," she came to realize that she wanted to "make a change." She asserted: "My compromise was to serve, all my life. So this is a work of God." While she had spent much of her youth working in wealthy Chilean homes, organizing domestic workers became an expression of sacred service for Aida, and a way to cope with the circumstances of her daily life. Her hope rested in making the lives of her comrade domestic workers brighter.

As Aida joined the informal women workers' movement in Chile, she chronicled her activism and her reflections in words. "I write. That is one of the things I like to do." As a writer and a poet, she also documented the workers' movement in Chile. For her beloved Confederación Latinomericana y del Caribe Trabajadoras del Hogar (CONLACTRAHO), the Central and South American and Caribbean regional confederation of domestic workers, she wrote:

> We always work together united
> We carry with us the history of our people
> Who have been through the oppression
> Of those that drew up the borders and our division[2]

Aida's poems consistently move beyond the circumstances of her life to speak to a wider women workers' movement, as well as her hopes to improve the human condition.[3] As she recounted, "All of my poems are in relation to the trade union, and my commitment to the Lord." She wrote about the shared story of "domestic workers in every country" as "daughters of peasant farmers, native Indians and mixed race people from this beautiful America," who organized without knowledge of "anything beyond their borders." The more contact she had with other domestic workers, the greater her motivation for collective activism. In the 1980s, Aida recalled, "they knew nothing of other employees who were also organized." Yet through her dedicated leadership, a national domestic workers' movement took hold in Chile, and eventually became the CONLACTRAHO regional hub. When her union turned 30, Aida reflected on its origins.

> Thirty years of life
> Small, half unknown
> As the wild flowers
> That grow in this land

While she celebrated the "big-hearted and united" stance of the organization, she recounted its original commitments to "struggle, serve and defend, the little or anything that you can manage."

In Aida's extensive autobiography and poetry collection, labor-activist organizing is at the center of her identity; it is the source of her strength. "For me," she contended, "the union is like my first child." Her commitment to activism eventually carried Aida beyond the borders of her own country. Pioneer scholar-advocate Elsa Chaney began working with Aida's organization to connect her local organizing with the growth of the global women's movement.[4] As she collected some of the earliest analyses on domestic work, Chaney continually practiced working in solidarity with domestic worker organizations. She wove her presence into the operations and daily struggles of activists on the ground and drew from the relationships she formed there to guide her writing on domestic work. As Aida Moreno contended, Elsa truly lived their organization's *Muchachas No More!* political conviction to bring dignity and respect to domestic workers. Her dual intention to document domestic workers' lives in rich detail and bring their stories to academic and policy circles captured her larger hopes of improving their everyday circumstances.

In 1995 Aida traveled to Beijing with Elsa to participate in a wider dialogue on women's rights. In her poem "En Route to Beijing," she writes:

> We started working for a better world
> United we will make it
> Alliances will strengthen our mission and
> Reason will strengthen our battles
> We will draw together our path to move together
> Oh glaring dawn in the sunrise

This relationship with Elsa became both personally and politically transformative for Aida. She recounted their last conversation, as Elsa reached out to Aida on the final day of her life. In her reflections on their relationship, Aida reminisced, "She has been my angel." In a poem dedicated to her friend, Aida captured the values Elsa modeled for her and others.

> Thank you friend Elsa, for all that you've
> Sown in all of us,
> Honesty, love and service,
> To work for the marginalized of the world.
> We will always work for a better world,
> And try to live it in all we do.

Elsa's legacy inspired in Aida a larger commitment to global activism for domestic workers' rights. Excited by the chance to step outside the geography of her own circumstances, she aligned with a transnational movement. As she entered the global arena, her political consciousness remained closely tied to these key relationships, of sisterhood, comradeship, and mutual engagement, that issued from her work as a Chilean activist.

Like Aida, so many of the domestic worker activist pioneers within the global movement spoke of allies who stayed with them even when they doubted their own capacity to lead. Many recounted the contributions of these "global sisters," who fueled grassroots organizations by investing time and resources and providing networking opportunities. Their shared commitments fostered a solidarity that gave the work meaning, as they envisioned domestic workers' eventual liberation and the radical social change that would accompany it. Across a range of relationships, these ally connections kept domestic worker activists in touch with larger movements for justice, rights, and recognition at the global level.

As Aida worked to build CONLACTRAHO, she turned her attention to the overlooked needs of aging domestic workers, contending that

> in general, in organizations, there is an issue of child domestic workers, but what happens to the old woman, the old domestic worker? She is abandoned. What happens? That woman, she can't work, but she still has

Figure 2.1. Aida Moreno

life. And that life that remains is very abandoned, very solitary and I am concerned about this.

After seeing so many of her *compañeras* struggle without means to attain decent housing and financial support when they were no longer able to meet the labor expectations of their employers, Aida decided to open a retirement center that would afford domestic workers proper means of day-to-day livelihoods, as well as a community of support, since so many had left their own families to care for the children of their employers. As she found, the intertwined nature of this occupation demands that rights travel beyond the household labor context, to consider the entire circumstances of domestic workers' lives.

Aida carried this cause, as well as 50 years of organizing experience, to the formative gatherings of the global domestic workers' movement. After traveling to Amsterdam in 2006 to form the first domestic workers' organization, she joined the 2010 ILO meetings as one of the most seasoned activists in the IDWN. She reflected upon her life trajectory— from the small domestic worker cooperative of her earliest efforts to her leadership in a global movement—with extraordinary optimism. "This is the second stage in the history of the movement of the workers. Not only in Latin America, in Africa, but everywhere. It is impossible to stop us now!" Aida celebrated the culmination of this struggle in a poem she dedicated to her sisters of CONLACTRAHO:

> We have managed to achieve visibility and to organize ourselves
> Our outcry reached the ILO
> This body heard our clamor from oblivion and invisibility
> After hundreds of years ignoring us.

Paying tribute to the "force and commitment of the thousands of workers who have supported the movement," Aida proclaimed, "This is the fruit of the seed that was sown in the beginning. We share that fruit today with the convention."

Why the ILO?

Aida's international activism takes place at the intersections of global government politics, international relations, and transnational civil-society mobilization. The ILO is the largest international institution dedicated to labor. Thus, it has both symbolic and strategic significance within the UN/international human rights hub, serving domestic workers' desire for access and influence in their pursuit of rights. Yet the ILO exists at some remove from the realities of the world's workers. As US government delegate Robert B. Shepard acknowledged, "It is always interesting, people don't know what the ILO is!" The organization's standard-setting role in international governance distances it from direct engagement with the majority of the world's workers. Yet this institution scripts the most encompassing terms for labor standards and practice, with the widest reach across national contexts. Its transnational scale makes the ILO especially relevant to today's burgeoning labor populations that migrate across state borders and therefore fall outside the scope of national protections. To fully understand domestic workers' struggle for rights, a basic understanding of the workings of the ILO is necessary, both to follow the organizing efforts and to appreciate the bureaucratic and procedural barriers the movement faced.

The International Labour Organization, a holdover from the League of Nations, is a specialized agency of the United Nations. Founded in

1919, 26 years before the United Nations itself, it is the largest and most overarching global body responsible for setting and evaluating the world's labor standards and practices. In 1946 the ILO became part of the UN as a specialized agency, yet it operates in a rather independent fashion. Unlike the broader UN, member states fund the ILO through both assessed regular contributions and voluntary support for particular projects and initiatives, accounting for annual revenues of $802 million in 2015. The main distinction is the ILO's guiding *tripartite* social dialogue process, involving the equal participation of member governments, employer representatives, and worker organizations in policy-making, procedures, and protocols.[5]

The ILO has two main functions: (1) to pass international conventions and nonbinding recommendations; and (2) to provide technical assistance to governments in their national efforts to implement such regulations. In the international law context, a convention is the strongest instrument with which to establish fundamental rights, with binding obligations for countries to report on their compliance practices. A recommendation outlines the mechanisms for implementation, and provides governments with suggested measures that go beyond the minimum rights prescribed in a convention. Even though these instruments are the most overarching standards of labor worldwide, ILO enforcement comes only from states' willingness to ratify them. Rather than exerting direct governance over states, the ILO relies upon states to develop legislative practices that uphold established standards. When national governments have the economic resources, commitments, and capacities to adhere to these standards, the ILO engages in direct relationships with states by requiring reporting and compliance with each condition of the adopted convention.[6] In the best situations, national unions support the standards set by the ILO. As one leader put it, "We don't have armies, just trade unions."[7] Thus, the instruments produced through the ILO rely on strong state systems of enforcement, and the support of national unions on the ground.

To achieve its mission of setting and enforcing standards, the ILO relies on a complex and well-staffed organizational structure, with units dedicated to legal standards, information gathering, labor conditions, and worker and employer relations. The ILO Governing Body oversees the leadership of the organization and sets the agenda for each year's priorities. In June the organization holds its annual International Labour Conference (ILC), where government and worker and employer representatives of all member states determine the policy agenda.

ILO legal adviser Martin Oelz describes the ILO as "a forum for the international community to collectively address . . . injustice."[8] Along with government and employer/worker groups, civil society organizations that meet registration and approval standards can observe policy negotiations. Officially recognized nongovernmental organizations (NGOs) may designate individual participants to take part in the discussions, provided they are approved for admittance into the ILC and follow the procedural rules throughout discussions. NGOs come to the ILO to influence global policymaking on a broad range of issues related to labor. Yet according to the ILO rules of order, they may offer input only during the broad organizational working group discussions at the annual conferences, and in the limited time allocated for civil society input at the opening and closing of each ILC session.[9] During the tripartite discussions, only the official labor and employer vice chair delegates and the official government delegates can speak, leaving very little room for NGOs to enter the official social dialogue process. Thus, NGOs must develop strategies outside the formal tripartite process to bring their concerns to the policymaking forum. As the domestic work negotiations exemplify, civil society partners have the potential to link the policy work of this institution to a range of wider social, economic, and political conditions that shape the terms under which workers exist, as well as their capacity to access ILO standards of protection.

Making National Movements

Aida's story of organizing from Chile to the ILO exemplifies the progression of movements at the center of this global activism story. Domestic workers' policy moment at the ILO followed years of national histories of struggle, solidarity, and endurance. Without the strength of national movements, and the many established victories across continents, domestic workers would not have developed a platform strong enough to stand in the international governance arena. In fact, the IDWN is a representative body of so many women like Aida, who built the strength of their local and national organizations before ever imagining they would take their movements global. Trinidad and Tobago's labor organizer Ida le Blanc contended that household workers' quest for universal rights only came about "after decades of struggling to get the rightful place for domestic workers in the world of work." Ida joined this movement largely because of her mother, Clotil Walcott, herself the daughter of a domestic worker, who founded the National Union of Domestic Employees (NUDE) and led the international Wages for Housework global movement in the 1980s.[10] Ida described her mother, who coined the term "global kitchen," as "a grassroots woman . . . with such a vision to try to free domestic workers from the slavery that persists with them all over the world." Thirty years later, in the most heated moments of the ILO policy debate, she invoked her mother's legacy in calling for the global recognition of domestic workers: "I feel the spirit of my mother moving here, in this ILO conference today." Myrtle Witbooi, IDWN president, also spoke of the personal and national struggles that laid the groundwork for this symbolic moment. "I have personally devoted thirty years of my life to organizing domestic workers in South Africa," she said. "Throughout these years of struggle, I would not have imagined that we would be here today, preparing to vote on an international convention for domestic workers."[11] Marcelina Bautista, lead domestic worker activist in Mexico and general secretary of CONLACTRAHO, reflected on the years of local, national, and regional activism that made a global movement possible. "During these twenty-three years, we as domestic workers have taken it upon ourselves to make our rights visible as workers, as women, and as citizens."[12] These bases of experience provided the source of domestic workers' strength within the ILO, and led to the pivotal strategies that helped them build a collective stance for domestic workers' rights worldwide, as discussed in chapter 5.

National platforms based upon legislative victories and civil society strengths served as vital sources of persuasion in fighting for the ILO convention. For example, Brazil's rich national history of domestic worker organizing was written into the nation's official statements in support of the convention.[13] State officials contextualized the long history of domestic worker activism, dating back to the 1930s, as part of larger race-, class-, and gender-equality struggles. By placing national organizing victories into a global context, Brazil made clear the urgency of protections for domestic workers, who serve as "the gateway for many families in their hope for a better life."[14] South Africa brought an equally impressive set of legislative victories in support of domestic workers.[15] With laws to protect basic work conditions, the right to organize, unemployment insurance, maternity protections, and even minimum wage standards, South Africa became a point of reference in the fight for global rights. If South Africa could pass such impressive domestic work legislation in the aftermath of apartheid, it was argued, so could the ILO in the context of a globalizing care economy. India also emerged as an exemplar of informal-worker organizing. Even though the Indian government's support for Convention 189 vacillated, the nation's Self-Employed Women's Association (SEWA) held such strong ground throughout the meetings that its call to bring domestic workers into larger protective frameworks resonated. With a strong history of involvement with the 1995 Home Work Convention,[16] SEWA connected the national informal-economy movements with a moral and timely claim for rights. In Hong Kong, domestic workers' demonstrated regional activism, even across diverse political affiliations, gave credence to the call for transnational protections. Finally, as an outspoken voice for protections, the United States presented an aligned government/labor front, with a leader of the National Domestic Workers Alliance, Juana Flores, gaining a seat within the US national labor delegation. During the first international deliberations in 2010, the national domestic worker movement achieved the most comprehensive legislative victory in its history. The passing of the Domestic Workers Bill of Rights in New York marked the culmination of years of national efforts to gain protections, and buoyed the IDWN in its fight for the first set of global standards.

State support and the histories of national domestic worker movements played a major role in the claim for global rights. When prominent countries presented their demonstrated capacities to organize domestic workers and bring them into the policy folds of the state, global rights became almost impossible to deny. For the ILO to turn its back on domestic worker rights would be to undermine national protections, policy victories, and activist movements within each of these countries. It was because of these national struggles, as Aida Moreno attested, that domestic workers' "outcry reached the ILO," making the institution's obligation to worker protections that much more "right, just, and long overdue."[17]

Crystallizing the Global Movement

Domestic worker organizations showed up in unity at the ILO after four prior years of organizing as a transnational network. The first such meeting of domestic worker leaders took place in Amsterdam in 2006 when the International Restructuring Education Network Europe (IRENE) brought together over 60 women leaders from Asia, North America, Africa, South America, and Europe. "Respect and Rights: Protection for Domestic Workers!" drew women like Hester Stephens, Aida Moreno, and Marcelina Bautista, who led efforts to mobilize household workers within their own countries.[18] Their goals took three forms: (1) to align national organizations, (2) to build an advocacy plan for domestic worker rights, and (3) to grow a global movement. As a critical outcome of this gathering, Dan Gallin asserted, domestic workers "became conscious of their own power" and "how widespread and well organized they actually already were."[19] In 2008, the same year the ILO announced that "Decent Work for Domestic Workers" would be placed on the ILC 2010 agenda, the IDWN established a formal leadership structure that set its sights on bringing its platform to the ILO. The formation of the IDWN allowed women labor activists to use the ILO as a site for both collective action on human rights and the growth of a global movement.

With the focus on a domestic work convention, the ILO broadened its perspective to look at labor through the eyes of informal workers. Since the founding of the ILO in 1919, over the course of 98 preceding International Labour Conferences the only other substantive consideration of policy protections for domestic workers took place in 1948 and 1965. Historian Eileen Boris describes these early ILO conversations as a way of testing the waters for women's rights dialogues and gauging institutional willingness to address gender-labor equity.[20] Forty years later, Luc Demaret, the lead domestic worker convention advocate within the ILO, attributed the organization's growing consideration of this sector to the pressure from larger political movements.

> It is true that as early as 1948, and then again in 1965, the ILO had already expressed its concerns about the poor working conditions and lack of rights faced by domestic workers. It is not that the ILO hasn't done anything since then, but there has not been enough pressure for it to take any

significant steps. It was around 2005 that more and more women domestic workers began to realize the need to organize. Women domestic workers' associations multiplied, particularly in Latin America and Europe, and as they began to feel the limitations on their forms of organization, they moved closer to the trade union movement. Furthermore, the [ILO] discussions on migrant labor in 2004, and the discussions on the elimination of child labor, also had an impact, as they strayed into the more nebulous territory of domestic labor each time. It was the convergence of all these elements that triggered greater awareness.[21]

Feminist analyses have expressed skepticism about the integration of issues of gender rights and protections by international institutions, mainly because of the predominantly male structures of leadership that have traditionally guided them.[22] However, as Demaret points out, pressure from larger movements held the ILO accountable to this predominantly female sector of informal labor. Furthermore, the wider UN focus on women's rights over the past 20 years pushed the ILO to bring gender equality into its labor policies, as aligned with a larger international development effort to "mainstream gender" by placing women and girls' initiatives within organizations' policies, priorities, and processes. The informal economy thus became an inevitable undertaking if the ILO was to demonstrate an authentic capacity to reach the "real world" of workers.

At an organizational level, the Domestic Workers Convention 189 amounted to a change of focus for the ILO, which in 1996 initiated a "human rights era of 'decent work'"—a prerequisite for discussions on this sector. As the ILO defines it, decent work "is based on the understanding that work is a source of personal dignity, family stability, peace in the community, democracies that deliver for people, and economic growth that expands opportunities for productive jobs and enterprise development."[23] This broader position stems from a guiding perspective that "productive employment and Decent Work are key elements to achieving a fair globalization, reducing poverty and achieving equitable, inclusive, and sustainable development."[24] Juan Somavía, former director general of the ILO, suggested that this notion of "fair globalization" requires that the ILO embrace those most marginalized, namely poor, migrant women workers.[25] Widening the standards of coverage beyond formal work relationships allowed ILO policies to include "precarious workers" in the informal economy.

With their framework widening to encompass "nonstandard work," beginning in 2006 key figures within the ILO and the larger labor movement identified domestic workers as the next group to be considered for a convention and accompanying set of recommendations. This inclusion pushed the ILO on two fronts—informal workers, and the household space as a site of regulation. The most substantive former attempt to cover any parallel group took place in 1995, when the ILO passed a Home Work Convention for home production/assembly workers,[26] which set the groundwork for inclusion of the private household as an appropriate site for ILO global regulations. With this precedent in place, to get domestic work on the table, advocates had to not only defend it as work in need of regulation, but also place this sector strategically within the new terms of the global "patchwork economy,"[27] where workers assume increased economic and personal burdens, global outsourcing severs employment relations, and the informal economy flourishes at the risk of human rights. Barbro Budin, chair of the Gender and Equality Office for the International Union of Food, Agricultural, Hotel, Restaurant, Catering, Tobacco and Allied Workers' Association (IUF), showed how the global economy affects care labor specifically. "The privatization of public services has led to increased demand for domestic workers and home care workers all over the world."[28] Because outsourced, nonstandard work was largely outside the reach of global standards, the appeal for an international convention on domestic work amounted to a larger call for the ILO to include the informal economy within its mandate.

As labor and women's rights advocates pushed the ILO to regulate this formerly excluded category of workers, internal players used their deep knowledge of the ILO, and its emphasis on rules and procedures, to carve out a space for dialogue on domestic workers. The 2008 ILO Governing Body decision to place "Decent Work for Domestic Workers" on the 2010 International Labour Conference agenda reflected an "attempt to bring the traditionally excluded group of domestic workers within the labor market formality."[29] According to the International Trade Union Confederation (ITUC), "This decision followed calls by the international trade union movement and received the unanimous

Figure 2.2. International Domestic Workers Network (IDWN)

support of the Workers' Group of the ILO Governing Body, which saw the decision to place the item on the Conference's agenda as an historic one bringing the ILO 'back to basics' by developing standards to effectively protect vulnerable categories of workers."[30] By connecting domestic work to basic human rights and exposing its vital role within the contemporary global economy, advocates within the system and those in close proximity in global unions strongly influenced the ILO's decision to take up the question of protections for this sector.

No other ILO process addressed the informal economy at this scale, nor did civil society play such a pivotal role in policymaking. In the history of the ILO, these negotiations drew the highest participation of "actual workers" and their allies, who brought a global activist movement to the policy process, fostering political solidarity among this large and formerly overlooked group. As Luc Demaret reflected upon the meaning of this symbolic occasion, he contended, "The call for a convention has become a rallying cry, as was seen during the recent trade union mobilizations on domestic work on May Day, international labor day." Even before the debates officially began, he asserted that "the mere prospect of a convention has had a major political impact."[31] Thus, far beyond the terms of its protections, the ILO convention served as the "anchoring movement" in a much larger global mobilization for domestic worker rights.[32]

"No Such Thing as 'Unorganizable Workers'"

In getting to the table, leaders of the domestic worker movement relied on a history of alliances, material resources, and ideological solidarity.[33] Behind this first global organization stood two core allies: the Women in the Informal Employment: Globalizing and Organizing (WIEGO) policy network and the IUF trade union federation. These established organizations gave the newly formed IDWN a foot in both labor and gender struggles for justice. As Ida le Blanc proclaimed, without these two support systems, "domestic workers and their organization from around the world would not have known where the ILO and the United Nations is, much less be able to speak out for themselves and participate at the ILC and side events."[34] Through these complementary allies, the IDWN gained substantive political and economic knowledge, as well as the means to "get in" to the ILC proceedings.

Over two decades before Convention 189, before any other global union or NGO embraced a commitment to building solidarity with domestic workers, the IUF extended its arms to disparate household-worker organizations around the world. This gesture stemmed from a defining Marxist political stance that placed the class struggle at the heart of the movement for social change. Dan Gallin, IUF general secretary from 1987 to 2005, spoke of the IUF's guiding historical ethos.

> The IUF has a long tradition. Actually, from its founding in 1920, it has been a radical organization, and an organization prepared to fight for underprivileged people that the rest of the labor movement might not have regarded as a priority, or as marginal.[35]

Originally, the IUF represented meat workers and bakers, predominantly male professions. Yet in the 1980s its membership grew to include hotel, food, and tobacco workers, traditionally feminized sectors. With this representation, the IUF built a pervasive awareness of interconnected gender and labor justice into its ideologies and practices. In his account of the IUF's history, Gallin contended, "The gender gap was never a real problem in the IUF. Taking care of the marginalized, that was our job anyway, from the beginning."[36] As the IUF debated the reach of its membership, leaders began to consider the large, underrepresented pool of workers who perform food, hospitality, and care labor in private homes. With its eyes on the possibility of organizing the informal economy, the IUF found its overarching ethos fully in line with domestic workers.

Alongside this original ideological solidarity with domestic workers, the IUF invested in a long-standing relationship with WIEGO—the global action-research-policy network that supports organizations of informal workers around the world. This organizational partnership stemmed from a shared commitment to domestic workers' right to organize, as well as the long-standing reciprocal friendship between the organizations' chiefs—Marty Chen, as the cofounder and international coordinator of WIEGO, and Gallin leading the IUF. As Juan Somavía reflected in his meetings with the IDWN in 2010, "Sometimes old friendships are helpful in getting the right people together."[37]

A development scholar and faculty member at Harvard University, Chen championed informal labor as a vital priority for any analysis of the links between economic growth, globalization, and poverty.[38] Given the extent and growth of informal employment, Chen argues for "a new economic paradigm: a model of a hybrid economy that embraces the traditional and the modern, the small scale and the big scale, the informal and the formal."[39] As a leader of WIEGO since its 1997 inception, she steered the organization through periods when major development agencies virtually ignored the informal economy, as well as, in many cases, women's activist contributions. Her commitment to WIEGO stems directly from having been raised in India. As the daughter of ecumenical missionary parents committed to interfaith dialogue, from her early childhood Chen lived among workers in the informal economy and witnessed the centrality of informal labor in the country that provided her most formative life experiences, as well as her first language—Hindi. Gandhi's teachings surrounded her, as her parents immersed themselves at the crossroads of religion and political struggles for freedom.

In 1961, when she traveled to the United States to study, Chen's connection to India and the economic conditions of its population only strengthened. She earned a doctorate in South Asian studies and returned to work in development and relief projects with the Bangladesh Rural Advancement Committee (BRAC), developing that organization's first women's program, organizing and promoting the livelihoods

Figure 2.3. Marty Chen (right) and Ela Bhatt (left)

of craft producers, poultry rearers, and silk weavers. Here, Chen pro-claimed, "I had found my calling—to promote the economic empower-ment and economic rights of working poor women through a mix of activism, research, and advocacy."[40] She later became the field represen-tative of Oxfam America in India, where she began working with the Self-Employed Women's Association (SEWA), focusing on the connec-tions between the informal economy and women's economic empow-erment. Alongside her friend and mentor Ela Bhatt, she developed an expertise in providing the "big picture" data sets for NGOs working to gain rights for vulnerable workers. Based at Harvard University, where she worked as a faculty member and policy expert, Chen brought grass-roots global realities to academe and used her organizational acumen to strengthen movements of women in the informal economy. In 1997, with the founding of WIEGO, Chen helped bring the collective voices and organizing capacities of street vendors, waste pickers, home-based workers, and domestic workers to public arenas to demand their eco-nomic rights and legal protections.

Chen describes WIEGO as "part think tank, part social move-ment"; it uses data and research to support organizations of workers in their struggles for recognition, rights, and protection in more than eighty countries. Its focus on recognition, rights, and representation for women in the informal economy guides the organization, comprised of invited members from three constituencies: member-based organizations of informal workers, researchers and statisticians, and development practitioners in governments, international development agencies, and NGOs. As the only advocacy network with a grassroots constituency and a statistical expertise, WIEGO's niche is "to put work, workers, and workers' organizations at the center of development discourse, policies, and processes."[41] With funding from large US foundations, as well as government development agencies, WIEGO's mission is to strengthen the capacities of the working poor, especially women, in the informal economy through increased organization and representation, improved data and research, and an enabling policy and regulatory environment.

The domestic workers' convention dialogues provided a framework in which WIEGO could see its vision to fruition—from the formative stages of movement making to a global network of care activists within the ILO. Although a long-standing ally of domestic workers worldwide, WIEGO's actions on behalf of this sector expanded rapidly when the organization received generous funding from the Bill & Melinda Gates Foundation. WIEGO's gaining of substantive resources and a fortified staff coincided with the ILO's commitment to investigate global standards for domestic workers. At the same time, the IUF provided support from its headquarters in Geneva, offering a space in which domestic workers could hold meetings, release time for its staff to invest in this cause, and financial support to get a global movement off the ground. Together, these two organizations supported the establishment of the International Domestic Workers Network. Yet, even with the serendipitous timing of resources, both organizations made substantive compromises to invest in the domestic workers' movement. In WIEGO's case, at a few critical junctures the organization borrowed from other funds to act in line with its moral position of support for domestic workers. In other instances, IUF leaders came under sharp criticism for their commitment to organizing a seemingly unorganizable sector. Yet both brought the force of their experience, resource bases, and political capital to the effort to build political, organizational, and economic support for their aligned vision at each stage of the journey. When the ILO began policy discussions in 2010, these partners stood behind this newly formed movement to galvanize support for informal workers in the global economy.

Dan Gallin refers to this alliance as "a textbook example" of an original social change "operation," where the women's movement, union movement, and NGO forces aligned to "produce a fantastic result, a big success story." His recollections on the origins of this movement reveal its organizational philosophies and approach:

> We were able to organize ourselves in battle formation. And then to the general surprise of the employers and of the unions, here all of a sudden was an international organization, which had been organized without asking anybody for permission and it was fighting. And in the end everybody was delighted. I mean, the workers' group was finally delighted. You see, all these women who had been considered unorganizable—I mean, I've seen this phrase "unorganizable" come up many times in trade union literature. The unorganizable—it's always informal workers, it's always women. And here you had all those unorganizable women, raising hell, being very organized, and unexpected allies.[42]

As the domestic worker movement grew through the ILO dialogue, these partner organizations provided resources, strategy consultation, and political capital, while developing an original model of social movement activism.

The Face of Domestic Work

In the highly visible venue of the ILO, domestic work came out of the shadows. By aligning testimonials across national contexts, presenting a unified front on rights, and demonstrating public solidarity, the IDWN built a larger identity for the global movement. At virtually every juncture in the policymaking process, the presence of domestic workers, with their personal narratives and national identities, put a "human face" on household employment. Take Shirley Pryce, for example, the former head of household for the prime minister of Jamaica, current leader of the Jamaican Domestic Workers Union, and the first domestic worker to gain an official vote within the ILO. In an interview, she depicted her journey from some of the most exploitative labor circumstances to her empowerment as the lead staff member for a head of state. In her worst employment experience, she recounted, "The dog had a bed, but not us."[43] Yet even under these circumstances, Shirley saw the possibilities for aligning with other domestic workers in her community as a means to alter the conditions of employment she had experienced, thereby confronting Jamaica's history of colonialism and servitude and the day-to-day working conditions of thousands of women like her. By attending the ILO meetings, Shirley placed her own experience within the larger global economy's reliance upon domestic workers to run the households of privileged families throughout the world. "Being here at the ILO, with the other domestic workers from around the world, and listening to all the discussions," she reflected, "I see so much more about all these abuses of domestic workers everywhere." Empowered by her participation in the IDWN, she drew on her own experiences to give voice to domestic workers within the ILO. Shirley, like so many of her sisters, used her own story to build a collective narrative of domestic workers' strength and resilience, bringing a compelling authenticity to their claims. As Shirley shared her leadership dreams, she proclaimed, "If I can help make domestic workers' lives *better*, then I will continue fighting for that."

As Premilla Nadasen, leading historian on domestic work, argues in her analysis of African American domestic workers' organizing in the United States, storytelling was a key unifier among women activists and played a defining role in building a movement.[44] In the formative years of this global organization, stories served two defining purposes: (1) they built ties across workers' diverse national contexts, and (2) they fostered a shared worker identity. Thus when Shirley Pryce recounted her early days of sleeping in a doghouse, other domestic workers shared their own stories of injustice, such as living "in the backyard" and sleeping in the garage, creating a shared experience of the dehumanization endured by workers in an unregulated labor environment.

In their struggle to win Convention 189, domestic workers harnessed the power of story in coming together as a transnational organization. When workers shared with one another their experiences of having to leave their home countries, and often their own children, to make a living for themselves and their families, the collective IDWN called

Figure 2.4. Shirley Pryce

for policies that would recognize the particular demands of migration, demanding that sending and receiving countries work together to address the reliance on exported care labor. Their shared public narratives enabled domestic workers to position themselves as a united front in demanding universal rights. As Myrtle Witbooi reminded, "We're fighting one goal. We are fighting one government and we are fighting the same employers. Let us come together." Collectively, the IDWN leaders made domestic work a common matter of global justice, rather than a national concern alone. As Witbooi contended, "Our suffering . . . it doesn't matter what color we are, if we are domestic workers, we do the same domestic work. There is no difference between us. Let us stand together, let us fight for our rights."

In their strategies to influence the international lawmaking process, the women of the IDWN wrote songs together, created group narratives to build continuity through the policy process, and performed stand-up skits about their own experiences on weekend talent nights. These bonding moments mattered, allowing IDWN members to build a collective identity that held the organization together as it faced the demands of policymaking within a highly formalized institution.

Professionalizing Domestic Work

While the IDWN's public presentation of domestic work centered on the experiences of "actual workers" in the field, the labor network relied heavily on professional advocates. In fact, of the original network at the 2010 ILC, only 28 percent worked full-time as domestic workers. The others had made their careers advocating for this underrepresented sector. Jill Shenker (United States) and Ip Pui Yu (Hong Kong), for example, held university degrees with a focus on social justice. They brought professional organizing experience to the table as leaders in national bodies of domestic workers. Vicky Kanyoka of Tanzania represented the Africa region, yet came to the IDWN with a strong union background and a quality of life that allowed her to employ domestic workers in her own home, as she advocated for justice in the field. During the negotiations, the organization's president, Myrtle Witbooi, referenced her experience as a domestic worker as a central dimension of her stance, even though she no longer worked in a household, rather as a national union organizer for over two decades prior to the ILO policy debates. As she often contends, "I got my degree in the employer's kitchen."[45] Thus, while the network spoke as a united front of domestic workers, its actual leaders varied according to the level of their direct dependence upon the field for survival, as well as their levels of education. Peruvian domestic worker activist Ernestina Ochoa recounted the conditions of domestic work in her public statements at the ILO. "We've had to leave our work in our countries so that we can come here to Geneva, so we can participate and be protagonists in this historic event."[46] Yet not every IDWN representative left work in a private household to travel to Geneva. Some were in professional advocacy positions that kept them on the road, speaking on behalf of domestic workers. In the ILO negotiations, however, the IDWN presented a unified front, as a representative body expressing the experiences of women employed in the field full-time. While solidarity and commitment to the rights of domestic workers universally aligned the network, the activist organization relied heavily upon professional advocates representing the marginalized women who depended on domestic work for their livelihoods. Thus, the IDWN came to the ILO floor through an alignment of domestic workers and professional spokeswomen, including those employed by unions and larger representative organizations as advocates for the sector.

IDWN representation must also be assessed in terms of the absence of voices from particular regions of the world. In many countries, domestic workers are not allowed to organize, let alone join a transnational movement for household-labor rights. No domestic workers from the Middle East could join the IDWN, given the dearth of organizations in countries with the highest levels of exploitation. In some cases, domestic worker leaders could not physically get to the ILO, as Switzerland denied visas in a few instances, while the cost and logistical challenges of traveling to and staying in the country prohibited others from getting to the meetings. Countries with high levels of support for domestic worker rights, and existing national structures, populated the global network, leaving countries without representation absent from the transnational organization. In other instances, language limited involvement in the IDWN, such as in the case of Brazil, where Portuguese interpretation was not part of the meeting processes. Thus, domestic workers with Spanish and English capabilities dominated the landscape of the network, as its formative processes could not account for the diversity of representation of domestic workers worldwide. These gatekeeping influences—the geopolitics of access to the ILO, economic resources, and language barriers—determined the composition of this first worldwide network of domestic workers.

The realities of this composition must foreground any analyses of the IDWN's participation as a transnational organization within the ILO movement. On the one hand, professional domestic worker advocates brought distinct rhetorical skills and organizational strategizing experience to the policy process, with a grounded capacity to link to larger social movements because of their full-time investment in this cause. On the other hand, however, the presentation of domestic workers' stances within the ILO relied heavily upon these professional advocates, whose life stories were very different from those of the "actual domestic workers" in the network. Thus, the voices representing domestic workers were very often trained by larger institutions and professional affiliations, creating an important cleavage in the standpoints, and in some cases authenticity, of domestic workers' public testimonials. As a central note of clarity about the terminology in this book, reference to "domestic workers" in the IDWN context assumes this fusion of full-time domestic workers and union/NGO advocates who held central roles in the organization. My intention is to reflect the perspectives of the organization as it was established in its diversity of members, rather than to present the IDWN as a homogeneous group of activists who also work full-time in the field. These representational factors are central to chapter 5's conversation on domestic worker strategies and appeals for protections.

The diversity of representation within the IDWN could prove challenging in the organization's efforts to align across these important divides. As Linda Burnham, one of the leading organizers and researchers in the NDWA, reminded, "We are human so there are tensions."[47] This is a slippery space for ally scholars of domestic work, who seek to strengthen a movement and bolster its capacity to influence systems of power. Yet to deny legitimate differences in domestic worker organizing risks reinforcing this sector as a "special category" of workers, in ways that dilute its capacity to engage with mainstream systems of power, and potentially patronize the movement. In the case of domestic worker global organizing, I bring these differences to my analysis to afford a more nuanced view of this distinct collective movement, in the understanding that such a view may contribute to its potential influence, as well as further the work of its ally scholar-activists.

Three predominant tensions arose over the course of the ILO process. First, the IDWN needed to come to terms with the extent to which it would speak as "one voice." Carmen Cruz, secretary general, CONLAC-TRAHO, Latin America, encouraged her sisters "*to unite in one cause, and plan with the same target in mind.*"[48] In a planning session, when another leader suggested that "at the ILC, we are all domestic workers," Jill Shenker of the NDWA challenged that notion, contending, "There are issues and complexities that we will need to bring to the discussion, to find the best practices for us. I do not personally agree that we need the same voice and the same position for all. We need to acknowledge the specificities in countries." Shenker's focus was on assuring that the organization would reflect "the industry and all of its manifestations around the world." Yet the demands of presenting a globally unified front limited the IDWN's capacity to speak to the realities of difference within the transnational sector.

Second, the varying work situations and national contexts characterizing the global market translated into differences within the IDWN. For instance, migration defined the needs of countries in Asia, whereas African activists dealt with a reliance on child work and family employment. In some national contexts, domestic workers align around identity networks rather than shared experiences in the destination country. For example, in Hong Kong, Malaysian, Filipina, and Indonesian domestic workers bring very different experiences to the shared dimensions of household work. In the United States, Caribbean and Mexican domestic workers bring language differences to the NDWA. Yet the global coordination of domestic workers could not fully embrace the complexities of these situations, nor could the organization bring such a diversity of representation to the formative work around the ILO convention. To work as a united front, it had to confront the limits of effective global representation, as more and more organizations sought to join the IDWN given the wide attention it gained in the ILO process. It faced the continual challenge of organizing across lines of language, identity, religion, culture, and class differences.

Third, the public relations activities that accompanied this movement required domestic workers' engagement with news media and related outlets. Like national organizations, the IDWN relied upon the voices of those members with training, and most often fluency, in English. Those who emerged as spokespersons for the movement gained global attention, becoming the "voice" of the IDWN. While the IDWN relied upon these voices, the women taking on this role shouldered the added demands of the spotlight. As one activist confessed, "I told my story like 1,000 times."[49] With the broad attention the global venue attracted, domestic worker leaders faced competing expectations to represent a transnational movement while tending to the demands of work in their own countries. In some cases, leaders dealt with highly sensitive employment issues in their home countries during the three weeks they spent in Geneva. These exemplar activists worked to advance a global movement at the cost of their own personal time and in some cases the needs of their national contexts. This tension peaked during the high-profile policy discussions, yet the demands on key leaders have continued to stretch activists' capacities to serve simultaneously at the global and national levels.

Unlike Any Other Movement

Among social change movements, this global organization of domestic workers stands alone. To go from formation to taking a central role in international governance in just three years is unprecedented in the history of collective action. In a very short period of time, domestic worker rights went "from impossible to inevitable."[50] How did this social movement achieve such accelerated success? Five critical strands underlie this unparalleled victory.

First, domestic workers established national and regional organizations that gave their movement credibility and the capacity to align on common ground. The organizations that formed the first global network had already seen policy victories at the national levels, organized regionally, and gained recognition as leaders in their field. These strong regional networks then built a coordinated domestic workers' infrastructure within the ILO, giving credibility and political capital to the IDWN once it reached this new transnational public space. When the opening emerged for "sectoral experts," the IDWN easily rose to the occasion, bringing experience, research, and strong testimonials to the policy stand.

Second, the movement emerged at a serendipitous time. Just as domestic worker leaders from around the world met for the first time, advocates within the ILO had gained substantive ground, with the 2008 agreement to place "decent work for domestic workers" on the 2010–11 agendas for new policy formation. Sociologists point out that social movements arise in part because of "opportunity at the top."[51] At the time the ILO provided an institutional opening, the transnational organizational structure was in place to encourage participation of "actual workers" in the informal economy and greater levels of inclusion for civil society organizations within the policymaking process. Thus, the ILO's consideration of the first global protections for domestic workers gave the newly formed network a very focused purpose and collective investment for their first undertaking.

Third, central to successful social movements, domestic workers mobilized a wide range of resources in making the most of a political opportunity. The IDWN took maximum advantage of the ILO's focus on "decent work" and its willingness to consider domestic workers' rights, in its newly defined role as a transnational organization. Part outsiders, part internal experts, domestic workers forged their way into the negotiations, forcing the ILO to engage directly with domestic workers and ensuring that their role became vital to the overall process.

Fourth, as part of this mobilization of resources, high-profile organizations, global unions, and related women's networks backed domestic workers, using their plea for rights as a demand for global governance to set a higher moral ground. By showing up and taking on this cause, global NGOs like Human Rights Watch and Anti-Slavery International pushed the ILO to address the needs of the world's most vulnerable workers. At the same time, the IUF and WIEGO gave domestic workers the backing of both a labor movement and an international women's rights campaign. In large part, these NGOs and ally organizations took on the work of putting domestic labor in a larger context. At the same time, their affiliated public relations campaigns made strong ideological arguments that bolstered domestic workers' political and social capital both within and beyond this global policy arena. Labor scholar Helen Schwenken claimed that "strategic coalition building" served as one of the core explanations for this global rights victory emerging from "a space of impossibility." Along with these ally relationships, she showed how "a fast-paced upscaling of the movement that brought different and more sympathetic political elites into the struggle" played a major role in the success of this global organization of domestic workers.[52] Indeed, as discussed in chapter 5, key government figures and "sympathetic" employers got behind domestic workers to embolden this strategic call for a higher moral ground through domestic workers' protections. For example, Betsey McGee, of Hand in Hand employers organization in New York City, traveled to Geneva to advocate for domestic workers' rights by linking fair employment to core benefits for employers. At one of the 2011 forums held alongside the meetings, she proclaimed, "A strong ILO convention can be used to change cultural norms, shape national policies, structure incentives for better care. This is a future we welcome." Thus, with key allies extremely well positioned in WIEGO, the IUF, the ILO, and ally governments, the movement was able to galvanize individuals as "bridge builders."[53] With these influential leaders and their "upscaling" of the movement, labor reforms for domestic work became a concern of moral necessity for the elite, for employers, and for the many related and well-resourced human rights groups.

Finally, the way this movement framed domestic work and linked it to related issues of justice played an important role in its success. Rather than presenting domestic workers as a special labor category, women leaders of this movement claimed that they were "workers, just like all other workers." Counter to ideas about domestic work as a fringe or special-interest sector, this movement repeatedly claimed its centrality in the global economy. As the National Domestic Workers Alliance mantra states, domestic work is "the work that makes all other work possible." In this framework, activists pushed the ILO to consider domestic work as "care labor." This is not just about the woman who occasionally cleans your home, they professed. ILO delegates were setting standards for the "valuing [of] the daily fabric of our lives."[54] Thus domestic labor encompassed child care all the way through to elder care, as the lines between health care and home care continue to blur while the "silver tsunami" hits the shores of so many nations. Through this wide construction of relevance, the domestic work movement cut across society, by exposing our collective human dependence on care in aging and end-of-life processes. Even those policymakers most opposed to human rights paradigms would have to confront their needs for such care, for eventually all of us become dependent on others. Thus, a vocal portion of the movement constructed domestic work as "the most vital work" in our reciprocal commitment to caring for one another, across generations and nations. Ai-jen Poo repeatedly frames domestic work as the "most universal and fundamental aspect of humanity; to uphold the dignity of another human being."[55]

Another core component of this movement's success was its capacity to make domestic work a composite instance of so many larger struggles for rights, justice, and economic restructuring. Domestic work became an "anchoring movement" that gave form, expression, and often emotion to a much larger people's resistance effort.[56] By claiming "domestic workers' rights are human rights," the movement built critical campaign ties to much broader concerns for migration, child labor, and women's rights. As Florencia Cabatingan, leader of the Trade Union Congress of the Philippines, contended:

this [domestic work] issue is too large and important to be tackled only by a single organization or sector because it is not only people's mindsets we have to change, but we have to dismantle existing structures and systems put in place to perpetuate the process of marginalizing domestic workers. And when we talk of marginalization, we are talking of curtailment of freedom, curtailment of human rights. Freedom has many faces . . . And because of globalization freedom has another face, that of human rights.[57]

In this analysis, the fight for domestic worker rights becomes a much wider struggle for redistributing resources and changing structures of domination. With the prevalence of globalization, as Cabatingan points out, possibilities for the resurgence of human rights expand, in a form reflective of the dialectic relationship between systems of power and control and individuals' capacity to alter these terms through collective action. Feminist scholar Nancy Fraser shows how different forms of struggle for recognition are in many cases closely interlinked.[58] With these vital connections, the "power of the people" is strengthened through broader social movements under core ideological human rights frames. Furthermore, this coordinated effort placed a moral imperative on the recognition of domestic workers in the larger system of policy protections. With this critical linkage, how could any decision maker deny human rights? María Luisa Escorel de Moraes, government delegate from Brazil, used this perspective to explain the great victory of the policy vote. "I think that, on that day, everyone was aware that these are human rights, and there is no longer any space in today's world to oppose this. Imagine how it would look to do that!"[59] Thus, by framing human rights as the core concern of this convention, domestic workers gained moral ground and created an umbrella demand for rights that reached far beyond the terms of their own labor. The movement capitalized on the capacity to draw in a much wider transnational network of vested interest, making domestic work an exemplar of both the failure to assure human rights for all and the hopes of redesigning a system that provides universal protections through the moral and applied guidelines inscribed through international policy. By foregrounding "justice for all," the movement succeeded in showing why "everyone should care about care work."

This seemingly impossible victory came at a particular moment in the arc of globalization. This contextual landscape of "in-betweenedness" provides openings for movements to gain important ground.[60] In this case, just as a collection of domestic workers from around the world began to meet in person to build a global movement, the largest labor institution opened up to consider informal workers in its policy protections. The timing of this intersection seems almost preorchestrated. Within this moment between activism at the state level and the coordination of a global movement, two related shifts took place as domestic work entered the ILO. As Schwenken points out, addressing the seeming "impossibility" of this movement, the ILO process reconstructed domestic workers' identities. Whereas formerly "the attitude of servitude inscribed into the very nature of domestic work, which does not allow domestic workers to display disobedience and it does not give them the self-confidence or authority to demand labour rights,"[61] the ILO forum allowed domestic workers to emerge collectively as global activists, demanding their long overdue dignity and rights with the backing of strong transnational coalition ties. Feminist social-movement scholars point to the dialectic relationship between individuals and collective action in ways that speak directly to this transformation of domestic worker pioneers.

> One of the recurring and most moving themes that one sees in the stories of women's public protest is how their very participation in movements changes their conception of themselves and their role in their communities . . . Social space is remade and women's lives are remade by protest action, sometimes at great personal cost.[62]

Thus, during the ILO process domestic workers went from "kitchen girls" to international policymakers. As their worker identities shifted, the household space itself was ideologically reconstituted. Formerly isolated domains of invisible labor, private homes became workspaces subject to state regulation and monitoring, "just like any other work."

Grounding Global-Care Perspectives

Convention 189 marks a critical moment in the feminist scholarship on domestic labor, centering on the value of reproductive labor and women's traditional work in the private sphere. Advocates of Convention 189 had to challenge core ideological assumptions about the devalued nature of domestic labor, as a result of its location within the private household and its traditional association with "women's work."[63] By placing conversations about labor in the (micro) household within a global (macro) institution, the Convention 189 process disrupted the public/private divide, as representatives of state and global governance created a volume of discourse on this growing force in the global economy. Central feminist theories emerged from the statements of domestic workers, governments, and even employers. For example, in her opening commentary, a representative of the government of Brazil made the following observation about the location of domestic work: "Because it is carried out in the home, domestic work is seen as part of the work carried out by women traditionally, and not remunerated. Therefore, domestic workers have been excluded from the main labor standards."[64] This speaker went on to suggest that traditional notions of women's work would need to be reenvisioned in order to assure fair working standards for this sector. The ILO process exposed pertinent questions about the relationships among domestic labor, the state, and the forces of globalization. The public debates on the most relevant protections for this formerly "invisible" sector also addressed the challenge of implementing labor standards in the home.

Analyses of the ILC proceedings allow us to examine the social constructions surrounding domestic labor, the movement to develop global gender-rights standards, and the role of international institutions in protecting the most marginalized. To evaluate the need for Convention 189, government, labor, and employer groups continually framed domestic workers as "poor" and "vulnerable" women and girls who generally lack agency as "victims" of global circumstances. Shireen Ally shows how governments portray domestic workers as "vulnerable" in their development of labor protections.[65] Drawing from the case of South Africa, which has the most sophisticated labor laws for this sector, Ally further illustrates how domestic workers themselves participate in this construction of vulnerability, so as to garner support from the state. Given that women represent over 93 percent of the sector worldwide,[66] the "decent work for domestic workers" campaign similarly plays upon such notions of gendered vulnerability in efforts to promote international protections for the "poorest of the poor"—most often migrant women and young girls.

As the ILO grappled with how to formalize regulations for the "invisible informal economy," the interconnections between domestic work and migration continually surfaced as challenges to the creation of regulations. Feminist scholars of globalization repeatedly show how the interdependency of global capital and demands for service labor have led to an escalating reliance on migrant women's employment in the informal economy generally, and more specifically within the domestic work sector. Sociologist Saskia Sassen illustrates how this growth of the service economy depends upon a global-care supply chain of migrant women of color, predominantly from the Global South.[67] Likewise, Kimberly Chang and Lily Ling posit that a "regime of labor intimacy" underpins global economic and technical growth.[68] During her opening speech at the 2010 ILC, Tanzanian activist and IDWN Africa Regional Coordinator Vicky Kanyoka argued that domestic workers are the "oil in the wheels" of the global economy. Michelle Bachelet, the leader of UN Women, joined the 2011 ILC closing discussions to speak of the critical role domestic workers play as the "lifeline to families at home and abroad." In this conception, domestic workers are conduits of globalization—connecting families, nations, and economies. Within the ILC dialogue, reliance on this transnational *care commodity* became a central rationale for the setting of domestic-work standards.

New Grounds for Transnational Women's Movements

The global domestic worker movement has charted new ground for international women's movements.[69] Over the past thirty years, women's transnational organizing has largely been influenced by the UN World Conferences on Women. The "Platforms for Action" that have emerged from these formative conferences have focused mainly on individual rights—such as education, health, and freedom from violence. Campaigns for global women's empowerment have focused mainly on gaining access to clean water, maternal health, and the right to attend school. Microlending gained wide popularity as a means to spur the economic empowerment of women in developing countries. These campaigns often took a familiar form in their construction of the girls and women positioned to benefit from the actions of international development agencies.[70] Yet the formative conversations and projects on improving the conditions of women worldwide rarely focused on the collective rights of workers, nor the organizations established to obtain shared labor protections. In most instances, development discourse failed to engage women's labor movements. Thus, labor and development discourse rarely intersected. Similarly, unions and NGOs developed separate ideological and applied practices to improve the condition of women, even in an economic sense. Leading labor sociologist Mary Margaret Fonow remarked on the prevailing tension between the collective labor standards priorities of unions and human rights and development institutions' focus on individual rights.[71] While a redistribution of resources is central to both, their paths and priorities have rarely come together to strengthen the potential to redress women's inequality from a labor/economic position.

The global domestic workers' movement transcended this divide in its coordinated effort to link development and labor priorities. In doing so, it shifted the terms of engagement, as well as the forums for interaction. Here you have a collective group of women who came together under the auspices of an international institution to demand protections for a group of workers on the margins of the global economy. They brought to the fore the central concerns of development and global-policy institutions, such as poverty, migration, and education, yet their interest was in collective standards for all workers in the "submerged economy." In doing so, domestic workers used the language of the ILO to demand collective standards. For instance, IDWN President Myrtle Witbooi contended that the "10 points plan" familiar to the UN rarely "touched the women on the ground." When she considered the women in her union, she asked, "When is the 10 points going to work for us?" When leaders like Witbooi stood up to the ILO in these ways, they generated new forms of connection that tied collective labor standards to the rights focus of the UN's original institutional efforts on behalf of women. Furthermore, during domestic workers' engagement in the International

Labour Conferences, NGOs met outside UN spaces on a range of topics of concern. In the ILO, domestic worker organizations were admitted to the central arena of policymaking, bringing the "women on the ground" into the formal governing chamber. As feminist sociologist Gay Young points out, women's organizations must continually balance engagement with macro-institutions, such as the UN and the ILO, with preserving their own autonomy and collective capacity to resist mainstream structures of power.[72] They must work both in and outside institutions, and weigh the potential outcomes of affiliation and confrontation. Unlike any other global women's movement up to this time, domestic workers effectively walked this line in their acquisition of collective rights.

3

Getting "on the Map"

Global Policy as an Activist Stage

This is a moment to take in and to celebrate. Milestones like this are few and far between. It still makes me breathe deeply when I think about the significance of this moment. Perhaps it was unusual in the history of the ILO, but my experience there is captured by the image of row after row of women worker leaders from every region of the world, following the discussion in at least eight languages, working together to champion the dignity of domestic work on an international stage.
—Ai-jen Poo, National Domestic Workers Alliance

A little step for the ILO, a big step for humanity.
—Luc Demaret, International Labour Organization

At the helm of the ILO, Director-General Juan Somavía pinned his hopes for "fair globalization" on efforts to bring policy protections to the informal economy. A Chilean former professor of economics and development with over 20 years of experience in UN leadership posts, Somavía has focused his attention on peacemaking efforts, social and economic development, and justice. After 10 years in exile, in 1983 he returned to his home country to take an active role in restoring democracy in Chile after the Pinochet military dictatorship, serving as the president of the country's International Commission of the Democratic Coalition. His compatriots included Colombian writer Gabriel Garcia Márquez, with whom he prioritized the value of national and international democracy, contending that "the diffusion of the power, concentrated in the hands of commercial or bureaucratic interests, is a worldwide necessity. This is particularly crucial in third world countries dominated by repressive minority regimes."[1] Somavía carried these values to his leadership of the ILO. In his early term as director-general, he initiated the 2002 World Commission on the Social Dimension of Globalization—"the first official body to take a systematic look at the social impact of globalization."[2] A few years later, he introduced his signature ILO initiative on "decent work in the context of fair globalization."[3] His commitment to labor justice brought a human rights paradigm to the regulation of work. In 2000 Somavía set up the Bureau for Gender Equality, dedicated to bringing a gender perspective to ILO policymaking.

Domestic workers provided the ultimate test of Somavía's "decent work" initiative. As he stated in his 2010 opening address to the tripartite delegation on domestic work,

> the essence of the decent work agenda is that work is not just the cost of production. It is not just a market concept . . . for societies and for people, it's *human beings*. And consequently, it's a source of personal dignity, of family and household stability, of peace in the community, of even the way you judge the results of public and private policies.

Somavía's statement addresses two core values in line with the ILO mission. First, human beings are the central consideration in any social policy. Second, public policies on decent work can be measured by the extent to which they have a positive impact on peoples' lives. Somavía's life trajectory as a global political leader and engaged intellectual had fully prepared him to bring a human rights perspective to the challenge of global labor demands, migration, and the increased informality of work.

Domestic Labor as the Floor of Human Rights

According to the ILO's 1919 founding constitution, "Universal and lasting peace can be established only if it is based on social justice." As an institution, the ILO sets the bar for the conditions of human engagement that take place in the work context. To the ILO, workspaces are where the ideals of equality, justice, and human dignity play out. They are also where individuals experience one another, through the day-to-day, face-to-face relations of work. Thus, labor-standards regulation is essential for the just coexistence of human beings. In its efforts to establish policy that would reflect the ILO's larger mission to bring a human rights framework to work, the domestic worker negotiations sought to establish a "floor" of social protections for this sector.[4] As expressed in the negotiations, "To do justice requires a minimum standard."[5] In turning to domestic work, the ILO set out to provide a global foundation of ideals and practices that would be adaptable across national contexts. Advocates within this process sought to assure the widest coverage possible for this massive sector of the informal economy. By working through this standard-setting system, they aspired to "make the floor as high as possible."[6]

This first negotiation on international domestic work tapped into the "final frontier" of the ILO's reach and impact. In essence, the potential to regulate labor in private households placed the greatest challenge on the ILO's capacity to apply its larger standards of universal peace and justice to the "invisible" work that comprised one of the largest sectors of the global informal economy. Policymakers referred to this task as taking the ILO "back to basics" in its efforts to guarantee fair labor to those most marginalized. Key human rights concerns, such as the protection of child and migrant workers, had to be taken into account when regulating the most vulnerable forms of labor in the global economy. Thus, the ultimate expression of the tripartite dialogue centered on agreeing upon the terms of a human rights foundation for decent work in the expanding terrain of feminized transnational labor.

The fruits of development are borne on the backs of migrant laborers and the world's poor—the majority of whom are women of color. As unprotected, informal labor floods the global economy, international institutions must be held accountable for those who travel, live, and work outside the realms of citizenship protections. Somavía situated the ILO as the preeminent front-line organization for addressing the human costs of global development. Given the global economy's dependence on migrant domestic work, only an international organization could respond appropriately to the call for "decent work for all." In Somavía's words, domestic workers are in the most serious need of the ILO's direct response:

> As we have seen with the crisis, we have been able to respond quickly and profoundly in moments that are serious, and we have a more serious

moment today, with probably some of the most affected . . . the domestic workers today.[7]

Given that forms of child labor, trafficking, and contemporary slavery are the direct result of unregulated household labor, Somavía contended that the negotiations on domestic work are part of a larger organizational mission to provide protections for those most heavily exploited in the global system. As he put it, "The ILO is trying to avert a human disaster."[8] ILO standards are intended to inject a global value system into transnational capital, recognizing that unregulated labor has led to the exploitation of the world's most marginalized due to their dependence on this system for daily survival.

Somavía heralded the ILO, alone among UN agencies, as "a place where the heads of state and domestic workers can come raise their voice." As those previously deemed "invisible workers" journeyed to this historic site to influence global policymaking, the ILO space became a concrete expression of Somavía's vision for democracy and his commitment to social justice. In that spirit, he celebrated the wide grassroots activist participation that made Convention 189 the anchor of a global movement for domestic worker rights. When asked what the inclusion of domestic work meant to him personally, Somavía professed that "the ILO is open to the grassroots organizations, and it understands and recognizes that a series of domestic worker organizations do exist in the world, that they have struggled for a long time, and the ILO listened to them. That's the most important thing."[9] This moment built Somavía's legacy, as the wide participation of civil society organizations and domestic workers themselves realized a policymaking process inclusive of those "on the ground."

When the negotiations began in 2010, the director-general sat down to meet with domestic worker representatives, receive their *Platform of Demands*, and recognize the origins of a global movement that grew through the ILO. He opened his conversation with the IDWN with the following words:

I'm very happy to receive you, and there are other networks as well, but the fact is that this organization has brought this issue to the fore . . . and I have been behind this for some time now, and finally, now this is happen-

ing, *this is happening*. So my message to you today is to continue to organize, continue organizing, expanding, use the national laws . . . I think it
is also very important that there was an acknowledgment that your voices
were necessary, and that many of you are part of official delegations, some
countries and another, some trade unions, et cetera, but the fact is that
you are here, and in different ways, you are present. So, again, I think that
also is very important. We have to continue, we have to get the discussion
going, we have to get as much going the notion of a robust strong instrument on this matter so that it can be reached.[10]

As he went on to encourage a space for social movements within the
ILO, Somavía emboldened domestic workers by recognizing their collective strength.

Thank you so much for being here, thank you for the struggle. You, more
than anybody else, know how difficult it is, and how, I won't go into the
detail, I won't explain to you what you know much better than me. But
just to know that, understand that, I think this is one of the most valuable
struggles that we have today, and I just want to be behind the ideas and
behind you and the organization that you are putting together.[11]

This public and symbolic recognition by Somavía aligned domestic
workers with his ideological commitments to global consciousness and
democratic social progress. When reporters asked if he had supported
the movement of domestic workers since its origin, he replied, "Deeply,
deeply. Always, always," as IDWN leaders around him clapped and
cheered, "Bravo!"[12]

The global recognition of domestic worker rights created a network
of coalitions and related UN agencies that joined the policy conversation
to emphasize the gender dimension of household labor, and the possibility of enacting policy that would redress historic imbalances. Michelle
Bachelet served as the executive director of UN Women between her
two terms as president of Chile. A physician and long-term advocate for
women's rights, she participated in the final sessions of the second year
of debates to support the convention and link it to the larger struggle
of eradicating the existing "decent work deficit" that disproportionately
affects women. In the US domestic worker campaign, a similar notion

of a "compassion deficit" drove activists' efforts to confront resistance to effective care-work policy in the global capitalist system.[13] Betsey McGee, an employer advocate who represented the New York–based Hand in Hand: The Domestic Employers Network at the 2011 ILO negotiations, asserted that global policy standards would result in changes at the national and household levels. As she contended, "A sound ILO convention on domestic workers will serve as a North Star, *l'étoile du nord*, for employers as well as advocates, opinion shapers, and policymakers." McGee identified the convention as one of the most pressing tasks of the ILO's charge to set and monitor global standards. Her position underscores an ILO ethos that policy sets the stage for social change. The daunting task of regulating the informal and migrant economy necessitated global standards that travel across nation-states.

The immediate task of setting policies and procedures for domestic workers charged those employer, government, and worker delegates as "custodians of a legacy" to establish moral human rights practices for those previously left in "no man's land." US government delegate Robert Shepard remarked, "This is something that nobody had wanted to deal with for a very long time."[14] Given this long-standing avoidance of regulating work in homes, advocates pleaded for a convention as a means to "set right a historic oversight."[15] Domestic workers themselves used this rhetoric of historic accountability as a framing stance in their demand for a convention. Narbada Chhetri, representative leader of the National Domestic Workers Alliance in the United States, contended, "As this is the 100th year for labor organization, and within the 100 years, our domestic worker sisters, they are not recognized as workers . . . This is the 21st century, and we are still demanding to be treated as human beings."[16] Thus, the ushering in of the first convention on domestic work symbolized a recognition of the impact of historic injustice, a pivotal moment in the ILO's role in setting the floor for human rights, and a groundbreaking practice of including "those who toil every day"[17] in the process of policymaking itself.

Key leaders in the ILO spoke of these emblematic components of the domestic worker policy process. Martin Oelz, the ILO legal specialist who played a central role in drafting the convention since its inception in 2008 and served as the legal adviser in both years of negotiations, remarked on the extraordinary nature of this process. He called it an example in microcosm of a potential global society in which "people that are from the bottom of the social hierarchy" come together with heads of state to craft the forms of a mutually agreeable and more equitable existence.[18] Oelz recognized domestic workers and indigenous peoples as two particularly marginalized groups who could "come to the ILO with their claims and say there is some injustice going on and we need to remedy it."[19] By bringing social protections to those formerly excluded informal economy workers, and including domestic workers in the process itself, the ILO lived out a core expression of its own highest standards: to create policies as instruments of larger human rights and social justice ideals. Oelz captured the larger intentions of the ILO mission, as he named "the ILO as a forum for the international community to collectively address . . . injustice."[20] In identifying its applied work of setting policies as the "human rights floor," Oelz referred to the ILO's social dialogue vision to reach consensus: "We do our collective work not only legally, but also mentally and philosophically."[21] Thus, within every technical dimension of the policymaking process, Oelz saw human rights values as guiding the ILO endeavor.

Louise McDonough, lead government representative from Australia, contended that the process of applying these principles to the negotiation of a domestic worker policy truly "gets to the heart of the ILO."[22] With domestic workers themselves in the room, an added layer of accountability seeped into every dimension of the process—from the conceptualization of the legal commitments of the policy to an analysis of its application to the real lives of the workers the IDWN represented. As one leading government delegate put it, "This seminal event for the ILO must be as significant for domestic workers."[23] Thus, the presence of domestic workers both reflected the ILO's visionary social dialogue process and ensured the policy's relevance to these workers in improving the conditions of their daily lives.

Making ILO Policy: People, Places, and Purpose

Tripartitism characterizes every aspect of the ILO's policymaking process. In the tripartite framework, each of the three social partners (workers, governments, and employers) enjoys equal participation. Figure 3.1 depicts this organizational framework. In policy negotiations,

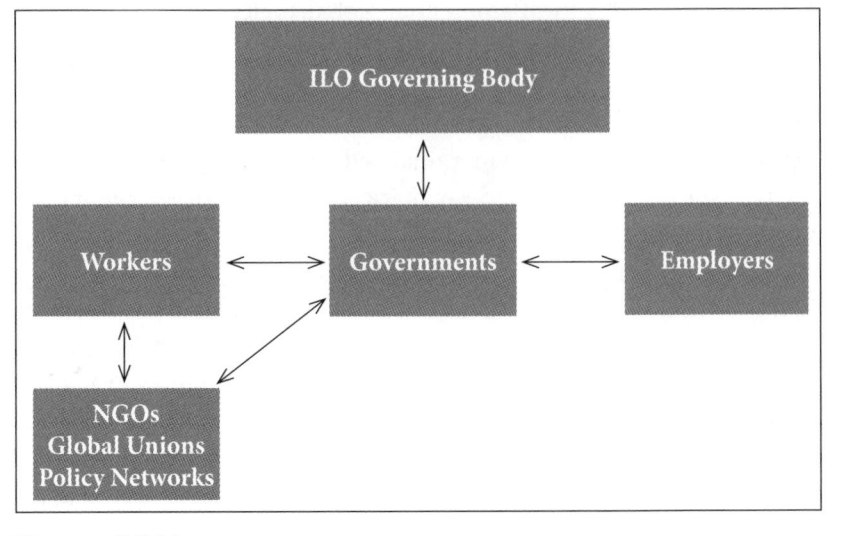

Figure 3.1. ILO Map

workers, government delegates, and employers talk across lines as social partners, while civil society observer groups lobby governments to represent their causes.[24] The tripartite model allows for equitable and mutually respectful engagement. Questions of where domestic workers fit into this process—and how they can influence global policymaking—parallel larger inquiries about how domestic workers are included in society more widely.

As the ILO negotiations addressed the technical dimensions of policymaking, positioning domestic workers within the organizational structure promised inclusivity for "actual workers." Ai-jen Poo, leader of the US domestic workers' movement, shared her observations of the ILC negotiations, and their inclusion of civil-society activists, in the following message to supporters of the National Domestic Workers Alliance.

I want to give you a sense of how the development of this kind of labor convention works. Picture a very large room, divided in three sections. One section is for workers' groups, and it is made up of representatives from the largest trade union federations in each country. Sitting behind them, there are representatives from NGOs representing domestic workers. Opposite them sits the employers' group, which is made up of delegates from the largest representative employer organization in each country. In between the workers' and employers' groups sit two to three representatives from every government member of the United Nations. Together, these three sections comprise the Committee on Domestic Work. The committee meets daily for several weeks in order to review, amend, and eventually vote on every article in the convention and every paragraph in the recommendation . . . The process involves long and generally diplomatic discussion about the controversial issues that domestic workers face every day in our work: how to count hours of work for domestic workers, particularly for live-in workers; whether standby time (that is, when workers are expected to be immediately available in case they are needed at any moment—whether it's to comfort a crying child who woke up in the middle of the night or to help ease the pain of a sick family member in the early morning) should be counted as official work hours; how migrant workers should be treated by employers and by governments; what it means to treat this workforce equally, or—in the technical terminology—"not less favorably" than other workers. Basically, these dialogues focus on developing a basic standard for what the conditions and terms of work for domestic workers should be . . . This is a challenging process for any industry, but there are particular challenges when it comes to domestic work. For most of human history, the work of domestic workers has been invisible, hidden away in private homes. It has been considered "natural" women's work, and it has been taken for granted. During this International Labor Organization process, governments, national trade union federations, and employer groups from every nation have had to sit down and think deeply about domestic work as real work that—like any other type of work—deserves basic labor standards. These delegates have had to reflect on the daily realities of domestic work and work to develop an instrument that can be ratified into law in nations around the world so that they can finally recognize and protect domestic workers.[25]

From her position as an NGO leader and observer to the negotiations, Poo captured the key issues that engaged representatives throughout the process. In the case of Convention 189, the presence of domestic workers themselves—bolstered by the strong national histories of activism and the transnational coalition that developed through the negotiations—served as one of the most powerful forces in the development of policy.

The presence of domestic worker representatives required delegates to "think deeply" about the "daily realities"[26] of women subjected to unregulated labor conditions stemming from the global outsourcing of domestic and care labor.

The presence of domestic workers also influenced the narratives of government delegates, who were placed in a position of direct accountability to the women who would be most affected by policy. In his 2011 opening statement for the US government, Robert Shepard reminded delegates of the potential for the ILO's signature social dialogue to make history.

> I would hope that two weeks from now we can depart for home knowing that we have taken part in a great and historic breakthrough, a moment when the three social partners, working together, determined that the time had come to afford domestic workers effective protections no less favorable than those provided for workers generally . . . And then all the members of this committee of this 100th Conference can return home knowing that we have opened the door to equal treatment and justice for domestic workers.[27]

This US government statement reflects the ideological principles of the ILO. First, Shepard references a guiding priority for *all* workers to enjoy equal access to basic conditions of employment. His emphasis on "protections no less favorable" than other sectors speaks to the ILO's central value of equitable standards and relevant application across fields. Second, he mentions the realities of workers' lives after decision makers "depart for home." The statement stresses that the outcome of the social dialogue process will be most accurately measured by the ILO's ability to ensure justice and labor protections for domestic workers beyond the Geneva debates. Such calls place a moral responsibility on the delegates, as part of the ILO vision to create policies that will assure social justice as a vital path to the larger UN value of "universal and lasting peace."

The overarching ideals of democratic engagement among worker, employer, and government social partners structure each stage of the policy process—from formation to adoption. To consider a new policy, the ILO begins with an extensive research and consultation process among member delegates. The domestic-work agenda followed the standard ILO "double-discussion" procedure, which affords two years of public negotiations on topics proposed for a convention or recommendation. In 2008, when the Governing Body decided to place domestic work on the 2010–11 agenda, it prepared a law and practice report and distributed a questionnaire to solicit comments on the national context of domestic work in all 187 ILO member states.[28] This first stage of data gathering for the policy negotiations resulted in 103 country responses, 46 of which involved consultation with workers' and employers' organizations.[29] These data informed the ILO's *Report IV(2): Decent Work for Domestic Workers*, which included a set of proposed conclusions that served as a draft for the 2010 discussions on the potential to establish both a convention and a set of recommendations for this sector. During the ILC social dialogue process, government, worker, and employer delegates introduce a series of amendments to the draft policy document. These proposed amendments are discussed one by one, as the employer and worker spokespersons express their willingness to compromise on particular measures. Government delegates weigh in on each amendment, thereby indicating the relative level of support and strength of potential policy revisions. As these negotiations are underway, advisory boards, advocates, and research experts supply representatives with data and arguments in support of their particular stance. In the case of the domestic work policy negotiations, the IDWN support network amplified this role with extensive research on national contexts, training domestic workers themselves to lobby representatives on particular amendments and assuring expertise at each stage of both rounds of negotiations. Through these informed discussions on each amendment, the social partners largely determine the formative structure of the emerging policy.

At the end of the first year of negotiations, the ILO releases a policy draft, which allows countries to garner input from relevant national bodies for the year between ILC negotiations. During this time, worker and employer bodies also have the opportunity to lobby governments and generate wider support for their positions on the instrument. During this stage in the process, the ILO proposed policy becomes an active working document in the political contexts of member countries. When the ILC reconvenes in its second year, key member-state constituents have already contributed to the document, thereby solidifying government positions on the eventual vote. In the second year of discussions, the document is revised into a final instrument to be put to a vote on the last day of the session. These processes of constituent input, draft revision, and public dialogue culminate in the adoption of a standard-setting instrument only if a two-thirds majority is reached on the final vote. The realization of any ILO convention thus follows years of prior political stage-setting, research, and negotiation.

Even though the domestic worker convention followed the ILO rules like any other proposed policy, it was unique in the way this victory for women, workers, and migrants was achieved. Dan Gallin spoke of the synergies that accounted for this formerly unimaginable event.

> Five years ago nobody would've imagined that domestic workers would become a major issue in the ILO or in the international labor movement. And I think it couldn't have happened as some aggregate, some total of national initiatives. It had to be an overarching camp.[30]

With global unions, international NGOs, research organizations, and a range of government allies standing behind the convention, the domestic worker victory story unfolded as a call to reconsider the human costs accompanying the world's dependence on migrant labor. Building on this discussion of the ILO's tripartite philosophy and processes, we turn now to the three ILO parties and the individuals who brought their expressions to life within the domestic worker debates. A look behind this pinnacle global policy reveals a seemingly serendipitous collision of forces—individuals, global politics, and institutional paths—at exactly the right moment in the organizational life of the ILO.

Workers

As the official voice of the workers' group, Halimah Yacob, a member of Parliament in the Singapore government, channeled the domestic worker cause. In her role as vice chairperson for the Committee on Domestic Workers, Yacob articulated the workers' stance through a grounded knowledge of the ILO tripartite system, well-honed argumentation skills, and true empathy for the domestic workers under consideration. An experienced negotiator, she used her history as a leader in the labor movement to legitimize the voice of workers, linking domestic workers' perspective to a wider labor and gender movement, strengthening her demands for rights. She opened the 2010 delegation meetings by rallying workers around this cause: "We all have a vision, and we will achieve that vision. We lead in solidarity together, in one heart, in one direction." Yacob's united front included her own vital link to the domestic worker cause. At the end of the 2010 negotiations, she acknowledged, "My mother was a domestic worker," bolstering her legitimacy as the spokeswoman for this cause, while testifying to delegates' own reliance upon paid household labor. Barbro Budin, IUF gender adviser and a leader of the domestic workers' movement, summarized the 2010 negotiations by highlighting Yacob's role: "[She] was brilliant all along. Her strong commitment and extraordinary advocacy of the domestic worker issues is certainly due to the fact that her own mother was a domestic worker."[31] For the domestic workers' network, Yacob became a pivotal figure in carrying their plight into the complex negotiation procedures of ILO policymaking. Even though she held high positions of power in her own national government, Yacob remained deeply connected to working-class struggles and gender-labor justice. As the voice of the workers' group, she clearly articulated domestic workers' needs and demands. As she disclosed, "When you spend three decades of your life in the labor movement, it is very difficult to forget who you are." Yacob combined her official position as an ILO spokesperson with her grounded place in labor activism to promote the power of a people's movement. Her public statements often referenced the social justice foundations of the domestic worker movement.

> I will call all of us the movement of the people. The movement of the people is a tremendous movement. That is where the real power resides. It doesn't reside in organizations, agencies, but it is a movement of the people. Power resides in the movement of the people, whether it is the trade unions, whether it is NGOs, that is where power resides. But with power comes tremendous responsibility, and that is something also we must not forget.

In her eyes, the domestic worker convention symbolized a larger moral turn toward justice, evident in the swelling number of voices behind

Figure 3.2. Halimah Yacob. Photo by Camilo Rubiano.

this policy process. Through the labor rights she promoted on behalf of domestic workers, Yacob repeatedly invoked a moral responsibility for global justice. Her persuasiveness stemmed from her repeated capacity to link the convention to a larger ideological position on workers' rights that has been central to the global labor movement since its inception. Yacob was not just fighting for Convention 189; she wanted this policy to turn the global tide toward justice and accountability to the world's poor, migrants, child workers, and women.

Yacob's role as the spearhead of domestic worker rights proved crucial to the final policy victory. Yet, in the critical second year of negotiations, her activities within her own government called into question her ability to serve as the workers' spokesperson. Just before the 2011 ILC, Yacob became Singapore's minister for youth and development, a promotion that could have compromised her vice chair role. The ILO executive body ultimately approved her leadership in the second year, a decision that bolstered the workers' group and ensured its continuity. Yacob assured the Domestic Workers Committee that her involvement in this vital labor struggle remained a priority. At the close of the 2011 Domestic

Worker Committee meetings, she shared her thoughts on first learning of her appointment to a ministerial position.

> When I was informed, the first question that I asked, honestly, this is the first question that I asked, I said that I have one last work to do as a trade unionist . . . I said this last piece of work is the domestic workers convention and recommendation . . . and I was told yes I can do it. And that was a source of greatest satisfaction for me.

Yacob's commitment to the worker's group during this second ILC is illustrative of the dedication of key individuals in shaping this historic ILO convention.

Throughout both negotiations, Yacob immersed herself in acquiring the most recent data on domestic work to build her arguments on solid national contexts. While her ideological position and experience in the labor movement provided a strong foundation to argue for domestic workers' legitimate rights claims, Yacob's contemporary examples, research, and testimonials backed up her arguments and elicited empathy for domestic workers. Among her core advisers were Myrtle Witbooi, president of the IDWN, a representative of the IUF-WIEGO alliance, and leaders from the ILO Workers Bureau, providing strategy consultation, background research, and contextual information that maximized the impact of Yacob's public voice on behalf of the cause. In many instances, she presented data on how domestic-work regulations functioned in various countries, such as South Africa, Brazil, and Uruguay, building the case for ILO global standards. Yacob's team of advisers enabled her to draw relevant examples and persuasive arguments "on the spot" during the negotiations. While workers' group members were unable to speak on the floor, the data, case research, and grounded evidence provided to Yacob made their way into the negotiations, serving to bolster the position of the workers' group. Through her consultation with those closest to the ground, she successfully humanized domestic work in both her public dialogues and her extensive meetings behind the scenes with government leaders, employer delegates, and ILO officials.

In her identity as a Muslim Singaporean woman MP with strong ties to the labor movement, Yacob brought delegates that much closer to the less fortunate women who "after all, work every day in our homes." As she positioned herself alongside the workers' movement, Yacob repeatedly injected into the policy negotiations the human component, by reminding participants that the convention discussions centered on the assurance of rights for "someone's mother, daughter, wife, [or] sister."[32] While the ILO structure grants only one official spokesperson role for the workers, Yacob continually positioned herself as the voice of a larger movement of women workers.

> It is in the interest of the more than 100 million domestic workers, who have waited for this convention. It is a great travesty if we do not do our work. The statistics we have mentioned are not just figures, they are *human beings*. We have a duty to protect. We have failed so far.

Embedded within this humanizing approach were Yacob's distinct feminist constructions of domestic workers as vulnerable, unprotected, and extremely marginalized. By asking delegates to vote with empathy for "poor, vulnerable domestic workers" who had been denied protections for centuries, Yacob posited a moral responsibility for the ILO to assure rights for "the lives of the 100 million domestic workers out there who depend on all of us to come up with an instrument."[33] She spoke of the high prevalence of migrants and young girls in the global profession, pointing to high levels of exploitation, physical and emotional violence, and sexual harassment as all the more reason for the ILO to take responsibility for this formerly forgotten sector.

By positioning herself in close proximity to domestic workers, Yacob amplified their moral and ethical demands for inclusion, protection, and universal rights. In her public rhetoric, she called upon the ILO's role as a social legislator to suggest that "moral and ethical" considerations be brought to the discussion of "contemporary forms of slavery"[34] that comprise global domestic labor. In ILO language, Yacob argued that domestic labor serves as a measure of our core and "floor" human value system. In other words, the treatment of those deemed most vulnerable in society reflects a culture's social value systems more accurately than any other indicator. Yacob used these moral-consciousness "hooks" to remind delegates of their responsibility to "set right a historic oversight."[35] Even though she acknowledged that the assurance of protections would be difficult to establish in the private household, Yacob continually relied upon notions of social justice and the "right" path in assuring protection through international standards. In strengthening the workers' case, she repeatedly pointed to the worldwide prevalence of domestic work to show how the issues in question transcend nations. She drew a contrast between the widespread reliance on paid household labor and the "lack of national standards of protection for domestic workers in most states." Whereas the employers' group resisted the establishment of universal standards, Yacob repeatedly put forth the position that the assurance of social protection should not be left to market forces. She made the case that it was the ILO's social justice mission to take responsibility for the establishment of work standards. By reminding governments that they were debating the lives of "workers who are after all your citizens,"[36] Yacob made it impossible for delegates to avoid this formerly forgotten and invisible sector of women's labor. She repeatedly contended that the ILO had a moral responsibility to assure decent work for those who have been left in "no man's land" within the global economy. After all, she proclaimed, "the whole world is looking at us."

The combination of Yacob's sharp negotiating skills, rooted connection to the domestic worker cause, distinct social position, and ability to call upon the moral consciousness of voting delegates enabled her to play a vital role in presenting the workers' position. Her leadership successfully integrated the domestic workers' plight within the formal negotiations of the policy arena. Domestic worker leaders repeatedly thanked "Halimah, who fought like a lion, not only for us but for all of the domestic workers in the world."[37] She garnered overwhelming confidence and support from the IDWN, who relied upon her skills to carry their voice. Narbada Chhetri of the US National Domestic Workers Alliance told Yacob, "You are the hero of the world for marginalized and voiceless people."[38] She took a central position in the convention negotiations, as she interfaced with the leaders of global capitalism representing the employers' body. Yacob continually referenced the longer-term goal of implementing ILO standards to underscore the need for producing actual change in the lives of those who suffer within the global capital system. As she closed the 2011 meeting, Yacob expressed this underlying motivation in her role as the voice of the workers' group. "I hope that together we will be able to improve the lot of working people, especially the domestic workers."[39] Yacob's authenticity and political influence emanated from her ability to speak from a position of authority as a leader connected to those women "on the ground." Ultimately, her casting as the "voice of" domestic workers demonstrated an evolution in the global political stage—where movements from the ground shape the policy-making institutions that articulate our global human value systems.

Yacob's role partially compensated for the gender politics of the workers' group representation on the floor. Her ability to carry the voices of domestic workers, as a leading woman in politics and the ILO system, gave these workers powerful representation, when national trade unions so often excluded them. The workers' delegation in the tripartite is comprised of leaders of larger unions and worker bodies from each of the member states. In the case of domestic work, male leaders of national unions comprised the majority of worker delegations for member states. Rather than domestic worker organizations serving as official worker representatives in these discussions, predominantly male leaders of large unions held the official positions, allowing them to "speak for" the interests of this feminized sector. Thus, representation at the ILO surfaced long-standing gender politics. As in many country contexts, mainstream unions have traditionally viewed domestic workers' unionization as "nonviable," largely because of their existence as a "scattered workforce" where the collection of membership fees is inconsistent with the employment models of factories and public institutions. At the global union level, however, the IUF countered this traditional gender-labor political struggle by integrating domestic worker rights in their larger ideological struggle for labor protections. The ILO focus on domestic work also reflected some shifts in national unions' willingness to include domestic workers in their leadership representation. For example, by the second year of negotiations, 16 domestic workers had been invited into the official delegations, largely the result of the political will backing this particular convention. Yet the domestic workers' real strength in terms of representation came from Yacob's position as their core spokesperson. Because of the distinct structure that emerged through domestic workers' presence at the ILC table, the official workers' group representative relied upon the IDWN and its ally civil society groups more closely than the national labor delegations to provide testimonials, arguments, research, and perspectives throughout the negotiations. The prominent role played by civil society in the ILO negotiations allowed for recognition of the multiple forms of work central to the global informal economy.

Employers

The ILO's tripartite negotiation structure attempts to simulate the actual relations of employment in the social dialogue process. Yet domestic workers could not speak in an official worker capacity because they came into the dialogue primarily as civil society observers. At the same time, the designated employer group represented wider employer bodies, rather than those who set the terms of household-labor relations. Thus, a complex configuration of representative bodies—a few steps removed from the circumstances of domestic work—sorted out the terms of global policy. The employer constituent within the tripartite is comprised of members of the International Organisation of Employers, which represents "the worldwide business community in international labor and social policy forums across the multilateral system."[40] The ILO frames employer organizations as representatives of "a key asset in any society: its enterprises." In the negotiations on domestic work, organizations like the United States Council for International Business, the All India Organisation of Employers, and the Australian Chamber of Commerce and Industry represented employers' interests in the household-labor industry. These groups, however, deal with standard labor practices in public organizations. Representatives' experience with the conditions of paid domestic work was limited to their own or others' private households, rather than industry management—a point that became a trump card for the workers and civil society representatives in their demand for policy protections. Furthermore, the employer group is comprised predominantly of legal advisers representing large employer organizations. Their emphasis is on the legal dimensions of the procedural processes central to ILO standing orders. Therefore, in the case of the ILO domestic worker convention, the face-off between workers and employers was somewhat mitigated, as national union representatives negotiated with public employer bodies within the tripartite process.

Over the course of the two years of ILC negotiations, leaders of the employer group forwarded an agenda that favored less regulation of domestic work. Given the interests of international businesses, the employer body generally frowned upon standardizing labor in the private household—and its requisite heightened costs and responsibilities for employer enforcement. In the opening 2010 ILC negotiations, the employer group took a strong stance against a convention on domestic work. Kamran Rahman, Yacob's counterpart as vice chairperson for the employer group, and a member of the Bangledesh Employers Federation, voiced resistance to what this group perceived as unrealistic rights-based standards. Rahman criticized the ILO's advancement of an idealistic policy that had no realistic capacity for implementation. On behalf of employers, he posited, "Our vision is not a flagship text which will never be ratified, but a tool that will be used."[41] The issue of implementation drove the employer position throughout the negotiations; in his opening remarks Rahman proclaimed, "I remind governments that they must support and uphold this convention." Rather than the "one size fits all" parameters of a convention, Rahman asserted that "flexibility is essential" and thereby expressed employers' preference to support a less binding set of recommendations for this "special category" of workers. While workers positioned household and care labor as a global industry that supports the flow of capital, Rahman repeatedly framed this work as outside the realm of standardization, and therefore beyond the purview of an ILO convention. As he repeatedly contended, "Hard cases make bad law."[42] Rahman asserted that the ILO would lose credibility if it passed a well-meaning instrument that could not be accompanied by tangible implementation measures. In later public statements during the negotiations, he suggested that some governments present in the ILC would ultimately refuse to ratify a convention, despite their public support during the negotiations. Thus, one of the employer strategies involved discrediting a potential convention on household labor by framing it as unlikely to be ratified.

In the opening ILC discussions, Rahman presented several employer arguments about why the regulation of domestic workers in the informal economy was unrealistic. First, he claimed the sheer number of workers in this field would overwhelm government regulating agencies. Even in remote locations, he claimed, "there could be hundreds of domestic workers skittering here and there."[43] Second, he argued that the diverse circumstances of domestic work made the enforcement of universal standards virtually impossible. In many countries, he stated, standards already exist. Thus, employers saw national legislative protections as the better vehicle for the creation and regulation of labor standards, rather than an ILO instrument. Third, as they referenced the state's requirement to uphold these standards, employers pointed to the difficulty of accessing household workspaces, given state protections of the private sphere. They asserted that states ratifying the policy under discussion would face an onus of responsibility in reporting to the ILO, emphasizing the burden on states of implementation.

This capitalist-oriented group also pointed to the potential negative effects of attempts to regulate the informal economy. They suggested that standardization would force employers to cut costs by seeking other forms of immigrant labor, thereby increasing worker vulnerability overall. As Rahman posited, in efforts to uphold this position in the public negotiations, "regulatory measures ignoring ground-level realities can cause further movement to informal labor."[44] The employer position viewed the regulation of domestic work as having deleterious effects on national and international economies as well as workers. Employers thus called for more investigation and a postponement of convention negotiations.

Even though the employers attempted technical maneuvers to delay the process, the conclusion of the 2010 ILC pointed to overwhelming support for the convention. Domestic workers and ally groups lobbied governments throughout the months between both meetings, while the ILO refined the proposed convention with input from the 2010 negotiations. Most noticeably, between these two sessions, Paul Mackay, an employer delegate from New Zealand, replaced Rahman as vice-chair for the group. Even though he shared many of the reservations voiced by his predecessor, Mackay conceded employers' willingness to recognize wider support for global standards on domestic work. Given the overwhelming "political will" of this convention, Mackay acknowledged that the pendulum had clearly swung in favor of an international policy for domestic workers. He opened the session with a statement in support of the tripartite process and a willingess to endorse Convention 189, given its majority backing.

> We argued last year, if you recall, for a recommendation alone. This year we said, given the will of everybody else, we will work with the structure that everybody else wants to work with, and we have got that now,

> we have got a convention and we have got a recommendation. There are
> some issues with it, and one of the things that we have said is that we will
> evaluate the outcomes on its own merits.

This statement showed the employers to be "good sports" in a game
that clearly favored their ideological opponents. Even though they were
resigned to the likelihood that the convention would pass, throughout
the second year of discussions Mackay held to the employers' core con-
victions around implementation as the defining measure of a policy
instrument's worth and purpose. After stating at the end of the 2011 discussions that employers would have "absolutely no reason whatsoever to
vote against either of these instruments," Mackay remarked on employers' consistent focus on questions of implementation. Employer support
for the majority consensus came with an emphasis on being "'pragmatic
and realistic,' the two words I said we would be all the way through."[45] In
his concluding speech, just before the convention vote, Mackay assured
the house that any employer abstentions would not be "for the purpose
of being negative," rather, "they are recognizing the real and practical
difficulties dealing with the very complex issues we have dealt with in
the last two weeks." The employer position also reflected the clear gains
achieved by the workers in this particular negotiation. In the face of
strong political will for the workers' cause, the employer group eventually accepted that its position would not prevail. The perception that the
convention's viability would depend on implementation made it easier
for them to vote for the instrument, allowing for a critique of the policy
in terms of its *application* across contexts.

Evolving employer support for the convention was achieved through
the tripartite model. Mackay's successful leadership of this group issued
from the public perception of him as a "reasonable employer" with a
realistic and flexible perspective.[46] Furthermore, employers used the
tripartite process to elicit support for their positions. In the first year
of negotiations, Rahman's resistance to paid household labor as worthy
of regulations led workers to see him as an embodiment of the power
differentials they experienced in the domestic-work context. They saw
this resistance as parallelling the oppressions they experienced in the
private household. As one leader stated at the 2010 IDWN's celebration,
"The way they treated us in there is the way they treat us at home."[47]

Yet Mackay put a different face on employer representation. This "good employer" recognized the needs of domestic workers and expressed a willingness to stand behind them. As employer representatives began to acknowledge domestic work as "real work," they opened a window onto the possibility of recognizing and protecting those workers who "make all other work possible."[48]

Governments

Government partners in the tripartite enjoy the opportunity to debate policy terms openly from the floor. Each member state appoints four voting government representatives for the committees that form the content of each ILC's focus. Unlike the worker and employer groups, whose perspectives are represented through the vice chairperson delegate, any government representative can speak throughout the policy debates. The 187 member state government leaders make public statements based upon the collective position of their country delegation, comprised of worker and employer bodies. They engage in the social dialogue process via official statements (typically at the opening and closing of the ILC), proposing policy revisions to documents in the making, debating suggested amendments, and offering statements in response to the worker and employer chairpersons' commentary. Their input forms the content of the debates, as particular countries espouse a range of values, conflicts, bloc affiliations, and perspectives relative to the larger geopolitical landscape.

Governments engaged in the debates on domestic work expressed two main areas of interest. First, they sought regulations that would provide guidelines for dealing with the proliferation of migrant domestic workers, and their requisite obligation to protect workers who travel across national boundaries. Robert Shepard, US Department of Labor representative, prioritized governments' needs to "have clear guidelines on what is reasonable and what is not"[49] in dealing with workers in the informal economy. In his public statement, he spoke of a shared interest in developing ethical standards across countries. "I believe that all of us in this room today support the core principles of equal treatment under the law for domestic workers. I do not believe I heard anyone from any party argue differently."[50] Shepard admitted that the potential application of the instrument fueled differences among governments. "We do recognize, however, that there is some disagreement about how these principles are addressed in the instrument and how they may be applied."[51] Governments, like employers, thus often had to balance ideological support for the rights of domestic workers and the complexities of policy implementation. Through government delegates' input, the negotiations revealed larger geopolitical relationships, as well as regional affiliations that clearly influenced the debates. Before the formal vote, the likelihood of a convention's passing can be gauged by the extent to which governments speak in favor of the proposed document. In the 2010 debates, employers tested the waters of convention support by making an unprecedented decision to call a vote that would reveal government positions on the central point in the draft policy: whether an ILO instrument should take form as a convention or a set of recommendations. Even though the house showed wide support for the ILO's development of standards for domestic labor, the difference between a convention and a set of recommendations held central importance for employers, who resisted the binding nature of a convention as international law. Rather, they saw a set of recommendations on domestic work as the most relevant instrument to set a precedent for regulation and fair working conditions, without requiring states to ratify a formal convention. When called to a vote, of the 108 government member states present, 62 voted against an amendment that would have changed the proposed instrument from a convention to a set of recommendations, 14 voted for the amendment, and 4 abstained (33 were not present for the vote).[52] The outcome ultimately revealed the longer-term direction of the negotiations, as employers and governments oriented their arguments to the ILO's efforts to draft a binding convention.

Not only did this barometer of respective government positions identify effective lobbying avenues for both employer and worker constituents, it also reflected a predominant pattern of government member states' alignment in both geographic and ideological blocs. The Arab states' position against a convention, for example, demonstrated evident shared political perspectives within a region that draws heavily upon the importation of domestic workers from Asia. Members of the European Union expressed similar shared concerns that a protective convention would increase migration—a topic of vital contemporary importance to the continent. Furthermore, power structures at play in the larger geopolitical sphere became evident in the persuasive capacities of particular member states' relative positions within the ILC negotiations. The United States and Australia, for example, aligned in positing shared perspectives to support a convention. As a power bloc within both the ILO and the larger world political system, these government positions held strong persuasive capacities because they set the tone for the level of support the convention garnered. Through their strong public statements, government leaders positioned South Africa and Brazil as two of the strongest advocates for the convention. In both cases, their extensive national legislative frameworks for domestic work served as a solid foundation for their promotion of global rights. These government positions also reflected core alignment with the workers' delegations, and the domestic worker leaders from those countries who joined the negotiations through the IDWN. In other cases, some bilateral relationships based upon various countries' relationships to domestic work played out within the negotiations. A prominent sending country, the Philippines, and its counterpart receiving Arab countries, took similar positions on the convention, while assuring that the particularities of their own reliance on third-party employment agencies would be protected throughout any standard-setting process. Similarly, the geopolitics of Europe emerged clearly in the discussions, as member countries' stances on the convention mirrored the range of positions on migration within Europe, with more progressive countries, such as France and Finland, coming out in favor of protections, while countries with stronger opposition to migration, such as the Netherlands and the UK, posed repeated resistance to the "promises that would come with such a convention." Here we see how the public forums of the International Labour Organization's tripartite procedures provide a lens into wider global political relations and positions on governments' and international institutions' appropriate roles in addressing concerns about the informal economy, gender inequality, and forced migration within the context of globalization.

Finally, some countries made obvious maneuvers to align with domestic worker representatives in the room. They referenced both the tripartite process and its outcome as core sources of the ILO function to reach an expression of world standards of human dignity and harmonious policy creation. In the close of the 2011 discussions, Australian government leader Louise McDonough captured this larger ideal through her voice as a central advocate for the convention.

> Australia has been very proud to have been part of the development of this historic convention and recommendation for domestic workers—we pay tribute to every one of the 100 million domestic workers across the world, including those who have attended these proceedings, we recognize domestic workers for the professional workers that they are, and we commend them for having the courage to stand up and seek this recognition as legitimate workers, often against all odds. Australia hopes this new international standard will make a strong and substantive difference to the quality of your working lives and mark a new era of decent work for domestic workers.

Within this statement, we see governments' ability to take strong stances on the ideals held within policy creation. In these particular negotiations on domestic work, however, governments enjoyed a new opportunity to align their positions in support of the "actual workers" sitting in the room. In doing so, they amplified their own positions, while garnering a wider moral stance for rights, dignity, and equality. Government representatives also provided the most available conduit for domestic workers to build alliances and lobby support for the convention. In the ILO space, domestic workers enacted their rights as citizens of their respective countries, while forming the relations of accountability that would carry their activism and lobbying beyond the policy negotiations.

Activist Observers: The Domestic Work Machinery

I believe that the fact that we're here in Switzerland, at the ILO, this is one of the first steps that we are taking. I know we're going to advance something. The fact that we even have a presence here is already a big step. I think nobody expected a thing like this.
—Aida Moreno, founding member of CONLACTRAHO, Chile

The transnational domestic worker network set about shining a light on those who suffer acutely under the existing global system. As the IDWN brought a strong activist participation to the debates, it stretched the role and impact of the observer group further than that during any former policymaking process in the ILO's history. Civil society representatives engaged with the institution to break with tradition in recognizing the participation of the workers who would be directly impacted by the policy under discussion. As she compared her many years of experience at the ILC, global union leader Barbro Budin recognized, "Rarely have there been so many true representatives of the workers that are concerned with a convention, sitting here, negotiating. This is exceptional! They have never seen so many real workers sitting in the UN."[53] While the ILO's core adherence to tripartitism relegates civil society participants to an observer status, domestic worker representatives and their allies skillfully expanded the reach of this insider/outsider role. These debates placed global unions, domestic worker organizations, and NGOs in a position of influence because of the particular legitimacy they held in their close proximity to the daily grind of paid household labor. In this context, domestic workers themselves made the imagined floor of human rights concrete as they formed a visual embodiment of policy's impact. Even though they entered the negotiations as observers, the influence and accountability they conveyed to all voting delegates reconfigured the social and political landscape of the ILO. This domestic worker machinery—comprised of worker organizations and their transnational allies—thus held real power in the determination of international labor policy.

In forming this first global policy, domestic worker representatives engaged directly with the most powerful international heads of state.

> MYRTLE WITBOOI, IDWN PRESIDENT: "I think that the ILO has
> never seen something like this before."
> JUAN SOMAVÍA, ILO DIRECTOR-GENERAL: "I can assure you."[54]

This exchange between the leader of the ILO and the president of the IDWN epitomizes the turn in ideological and practical engagement between the ILO and workers on the ground. In the public representation of the transnational domestic workers' movement, Witbooi's rhetorical strategy embodied her 30 years as a domestic worker activist in South Africa, combined with her savvy knowledge of political systems. Her public speeches pierced power structures—combining union-mobilization rally calls dating to her time in the apartheid struggle, unchallengeable testimonials from her "white apron"[55] days as a domestic worker, and an unwavering demand that the elites she was addressing recognize their moral accountability to "the women in the backyard."

In her signature style, she passionately defended the legitimacy of workers' demand for rights. "Listening to the speakers, there is such a lot of emotion going through me." Describing "domestic worker rights as women's rights," she framed Convention 189 as a moral fight.

> We are going to win! We are going to keep you all accountable. We are going to say if we fail, you have failed us. Since the beginning of slavery, we were there . . . We say a simple message, support us in our struggle. The whole world is on a fever and now we need to give antibiotics. And this is where we are going to get it. We only want what the other workers got. When we go into battle, we put up our arm, and we are at war. I *thank* you.[56]

Witbooi became the face of a worldwide movement, as she positioned delegates as a core source of accountability and moral persuasion. Throughout the negotiations, her compelling presence attracted global media coverage and garnered widespread support for creation of a "policy for the people." She convincingly connected state-level victories to the promise of transnational solidarity. At the opening 2010 ILC meetings, she took every public stage possible to expand the political strength of the domestic workers' network and bolster the influence of civil society within the negotiations. Here, she addresses the Gender Commission of the ILO during the first days of the meetings:

> You clearly have seen the unity among the domestic workers here today. And I want to say to you today, we are going to make history at the ILO. As you all know, trade unions always have a slogan that says "An injury to one is an injury to all." Now we have come here to make that slogan a reality. We want everybody here at the ILO, all women, all labor, all business, all governments, to know that we have come to claim what is our

rights. To be recognized as human beings, to give us back our dignity as women, because after all the women that we work for sometimes don't see us as a woman. And we want to restore that dignity and that pride, and when we walk away from this conference . . . we want to walk away with that thought, with our government and a convention. But on our own, we can't do it. We need you, and we need everybody at the ILO. So from tomorrow, the ILO is going to see something that has *never happened before*. On every corner and on every street, you are going to see domestic workers popping up. So be prepared. We are taking the ILO *by storm* from tomorrow.

It was the IDWN's strategic vision to be seen and heard as a persuasive collective force. Not only did domestic workers show up—they faced off with employers, governments, and even representative labor leaders by holding them accountable to their own household-employment practices. This activist "storm" forced the ILO to recognize its most direct constituents and carve out a space for their participation in the process.

Each tripartite partner recalibrated its engagement in relation to domestic workers' active presence throughout the process. For employers, the domestic worker–NGO alliance represented a fourth-party bias that disrupted the tripartite structure of the ILO. Employers pointed to this perceived compromise in voicing their initial opposition to a convention. A disrupted process, in their eyes, could not be tolerated to justify any policy outcome.[57] Yet in the second year of negotiations, the bolstered strength of domestic workers and their groundswell backing led employers to reframe their opposition into qualified support.

The labor group unanimously stood behind domestic workers in terms of ideology. Yet the women activists within the IDWN called their comrade delegates to task by interrogating their representation in the voting delegation. Even though the workers' group supported more regulation and protection, in national unions, women in the informal economy have often been considered "nonviable" and difficult to organize. While domestic workers sat on the fringes of national unions in their own countries, their active presence in the ILO and growing support from international allies put pressure upon national unions to rethink their exclusion of the very workers whose protections were being debated in these sessions. Hong Kong activist Ip Pui Yu positioned the IDWN prominently to "show to other workers the presence of domestic workers." As she directly appealed, "I call upon the trade union brothers and sisters. We really need to bring more domestic workers here to the ILC."[58] These statements pushed for a reconfigured ILC worker representation that would reflect the composition of work in the "real world" and integrate women into the trade union leadership structures.

For governments, the ILC negotiations made public their own relationship to "such workers who are after all your citizens."[59] Australia, a leading advocate for the convention, took on this challenge by emphasizing the central relationship between global policy and national practice. As the Australian government pointed out, "If national law and practice was already adequate, this house would not have been charged with developing international instruments for domestic workers across the world who largely work in the informal economy." National governments had to consider both the construction of the policy and the practical level of implementation that would make the convention meaningful as a working set of laws and practices across locations. The Australian government went on to reinforce this priority by stating, "Our approach should not be that we can't ratify, but rather how can we ratify. Because if countries don't amend their laws to meet the international standard, the situation for domestic workers around the world will not change." These governmental statements often responded directly to domestic workers' persistent call for both advocacy in the creation of international standards and assurance of ongoing commitment through ratification.

Domestic workers' power to influence the ILC stemmed from three main sources. First, the "first time" status of workers in the ILO drew social and political capital to workers "on the ground." Second, their alignment with NGOs, unions, and policy organizations brought them global recognition. Third, domestic workers capitalized on the nature of their labor in the private household, and on delegates' personal dependence on such labor, in making their appeals for rights and accountability. Thus the "subjects" of policy were brought into the very process of debating, formalizing, and eventually attaining their own rights.

First Workers in 100 Sessions

This is the 100th conference of the ILO; I think things never-
theless happen for the first time.
—Frank Hoffer, International Labour Organization

Simply getting to the ILO marked an extraordinary victory for domestic workers in their quest for international recognition. Yet once in the
chambers of the largest international forum for labor policymaking, the
IDWN drew upon this wider recognition to demand a central place in
the ILO's efforts on domestic workers' behalf. Leading Latin American
activist Marcelina Bautista asserted, "In our experience, one aim is that
domestic workers should be the protagonists of their own rights."[60]
Recalling domestic workers' history of exclusion, she said, "We have previously been seen as part of people's private sphere, and now we want to
have a much more public role."[61] Severely isolated workers were coming
to a transnational arena for the first time. Shirley Pryce, president of the
Jamaican Household Workers delegation, spoke of her role as a voting
delegate to the ILO. "I was a domestic worker. I have been in the field
for over 20 years, and I was in a cage also, and I came out. And I am here
now working to enlighten others to come out of the cage also."[62] Media
attention focused on the symbolic significance of domestic workers sitting at the table with the world's political leaders. Lead international
reporter Isabel Garcia-Gill contextualized her coverage of the 100th ILC
by stating, "Seventy-five cooks, nannies, and household workers took
part in the negotiations and made their voices heard in the Palais des
Nations, with the same titles as experienced diplomats."[63] Thus, this
historic session of the ILO proved a turning point in the struggle surrounding the rights of women workers and migrants in the informal
economy.

Juan Somavía celebrated this moment by paying tribute to the extraordinary capacity of the ILO to bring domestic workers and heads
of states together at the same table, to negotiate the terms for the future
of labor. His 2010 opening statement to the Domestic Work Committee
framed this moment with a moral charge to protect the rights of the
world's most marginalized.

First of all, it is impressive to see this room, that there is so much interest. And I think this reflects the significance of the importance of the
work that you are doing. I'm also happy that in different ways, domestic
workers' activities are in fact present here in the room also, which I think
gives it an important capacity to come down to the reality of what you
are discussing today. What I wanted to do is simply to accompany you
for a moment, at this first stage of your debates. I honestly think that you
have in your hands the potential of a historic instrument, of that moment
in which you deal with the question that we know is out there, and we
haven't really dared to tackle it in honest dimensions. And that is what
you are going to do this year and next year, and what I want to say is to
stimulate you, really, to go as deep as possible in the common understanding that behind the discussions here, you know you have an enormous amount of people, in which what we are doing now generates hope.

Somavía's statement highlighted two critical aspects of the domestic
worker-activist story. By acknowledging that the ILO had not "dared to
tackle" this issue since its inception, the director-general recognized the
magnitude of this landmark policy as a means to acknowledge, integrate,
and generate hope for informal workers throughout the global economy.
Second, in his recognition of domestic workers' presence as a means to
come "down to the reality" of policy discussion, Somavía acknowledged
a critical turn in the ILO process, in which domestic workers and their
social partners would play a part in the policy discussions. Furthermore,
this inclusion of domestic workers changed the tone of the ILO from
one of exclusivity to one of representation. The real struggles of organizations on the ground would be visible. Outside the UN press room,
when the media asked Somavía about what he thought a domestic work
convention symbolized, he said,

I believe it's that the ILO is open to the grassroots organizations, and it
understands and recognizes that a series of domestic worker organizations do exist in the world that struggled for a long time, and the ILO
listened to them. That's the most important thing.

Thus, while domestic workers heralded a major "win" in the history of
the global struggle, they also brought accolades and global attention to

the ILO—shifting it from an iconic high-level Geneva policy forum to one willing to embrace one of the most challenging labor struggles in the existing global economic system. Employers, workers, and governments would come together for the first time with the aim of establishing a viable system where human rights would be assured in the wider context of "fair globalization."

United We Stand! Domestic Workers' Justice Network

Never forget that justice is what love looks like in public.
—Cornel West[64]

Throughout the ILCs, the civil society network demonstrated a united front, with a common purpose to support domestic workers. Maysoon Qara, leader of the women's movement in Jordan, described the unity and overarching kindness she felt within this larger effort in support of domestic worker rights.

> This is different, the spirit of the people who are sharing and the power that they have. They have a goal, and they insist to reach that goal. It is very nice to feel that. And they are warm for each other, they are like brothers and sisters. It's nice to meet such kind people like that, and they believe in what they want. It is very important to believe in what you want.[65]

By showing up, aligned and in large numbers, domestic workers forced ILO policymakers to take them seriously. At the same time, civil society observers voiced unity in their support for worker participation in the negotiations. Migrant Forum in Asia (MFA), one of the strongest NGO advocates, took the floor on several occasions to validate the importance of domestic workers in the ILC process.

> We emphasize the urgency of having domestic workers themselves centrally and critically involved in this process. Otherwise the ongoing position and marginalization of domestic workers will be reinforced. We recognize domestic workers who are with us today, who will be directly affected by what is done or not done in their name in the 99th session of the ILC. We stand in solidarity with the domestic workers who cannot be physically present

here, but who engage in the various national and regional partnerships. We assure their voices are heard and their demands for rights and recognitions are considered, recognized, respected, and protected.[66]

With its identification as a human rights monitor, MFA linked the recognition and legitimate involvement of domestic workers to a wider call for justice for marginalized workers. In essence, this organization positioned the ILO as a microcosm of larger societal relations, suggesting that what happens in dialogue and policy outcomes would parallel larger global structures and practices. If the ILO could include domestic workers as part of the policymaking process, NGOs contended, that process would set the example for a larger democratic shift in power relations and inclusive representation.

Along with a united body of civil society organizations, the IDWN bolstered its stance through key union leaders, some of whom sat inside the official workers' delegations. Florencia P. Cabatingan, executive board member of the Trade Union Congress of the Philippines, spoke of the central role of domestic workers in establishing the ILO as an exemplar of humane policymaking.

> They [domestic workers] are challenging the tripartite sectors in the ILO, who are considered instruments of change to prove our value for freedom and human rights. How we respond to the challenge would reflect our own values on how we look at freedom and human rights.[67]

This civil society network connected domestic workers' demands to a wider commitment to the eradication of contemporary slavery, migrant justice, and human rights. Thus the negotiation of domestic worker rights took on a global human rights cast. This policy held the potential to improve the conditions of the world's working poor, protect migrants, and set standards for a larger recognition of women's work in the private household. Spiritual leaders and faith-based organizations joined their voices to a cause that would hold the world closer to values of compassion and care for the poor. Sister Escaline Miranda, a Catholic nun and leader of the National Domestic Workers Movement in India, became involved in the negotiations and the related public demonstrations. Her

Figure 3.3. IDWN quilt

personal reflections on the policymaking process reveal the spiritual foundation of her activist framework.

> Every human being has a right to live. And every human being must give that respect to others, especially the domestic workers. So far they are considered like slaves. Today I feel that we have a different path and different hopes. Our dream will be one day fulfilled.[68]

At a public demonstration in downtown Geneva, standing before a large quilt in the form of an apron that included the handprints of 3,500 Asian domestic workers, Sister Escaline pronounced that these hopes and values would be expressed in the attainment of global law.

> If we have a real law, so that domestic work will be work that gives dignity, and the work will get dignity, and the workers also will be treated as a human being, and a human life, a better life. This work will come to be like any other work. This gives us hope that in any other country they will join together and stitch the apron that means that we are all locked together.

Thus with faith-based leaders, international NGOs, grassroots organizations, global unions, and policy organizations behind them, domestic worker representatives had behind them a much larger global movement for the rights of women, workers, children, and migrants. Their call: to hear the voices of those on the front lines of the injustices that had emerged with globalization and its inherent reliance upon unregulated, feminized, migrant labor.

Bringing Justice Home—Policy as Prevailing Consciousness

Domestic workers' power in the ILO stemmed from a particular strategy they employed—to frame the guarantee of domestic worker rights as a moral responsibility for this largest global policy body. In her opening speech at the 2010 ILC, Vicky Kanyoka, worker representative for the Africa region, reminded the house that it held a responsibility to protect the world's most marginalized workers.

> On behalf of the International Domestic Workers Network and the millions of domestic workers who are watching your actions over these few weeks and are counting on you, we appeal to you all—governments, employers, and workers, men and women—to support us by agreeing to this vital and historic convention. Please read our *Platform of Demands* and see if you cannot agree that what we are asking is both right and just, and that it can be done. And, by the way, do you have a domestic worker in your own home?[69]

Kanyoka's closing line shrewdly calls out policymakers, putting their own homes on the ILO's "decent work" agenda. Because so many government, employer, and worker delegates themselves employed domestic workers, the IDWN and its allies could challenge delegates about their own relationships to household labor. Rather than determining policy for workers "out there," domestic workers asked delegates to think of their own households as they considered the issues in front of them. If decision makers were not willing to protect the individuals in their personal employ, activists asked, how could they legitimately take part in the ILO process as an exemplar of its policies and underlying beliefs in worker rights?

The presence of domestic workers forced delegates to consider their own private lives as a measure of moral accountability, making it difficult to overlook this group and deny it protections. María Luisa Escorel de Moraes, government delegate from Brazil, spoke of the irony of delegates' opposition to the convention. "We are all employers in this sense, so why would they oppose this? I'm an employer, you're an employer, all of us are employers, right?"[70] Awareness of delegates' dependence upon household labor advantaged domestic workers in their demands for protections, adding a bit of theater to the dynamic between the IDWN and policymakers. On behalf of the workers, Myrtle Witbooi played a leading role in this performance, as she so often confronted delegates directly by bringing the realities of their own lives into the policymaking process. As she confidently posed, "We have built the economies of the world, by caring for your families. You can reward us by voting in favor of the convention."[71] It was evident that to vote against rights for the women who cleaned their own homes, cared for their children, and nourished their families would render the ILO hypocritical, elitist, and detached from the workers who were "the backbone of society."[72]

This issue of moral accountability was present in the larger discourse framing the domestic-work convention as an anchor for human rights and the protection of the world's "most vulnerable workers." The Brazilian delegates spoke of the responsibility to address a much wider human rights struggle.

> There are a great number of workers in this profession. In the 21st century, we need to fight for women's rights. The women and men in this convention cannot fail to vote for domestic worker rights around the world. If we do so, we will be failing the rights of women who go out and do this work. We are the enablers for others who are then free to go out and work. We have a great deal of hope from this conference.[73]

The closing report of the 2010 conference situated the ILO's efforts toward achieving a domestic worker policy within a larger moral context. It stated, "In adopting these conclusions, we have shown that we have the moral courage and conviction to do what is right." While the report went on to acknowledge that "we do not pretend that these conclusions alone and the convention and recommendations to be adopted next year will in themselves bring an end to the suffering of our domestic work,"[74] it continually pointed to the creation of this first global policy as a moral compass on human rights. As labor leader Dan Gallin stated, "With domestic workers, it's extremely easy to conquer the high ground and keep it. They're treated so badly. It truly is a moral issue."[75]

The IDWN represented "the 100 million domestic workers out there who depend on all of us to come up with an instrument."[76] As advocates repeatedly urged policymakers to consider how their "actions could change the positions of millions of domestic workers,"[77] a spotlight was placed on an international human rights crisis that leaves so many workers in the global economy without protections, rights, or recourse for their suffering. Given the pressing need for regulations to address this condition, the ILO discourse often referenced the opportunity tripartite members now had to make a real difference in the lives of the "world's most vulnerable workers."

The IDWN in particular asked delegates to look "deep in your heart and conscience"[78] in considering the women workers behind this policy formation. Vicky Kanyoka opened her public statements at the first negotiations with a call for delegates to engage with empathy. "I ask you to imagine yourselves in such situations. How would you feel?" Representatives of the US National Domestic Workers Alliance appealed to delegates to support the convention, contending, "We know you have a heart."[79] Domestic workers' policy demands thus often accompanied calls for moral accountability. Through voters' abilities to act "from their hearts," leading US domestic worker activist Guillermina Castellanos assured, "We have a chance to correct this injustice and to leave a legacy to our children, showing that women's work is valuable, just like any other work."[80] Voting members were continually reminded of their dependence on household labor in assuring a high quality of life for their families, and of their responsibility to domestic workers, whose future, and whose children's future, depended on the outcome of the labor negotiations.

Institutional Revolution: The Activist-Policy Edge

Domestic workers realized this historic policy victory by working on the activist edge of the ILO institution. They played by the rules while pushing the boundaries to bring social change to a rule-laden policy arena. To get to Convention 189, domestic workers drew on activist strategies to build ties, influence decision makers, and bolster their demands. They interfaced with the ILO as both an ally and a bastion of traditional power. While working within the system, their unconventional politics of resistance often collided with the ILO's guiding ideologies and practices. Their activist stance within the staid policymaking arena raised tensions throughout the negotiation process. As domestic workers navigated the system, their relationships to people and processes demonstrated both accommodation and resistance.

Domestic worker activists knew the importance of building relationships with those in positions of power. In the negotiation of a convention, they needed allies with established links to the ILO to advocate for their cause. The institution's tripartite negotiation structure limited the extent to which officials could carry the torch for the plight of domestic workers. Yet two key figures within the ILO paved the way for domestic workers in the formal ILO process. Because of their knowledge of the system and their commitment to workers' voices, these leaders played a central role in opening the ILO to worker activists. Their support proved crucial during the formative conversations surrounding the consideration of a domestic worker convention.

Luc Demaret led the domestic worker portfolio within the Bureau for Workers' Activities (ACTRAV), the labor side of the ILO's tripartite organizational structure that put the domestic worker convention on the agenda. A former leader of the International Trade Union Confederation (ITUC), the central global union partner to the ILO, Demaret sat down with IDWN leaders to discuss how their needs could take form in ILO policy. As the lead internal advocate, he then prepared the first domestic worker document for consideration in the ILO's Governing Body. His goal: to "sensitize the ILO from the inside."[81] Like the IDWN strategy, from within the workers' side of the negotiations, Demaret could draw upon the sector's history of exploitation to make stronger claims for a convention. Through public dialogue on domestic work, he claimed, "you can speak to the heart of people."

Demaret rallied the players in his wider labor spheres by prioritizing the crisis of this growing category of workers and then positing the ILO as the only organization capable of responding to their distinct needs.

He showed how historically, at both national and international levels, domestic workers were a "favorite category of workers to be excluded." This placed a moral responsibility on the ILO to fulfill its mission to protect *all workers* by addressing this historic injustice. Demaret put this institutional responsibility into the language of rights to legitimize domestic work standards as part of the ILO's mandate.

> The fundamental objective is to give these workers back their dignity, to transform an exploitative relationship into a legal relationship. The principal issue that motivated the ILO to take action was the realization that tens of millions of people are excluded from any form of recognition and protection and that exclusion means exploitation. Exclusion is the root of all the problems faced by domestic workers, notably the very negative image they have in our societies. Legal recognition would give them the means to achieve their emancipation and restore their dignity.[82]

From this perspective, global standards would move domestic workers "from a world of exploitation to one of dignity." Demaret repeatedly contended that domestic workers' demands would be met by an ILO policy. "An international convention can make a difference. That is what domestic workers are asking for. This isn't theory, it is a tool for real change."[83] Demaret's position at the helm of the domestic worker agenda made him the workers' liaison to governments, employers, and global unions. To achieve a convention, he would need wide support among the various players. At the same time, domestic workers placed a great deal of hope and trust in Demaret's ability to represent their cause within the ILO. He was both a power figure and a comrade. As they acknowledged, "Luc has come with us a long way."[84]

Demaret's solidarity with the plight of workers is grounded in a genuine empathy for those who make a living by cooking, cleaning, and caring for others: His own mother, sister, and sister-in-laws were domestic workers in Belgium. This personal history gave Demaret an appreciation for the profession that guided his policy work. After the final negotiations, Demaret claimed he had learned more from the domestic workers' campaign than from any other part of his career. Just before his retirement, Demaret shared that his greatest professional satisfaction came from contributing to the ILO's negotiations of domestic worker rights.

Figure 3.4. Luc Demaret. Photo by Camilo Rubiano.

"To think that you can contribute to something that will remain for people. What more do you want?"

Demaret's role as a bridge builder across the tripartite, coupled with his long-standing history of leadership in the ITUC, placed him in an ideal position to carry the flag for domestic workers. Part diplomat, part ILO expert, and prevailing union comrade at his core, Demaret became a key figure in advancing the domestic worker convention. His ties to domestic workers expanded throughout the negotiations via the efforts of his colleague, Claire Hobden. An activist with dual Swiss-US citizenship, granddaughter of an ILO official, and former National Domestic Workers Alliance staff member, Hobden's home office, Bureau for Workers' Activities, loaned her to Demaret's central team to facilitate ACTRAV's work on the convention. Her experience with domestic worker organizing and advocacy, along with her grounded connections to leaders within the IDWN, infused another layer of trust, authenticity, and advocacy into Demaret's leadership. While they spoke for domestic workers within the sessions, their input stemmed from the direct experiences of the IDWN representatives. They built a consultation team for Halimah Yacob, to provide her with the most persuasive arguments on the lived experiences of domestic workers. The structure of this leadership included Myrtle Witbooi, who was the voice of domestic workers and allowed for the inclusion of this civil society group in the central workers' team. Witbooi brought the IDWN perspective directly to the

Figure 3.5. Claire Hobden and Ai-jen Poo

ILO representatives, who would speak on behalf of domestic workers. This process issued from Demaret's commitment to working inclusively. Even though they could not speak in the formal sessions, the advisory group provided a forum in which domestic workers could voice their concerns to the central workers' body, allowing domestic workers to build relationships at the center of the ILO.

Once the ILO decided to place domestic work on the 2010 agenda, then director of the Conditions of Work and Employment Programme, Manuela Tomei, became the point person for domestic workers in the convention process. She led the extensive process of establishing background research, surveying governments, and assuring that the discussions followed ILO procedures, championing the institutional capacity to embrace the informal economy through the practice of social dialogue. It was her job, then, to mainstream this sector and align it with other ILO policy discussions. As domestic workers celebrated their victories along the way, Juan Somavía stated, "The person you need to thank is Manuela Tomei! Viva Manuela Tomei!" The ILO's institutional ethos centers on documentation, and the production of extensive reports that allow for thorough review by member states. Once the ILO's Governing Body decided to place domestic workers on the 2010 agenda as a "double discussion" for a possible convention with recommendations, Tomei pulled together a central team of experts, including legal scholar Adelle Blackett and ILO legal adviser Martin Oelz to build the foundational research and report documents that would lend the necessary credence and legitimacy in the ILO's heavily formalized structure. Alongside these experts, she created the foundational report on the status of domestic worker rights. This exhaustive ILO document, *Report IV(1): Decent Work for Domestic Workers*, summarized the "specificity of domestic work in the contemporary global economy," surveyed all existing national and international laws, and overviewed the existing organizations of domestic workers worldwide to set the stage for discussions on international standards.[85] The comprehensive nature of this report aided governments in responding to the closing questionnaire, which asked for member-state input that would inform the first discussions at the 2010 ILC. The questionnaire had the highest rate of response of all such surveys in the previous 15 years, according to Tomei. Through her efforts to document domestic work globally and spearhead the ILO process, Tomei gained the respect and attention of domestic workers, who saw her as both an executive of the ILO, a sister, and an ally. Her international reach, with fluency in Spanish, English, French, and Italian, a graduate degree in sociology from the University of Turin, and close professional focus on issues of poverty, economic rights, pay equity, and indigenous populations, won her wide-ranging respect. From the beginning, domestic worker representatives found their place in the ILO through vital ties to this symbolic ILO ally, as a "way in" to the larger organization.

Tomei's role required a tripartite approach that engaged all social partners in the domestic worker convention process. She walked this line with sophistication, as she shaped the dialogue and institutional processes in ways that resonated with workers, employers, and governments. For example, in outlining the main issues of a prospective domestic-work policy, Tomei pointed to global-economy shifts that made domestic work a growing sector with potential for job generation that would be "good for business" if regulated through proper employment channels. She praised the efforts of some governments for their existing regulatory mechanisms, while calling for innovative thinking to respond to the millions of workers at the margins of the global economy.

In all of her efforts, Tomei framed domestic work as "an essential part of our lives" and "critical for life outside of our household to function,"[86] emphasizing the importance of domestic work to all parties, not just the domestic worker representatives in the room. In reminding delegates of their own reliance upon domestic labor, she raised the issue of moral accountability. As she stated, "We are all employers of domestic workers."[87] Throughout the convention process, Tomei gave critical support to domestic workers. Even though in her ILO role she had to remain neutral, IDWN delegates were grateful for the solidarity they shared with this feminist-leaning diplomat, or *femocrat*.[88]

These two key ILO figures provided the most direct bridges between domestic workers and a complex policymaking institution. Demaret and Tomei's efforts within the ILO were crucial, as they headed the two bodies most directly responsible for the consideration of a domestic worker convention. Yet their status as ILO officials, adherent to the tripartite model, limited the extent to which these players could be public allies of domestic worker advocates.

For this role, a series of international NGOs, faith-based organizations, and policy institutes aligned with the IDWN in an advocacy role throughout the convention negotiations. As an aligned force, they brought a new level of engagement to civil society participation within the ILO. With the domestic worker discussions, these allies walked a fine line between activism and accommodation, as discussed in chapter 6. When NGOs and the IDWN entered the policymaking world of the ILO, they encountered a formal bureaucracy with entrenched procedural rules. A clash was inevitable—mainly with respect to forms of process and participation.

Behaving

The ILO's policymaking process conforms to a detailed set of rules and procedures that ensure the efficiency of the negotiations and the equitable engagement of all social partners. The rules of order define participation according to the task at hand, the roles of parties, and the hierarchies that oversee negotiations. With two years of preparations in place, domestic workers entered the ILO process aware of the rules of order that would govern the formal dialogue. They sat in the observer role, deferred to the appropriate representational leaders during the formal sessions, and closely followed the rules surrounding civil society input. Yet part of the strategy of domestic worker representatives was to put a human face on domestic work. And they came to this forum energized by the prospect of finally receiving international recognition. At times, their clapping, cheering, and overt expressions of enthusiasm led to public reprimands, which had the effect of reinforcing their outsider status.

Again and again, ILO official delegates told domestic worker representatives to "behave." Their activist responses would not be welcome within the hallowed halls of ILO policymaking. Lourdes Trasmonte, chair of the Committee on Domestic Work in 2010, scolded the civil society organizations for their frequent outbursts. "We do not allow clapping here. We are still starting. Please refrain from clapping and showing your emotion."[89] For Shirley Pryce, the first official domestic worker voting delegate, this was one of the key memories of her participation in the ILO.

> As the first negotiations got underway we expressed our enthusiasm or disappointment at things said during the discussions, with claps and cheers, or sighs and groans. This caused the Chair of the Committee to issue a warning that this was against official procedure. We continued to watch, in silence, but still making our presence felt.[90]

Domestic workers repeatedly referenced this moment, when the stifling of their voices symbolized the larger power struggles they faced: "The way they treated us in there, is the way they treat us at home."[91] In their eyes, it was akin to being forced to "swallow our emotions" in their day-to-day experience as household laborers.

As a response to this power dynamic, domestic workers used song to find strength in their collective history of struggle. While they tempered their expressions of emotion within the formal sessions, they broke into song, and often dance, as soon as the gavel closed a session. Shirley Pryce recalled how song gave her colleagues strength and endurance.

Between sessions, as the Delegates were leaving for meal breaks or at the end of the day, we would break out into singing and clapping and cheering. Sharing songs also gave us spirit and motivation to keep going through the long, formal sessions.[92]

As chapter 5 discusses, such emotional responses emboldened domestic workers within the policymaking process. As they realized empowerment in these acts of resistance, however, they collided with the ILO's rules of order.

For employers, "disruptive" expressions on the part of domestic workers and civil society organizations became grounds to question the policy process and express resistance to the convention. They contended that in a legitimate tripartite process, they would "avoid being disturbed by NGOs."[93] In the view of some delegates, domestic workers' inability or unwillingness to follow the rules delegitimized their claims. Yet for others, like US government leader Robert Shepard, these disruptions represented growing pains, as the ILO gradually opened to the presence of NGOs. At the same time, domestic workers and other civil society organizations continued to orient to the ILO and learn its complex rules. As Shepard contended, "I don't think NGOs are used to the ILO."[94] Ultimately, the domestic worker convention became a space where expressions of "enthusiasm," and the policing of same, represented the evolution of the ILO's more inclusive policymaking processes.

For domestic workers, emotional expression became a marker of their place within the ILO. As IDWN leaders recounted their experiences from 2010 to 2011, they pointed to their expressive nature as a key component in forging an identity within the ILO. By demonstrating a capacity to "be disciplined,"[95] domestic workers expressed their ability to work within the policy realm. Yet self-expression continued to characterize their distinctive presence in the ILO. As Myrtle Witbooi steered the IDWN to its second year in the negotiations, she emphasized the importance of workers' emotional stance in making their case.

We can assure you that next year, we will be back here, and the ILO is going to experience even something much greater than what it has been this last year. And we are going to appeal . . . [to the ILO] to let us show our emotions next year.

In 2011, she professed that, unlike in 2010, when "we were very quiet because we said we were going to be disciplined," on the day of the convention vote she assured, "You will just hear our shouting and screaming here."[96] Affective performance became a vital tool for domestic workers in bolstering their stance, demanding the moral accountability of delegates, and pushing the boundaries of the ILO. Chapter 5 takes a closer look at the coalition strategies employed by domestic workers and their ally organizations in achieving their policy victory.

Summary

This is the ILO at its best.
—Manuela Tomei[97]

Convention 189 marked a shift in how the ILO accommodated workers, civil society, and activists. By "bringing social justice to those who are lacking it" through a "robust convention,"[98] the ILO reinforced its commitment to building a social floor of protections for those who had long labored without the benefit of legal protections. Domestic workers held high hopes for how a convention would change their lives for the better.

> These international instruments will truly break new ground. They will take a huge step forward in human history to combat the exploitation, abuse, and lack of respect endured by many of the world's domestic workers. Some of us work in conditions of forced labour or slavery, with no respect for our rights as fellow human beings. Others may work for relatively good employers. But all of us are in a sector of the world's workforce that has been overlooked and ignored for far too long. Almost everywhere we do not enjoy the full rights and legal protection that other workers do. . . . It is an injustice that has lasted too long.[99]

To redress this injustice through policy work, the ILO expanded its tripartite dialogue to include domestic worker representatives in the process of determining a common set of standards. Most prominently, the institution had to find space for civil society, when domestic worker representatives and ally NGOs showed up in numbers often larger than the UN venues could accommodate.

The consideration of domestic worker rights required new negotiations of voice. While workers themselves could not speak on their own behalf, the IDWN found channels to make their voices heard, through activist maneuvers, the infusion of expertise, and the strategic use of allies in the NGO network. When the formal procedures allowed for civil society input, domestic worker representatives took to the stage and used the language of the ILO to advocate for their own rights. As Vicky Kanyoka's 2010 opening speech professed, "We hope that an ILO convention will stop this race to the bottom and will help us to achieve decent work and a decent life."[100] As domestic workers took a prominent place in the negotiations, employers and governments had to account for their own positions directly—recognizing that while they represented official bodies they also employed domestic workers in their personal lives. At the same time, the groundswell of support behind the convention on the part of NGOs tipped the power balance in favor of the workers' group. The ILO space and convention negotiations became the site of a larger mobilization for global human rights, not only for domestic workers, but for migrant workers and informal workers throughout the world.

While the tripartite structure remains the binding framework of this organization, the questions and challenges raised by those who may be most impacted by global policy in their daily lives forced this historic institution to look at how to actually establish "floor values" of labor for this massive and previously unrecognized sector of the informal economy. Even given the constraints of the ILO organizational structure, they moved the convention agenda forward on moral grounds. Only through their physical presence could they hold policymakers directly accountable. For example, Myrtle Witbooi's statement places delegates in a global system that benefits from the exploitation of domestic workers and calls ILO leaders to take responsibility by establishing the first set of global rights for household labor: "We have built the economies of the world, by caring for your families. You can reward us by voting in favor of the convention." This engaged the international community's capacity and willingness to recognize the feminized, outsourced migrant labor that "makes the world go round."[101] The ILO drew from these ethical grounds to promote the convention as a groundbreaking global policy and a necessary turn toward new forms of human rights and labor recognition worldwide. As the 2010 ILC report stressed, "In adopting these conclusions, we have shown that we have the moral courage and conviction to do what is right." Only with domestic workers in the room could delegates be as closely in touch with the realities and outcomes of the ILO's capacity to do right, in policy and practice.

As the ILO debates developed, they expanded to accommodate the larger consideration of "how the convention is brought within the discourse of civil society." Domestic workers continually demanded a "convention with teeth" that would move beyond paper into tangible practice. Through their eyes, this ILO policy symbolized the largest attempt to redress centuries of exploitation and set in place new standards of recognition, respect, and dignity for domestic workers. The particular contexts of workers' lives, their historical exclusion, and the global dependence on paid household work demanded of the ILO the articulation of a global ethics of accountability. Juan Somavía framed the policy as a way to redefine the value of domestic work. "We have to get as much of the good practices in, now, but maybe we have to go beyond good practices, because good practices represent the prevailing consciousness." Thus, the creation of policy shapes practices enforced as part of a larger social code of conduct. These standards have the potential of effecting a shift in how society values care workers at the macro level and (ideally) at the micro level as well. Even if such a shift is slight, or gradual, it holds out the promise of a better and more humane world.

4

"First to Work; Last to Sleep"

Central Policy Debates

Employers give orders. We must work. No holiday. Every day work. No schooling. No good food. No good rooms. Child domestic workers are sleeping in doghouses. No light. No wind. Some sleep. Another is caring. Many abuses. Many daughters . . . We want to solve the problem together, internationally and nationally.
—Narbada Chhetri, National Domestic Workers Alliance

We get up to work before sunrise.
Work in home at the door's behind.
We've made the comfort in your home.
Why our work's never recognized?
—Korean domestic workers' song

At the age of seven, Sonu Danuwar Chaudhary began her career as a domestic worker in Nepal's southern Jhapa region to pay off the debt of her father's 13-day death ritual. It took her three years to cover these costs, yet her first employer insisted that she continue to work full-time. She recollected, "After my father died . . . I ran away from that house and never stepped there ever again. Then I came to Kathmandu." At age 12, Sonu sought better employment, leaving her own family behind. As the middle child in a caste ascribed to live-in domestic work, she had not yet met her older siblings, as they had assumed jobs as servants at similarly early ages. "I learned I have an elder brother and sister only after I grew up," she explained. "I never knew them. They left to work when we were very small and we never saw them while growing up and sometimes they were not allowed to come home during Dashain [family gathering festival] so it never registered." In a family of seven remaining children, all are domestic workers. Sonu's departure from school and relocation to the city reflected the limited options dictated by her caste standing and her life trajectory as a live-in domestic worker. As she recounted, her transition to a brand-new family in Nepal's capital was traumatic.

> When I came here first, I came in a car with a brother of the mother of the house. It was my first time in the bus. I remember I had a coke for the first time and I cried that it burnt my throat. I came here, I was made to shower and was asked to mop the floor. I started crying in the passage. I felt like where am I, as I had never been away from my house. I mean I had not traveled out of Dhulabari and when I came here, all were new faces.

Sonu worked for a big family; the head of household had two wives, many siblings, and three generations under one roof. In the beginning, her employers were strict, yet after many advocacy visits from the General Federation of Nepalese Trade Unions (GEFONT) and the Children and Women in Social Services and Human Rights (CWISH), Sonu's employers agreed to allow her to attend school for three hours per day. In her efforts to become literate, she met other child domestic workers with whom she shared a common bond. Sonu was able to continue her schooling even as she performed her domestic duties. She recollected,

> I knew nothing. Also I knew no alphabets. But the teacher taught and she gave Nepali alphabets and numbers as homework. I don't remember all but she started with writing. After I came home, I kept looking at alphabets while preparing tea or doing anything. The didi [older sister] of the house, who died of uterus cancer, she used to hold my hands and help me write and speak up. Within a week I left everyone in my class behind. That didi used to teach me until very late at night. All the time she would ask me to read. Even in the cooking place, she pasted alphabets for me to read while working. I looked at them while doing all work. In my mind I was like I must read and read.

In her late teens, Sonu practiced writing via Facebook, where over a period of five years she met and courted her future husband, never seeing him face-to-face. After her marriage, Sonu's husband returned to work in the Middle East. Besides their "love come arrange" relationship, their life circumstances as migrant service workers served as a bond. She continued her education and enrolled in college, studying English and sociology, with the intention of mobilizing domestic workers in her country.

In 2010, based upon her work as a leader in GEFONT and her acquired literacy and study of English, Sonu traveled to Geneva to take part in the ILO policy negotiations. She carried the torch for domestic workers' empowerment, as a former child worker from one of the poorest countries in the world. During the 2010 protests, she demanded domestic worker rights using her own story as a rallying cry for compassion and justice. Sonu returned to Geneva in 2011, and now holds a major position in the global domestic workers' movement. When asked if she wanted to have children of her own, she stated that she would not embark upon this life dream until her country put in place legislation to support domestic workers. As she expressed, "I am waiting on that bill before I have a baby."

The global policy that emerged from Convention 189 had to cover domestic workers like Sonu, as well as those involved in professional care work in countries far beyond Nepal. In the "nitty gritty" of the policy debate, the value systems, complexities, and struggles for fair labor protections reflected the key stakeholders representing governments, workers, and employers. Core dimensions of daily work formerly left to the whims of employers and their willingness (or lack thereof) to treat domestic workers fairly were now under scrutiny by a policymaking body. Director-General Juan Somavía launched the 2010 discussions by encouraging delegates to "go as deep as possible in the common understanding that behind the discussions here, you know you have an enormous amount of people, in which what we are doing now generates hope."[1]

This chapter breaks down Convention 189 into its most important and contested terms. At the heart of the debate was the pervasive challenge to construct a policy that is both universal and adaptable to diverse national contexts. The instrument needed to work across state contexts, yet not allow for so much flexibility as to be meaningless. Furthermore, the policy had to be approved by the very diverse parties in the

Figure 4.1. Sonu Danuwar Chaudhary

tripartite—with the interests of labor, capital, and governments invested in realizing concrete work standards for this formerly excluded group. In the larger struggle for domestic workers' rights, many of the articles that appeared in the final policy instrument had to confront overarching ideologies and deeply embedded histories that created a wider context for what Jo Becker, lead advocate for Human Rights Watch, called the "protection deficit."[2]

From Slaves to Workers

So long as entrance into domestic service involves a loss of all social standing and consideration, so long will domestic service be a social problem. The problem may vary in character with different countries and times, but there will always be some maladjustment in social relations when any considerable part of a population is required to get its support in a manner which the other part despises, or affects to despise.
—W. E. B. DuBois[3]

In making their case for an ILO convention on domestic labor, advocates laid the groundwork by situating domestic labor in the context of accepted occupations. Rather than servants, slaves, or maids, domestic workers claimed their profession as "real work," worthy of rights, standards of practice, and global protections. On the day they won the convention, IDWN leaders proclaimed, "Our dream became a reality, and we are free—Slaves no more, but workers!"[4] The strongest platform for access to rights came from this framing of domestic workers as "legitimate workers" deserving of the same protections as any other workers. This reenvisioning of domestic work dovetailed with a moral call for human rights for women employed in households worldwide. As activist Narbada Chhetri contended, "We don't want slavery and dehumanizing work. We want respect and rights, we are human beings." Describing the plight of domestic workers in the absence of national or international standards, Chhetri recounted, "Some domestic workers are not allowed to sleep on the bed! And this is the 21st century, and we are still demanding the right to be treated as a human being."[5] The ILO discussions surfaced deeply embedded histories of slavery and colonial servitude as the origins of domestic worker exclusion and abuse. At the same time, the organization's priority to set human rights standards provided a very public international space for new discussions that would redefine, and ideally revalue, domestic work.

To standardize domestic work required loosening individual employers' control over the employees in their private homes. The prevailing links to colonial constructions of "maids" and "house girls" came under scrutiny, as workers themselves called out this historic exploitation, while the consideration of standard global regulations elevated the status of domestic work as not only legitimate, but honorable, work. Fataou Raimi, a prominent domestic worker activist from Benin and the only male to join the IDWN for the ILO conversations, asserted, "Je ne suis pas un boy mais un travailleur!" (I am not a boy but a worker!)[6] Raimi found being called "boy" humiliating. For him, domestic labor is a "profession of dignity" that made him "proud." María Luisa Escorel de Moraes, a Brazilian government delegate, put the relationship between legal rights and employer attitudes into perspective.

Figure 4.2. Kenyan activist Evelyn Mulo and
Ip Pui Yu promote the value of domestic work.

Look, on one hand, you have the governments recognizing that it's important to establish fair legislation for this group of workers. Another
thing is the parts of society that may resist this due to outmoded, old
ways of thinking; it's not that they are bad people necessarily, it's just that
they are from the colonial era, things were always that way, so first, the
law needs to be established and then one must guarantee that the law
is followed, and, little by little, this minority, because I do think it is a
minority, will adapt itself to the new world, a new reality and new times.

In Escorel's view, the implementation of laws and global standards
would reinforce the vision she held for a more democratic household-
work environment.

May it be a relationship based on mutual respect, I've always said that, on
trust and mutual respect, reciprocal, that's how it needs to be. A person
works in a home, she needs to respect the home also, the home needs to

respect the worker and have respect and trust on both sides; that is the only way it can work.[7]

Yet the power relations that have defined this sector since the colonial period so often inhibit domestic workers' capacity to demand or fully access reciprocal levels of respect. Thus, the capacity of the law to provide a leveling instrument within the workspace becomes even more important in the case of domestic work and private households, where the labor relationship is traditionally one of disempowered workers and families privileged by class, race, caste, and ethnicity.

In the absence of laws and standards, domestic workers' ability to realize a fair labor existence hinges upon individual circumstances and "benevolent employers." While social reproduction work is fundamental to everyday existence, across the world domestic workers have been viewed as merely an "adjunct" to the workforce.[8] This pervasive perception served as a serious barrier to legal protections and discouraged standardization. As one domestic worker activist recollected:

> This work in our home has not been recognized; this is why the abuse has increased. There is no recognition of domestic workers as well. If you left the house with a little bit of dust, they will say that you did not do this well. But no one said you did things well. We must work on this as children from our own homes, because it has been a long time since we have been recognized. We need to work from the base so that we can continue the struggle for our rights.

Along with policy development, changes in attitudes within household relations are the real measure of progress toward addressing social injustices that devalue and marginalize domestic workers. To move from the prevailing mentalities that justify domestic work as informal labor not subject to regulation requires not only a formal recognition of standards, but a raising of social consciousness in the household. Children grow up with daily examples of stratification as they witness who cares for and cleans up after whom. The law alone cannot redo these powerful systems of socialization. Yet policy standards are an important starting point for potential change. With laws in place, standardization of this sector increases the likelihood that a recalibration of household social relations will follow. Thus, legal protections, social power relations, and everyday attitudes must all be addressed together in order for any meaningful change to occur.

Spelling Out Standards

Beginning from a virtual vacuum of standards, the domestic work negotiations set out to develop codes of conduct for dignified work. But how would policy ensure that domestic workers receive decent food, a proper place to sleep, fair wages, vacation time, and long-term security? Since domestic labor is performed in private households, often impeding on the private lives of domestic workers, this policy required a reach beyond the terms of most standard labor protections. At the same time, by regulating an outgrowth of colonial relations, in the nitty-gritty of policy negotiations much larger ideological struggles surfaced.

In the first conversations on this policy at the 2010 ILC, the following draft terms served as the foundation for the debates that eventually defined Convention 189. This condensed version conveys all of the points raised in the draft policy.[9] In its content and level of detail, the prevailing conditions of domestic work, and the serious gaps in its protections, come into sharp focus.

SUMMARY OF PROPOSED CONCLUSIONS
  A. Form of the instruments
    1. The ILC "should adopt standards concerning decent work for domestic workers."
    2. The form of the instruments will be a Convention, supplemented by a Recommendation.
  B. Definitions
    3. As the terms are used in these standards:
      (a) "'domestic work' should mean work performed within an employment relationship in or for a household or households;
      (b) 'domestic worker' should mean any person engaged in domestic work for remuneration."

C. Proposed conclusions with a view to a Convention

This section makes a case for the need for protections and sets specific terms to be included within the Convention. The most salient items include the following:

4. The Convention's preamble lays the foundation for the conditions of domestic work worldwide through the following key statements:

   (b) recognition that domestic work "continues to be undervalued and invisible and is mostly carried out by women, many of whom are migrants or members of historically disadvantaged communities, and therefore particularly vulnerable to abuses of basic human rights and to discrimination in respect of employment and working conditions";

   (c) acknowledgement of the "significant contribution of domestic workers to the global economy";

   (d) a recollection that "international labour Conventions and Recommendations apply to all workers";

   (e) a recognition of "the special conditions under which domestic work is carried out that make it desirable to supplement the general standards with standards specific to domestic workers, to enable them to enjoy their rights fully";

   (f) a reference to other UN instruments, such as the Universal Declaration of Human Rights, the International Convention on the Elimination of All Forms of Racial Discrimination, the Convention on the Elimination of All Forms of Discrimination Against Women, the Convention on the Rights of All Migrant Workers and Members of Their Families, as a case for the moral claim for rights.

5. The Convention must apply to all domestic workers once a country has ratified it.

   States must take responsibility for exclusions of particular categories of work and report these to the ILO.

6. "Each Member should take measures to ensure that domestic workers enjoy the fundamental principles and rights at work, namely":

   (a) freedom of association and recognition of the right to collective bargaining;

      (b) "the elimination of all forms of forced or compulsory labor";

      (c) "the effective abolition of child labor";

      (d) "the elimination of discrimination in respect of employment and occupation."

7. "Each Member should set a minimum age for admission to domestic work," which should not be lower than that stated in national laws and not less than 18 years.

8. Each state should take measures to ensure "fair terms of employment," "decent working conditions," and "where applicable decent living conditions respecting the worker's privacy."

9. Domestic workers must be informed of their terms and conditions of employment, in particular hours of work, duration of the contract, and the provision of food and accommodation.

10. Each Member should take measures to assure domestic workers' "protection against all forms of abuse and harassment."

11. Each Member should take measures to ensure that domestic workers:

      (a) "are free to negotiate with their employer whether to reside in the household";

      (b) are not bound to remain in the household during times of rest or leave;

      (c) "are entitled to keep in their possession their travel and identity documents."

12. "The normal hours of work, overtime compensation, periods of daily rest, weekly rest and paid annual leave of domestic workers" must not be "less favourable than those applicable to other wage earners." Domestic workers are entitled to "weekly rest of at least 24 hours in every seven-day period." Hours in which "domestic workers are not free to dispose of time as they please and remain at the disposal of the household in order to respond to possible calls should be regarded as hours of work."

13. Member states must "ensure domestic workers enjoy minimum wage coverage, where such coverage exists," and that such rates are not subject to sex discrimination.

14. (1) Wages must be paid directly to domestic workers, in regular intervals, not less often than once per month. (2) Limited forms

of payment in kind may be included in compensation. This form of allowance "must be appropriate for personal use and benefit of the worker," with a fair and reasonable added value.

15. (1) Each Member must ensure working conditions that are "not less favourable" in terms of occupational safety and health, social security, and maternity.

16. (1) Migrant workers must receive a "written contract containing minimum terms and conditions of employment that must be agreed upon prior to crossing national borders." (2) Each country "should specify by means of laws, regulations and other measures, the conditions under which migrant domestic workers are entitled to repatriation upon the expiry or termination of the employment contract." (3) Member states "should cooperate with each other to ensure the effective protection of migrant domestic workers' rights under this Convention."

17. "Each Member should take measures to ensure that domestic workers have affordable and easy access to fair and affordable dispute settlement procedures."

18. Each Member should make arrangements suitable to the specific context of domestic work in their own country contexts.

19. Domestic workers recruited by agencies should be effectively protected against abuse.

20. The Convention should be implemented by laws, regulations, and collective agreements, with specific adaptations or extensions to domestic workers where needed, in consultation with domestic worker organizations.

21. The "Convention should not affect more favourable provisions applicable to domestic workers under other international labour Conventions."

D. Proposed Conclusions with a View to a Recommendation

22. The Recommendation should be "considered in conjunction with those of the Convention."

23. In order to ensure domestic workers' freedom of association, Member states should provide support to strengthen domestic worker organizations.

24. Work-related medical testing must ensure confidentiality.

25. With regulations, Members should pay "special attention" to the needs of young domestic workers.

26. The terms and conditions of work should be provided in writing, with appropriate assistance when necessary. These terms should include the following: specific terms and conditions of employment, list of duties, leave and rest time, payment procedures, in-kind payment and accommodation details, ideally an established model contract.

27. Hours of work and the terms of their calculation must be freely accessible to domestic workers.

28. States must establish laws and particular conditions for standby time.

29. Night work must be appropriately counted and compensated.

30. Domestic workers are entitled to rest periods, meals, and breaks each day.

31. The day of weekly rest should be fixed.

32. National laws must define the grounds on which domestic workers would be required to work on their fixed time off, and make measures to compensate in equivalent rest periods.

33. Holiday time with employers may not be counted as annual leave.

34. Payments in kind must be limited, not considered as a replacement for cash remuneration, and fairly calculated. These compensation forms must be limited to the personal relevance and use of the domestic worker, such as food and accommodation, and are prohibited in the form of items required of work, such as a uniform.

35. Payments must be accompanied by a clear record and history of remuneration.

36. Workers must be protected in the event of insolvency or death of the employer.

37. Accommodations must include a separate or private room, which is suitably furnished, adequately ventilated, and lockable, access to suitable sanitary facilities, adequate lighting, heating and cooling mechanisms, and meals "of good quality and sufficient quantity, adapted to the cultural and religious requirements of the domestic worker concerned."

38. In the event of termination, "domestic workers must be given a reasonable period of notice and time off during that period to seek new employment."

39. Members must take measures to identify, mitigate, and prevent occupational hazards and provide training for occupational safety.

40. Members should "facilitate the payment of social security contributions by employers, even when domestic workers have multiple employers.

41. Members should assure "additional measures" to ensure the effective protection of migrant domestic workers' rights such as: visits to the household of employment, the establishment of emergency housing networks, and the provision of information in the relevant languages. Member states that are countries of origin for migrant domestic workers should assist in the protection of the rights of these workers through rights education, legal assistance funds, and social services as most relevant.

42. Members should work with domestic worker and employer organizations to encourage training and development in literacy, "address the work-life balance needs of domestic workers," and "ensure that the concerns and rights of domestic workers are taken into account in the context of more general efforts to reconcile work and family."

43. Members should "cooperate at the bilateral, regional and global levels" to enhance the protection of domestic workers, "especially in relation to social security, the monitoring of private employment agencies, the prevention of forced labour and human trafficking, the dissemination of good practices and the collection of statistics on domestic work."

This policy draft outlined the conditions of decent domestic work across contexts. In the colonial period, domestic workers relied upon "benevolent employers," who could partially mediate the prevailing inequities by providing for the school fees, health care, and related needs of the women who labored daily in their households. In the existing context of globalization, the precarious nature of domestic work is a defining factor. As one domestic worker activist contended, "All of us face the same problems: exclusion and exploitation."[10] The very need to set standards ensuring the most fundamental aspects of decency and human rights revealed pervasive labor exploitations, where in the worst scenarios domestic workers are not assured a private place to sleep or bathe, reliable meals, regular leave time, monetary compensation, social security, or the right to organize, among other basic protections. To redress this situation and build respect through rights, this policy called for standards "not less favorable than other workers." The workers' group built their case around demands to consider household labor "just like any other work." Yet the nature of the work in the private household also required particular protections. Thus, article by article, the tripartite dialogue repeatedly walked the line of establishing household labor as standard labor and calling for protections to address the pervasive asymmetries specific to this sector.

As the policy negotiations began, governments, workers, and employers could propose amendments to each of the 43 terms within the proposed draft. The discussions then issued from various government delegate responses to the proposed amendments, worker and employer debates between the vice chairs, followed by the chair's final determination of the majority response to each item. Many revisions passed easily because a consensus had been achieved among all parties. Who could refute, for example, domestic workers' rights to regular time off, a contract of employment, and protection against abuse and harassment? In these cases, model countries with existing structures for such regulation easily demonstrated the ILO's capacity to take regulations to the global level. Yet several proposed protections generated lengthy debates because they required a notable shift from traditional conceptions of domestic work. The most heavily debated items exposed prevailing assumptions about the value of domestic work, repeated resistance to standardization, and persistent questions about the ILO's capacity to protect such a "scattered"[11] informal migrant sector.

The ideological perspectives of labor, employers, and governments became clear during the negotiations on the policy terms. The workers' group held to three foundational arguments to widen the rights platform, as Toni Moore, labor leader from Barbados, summarized in her final statement: "1. Domestic work is work performed in private homes; 2. As a consequence, domestic workers are more vulnerable to abuses, and 3.

Domestic workers lack the legal protections afforded to other workers."[12] According to workers, policy protections were necessary to redress the substantive consequences of exclusion and exploitation. Employers focused on monitoring and implementation in their attempts to minimize regulations. Framing domestic work as an informal sector in the private household, employers generally resisted standardization by scaling back the level of protections in the majority of the amendments, and introducing language that allowed for the exclusion of domestic workers. While governments held a range of positions on the policy measures, in general their focus was on the obligations of the state once ratification took place. These national leaders faced domestic workers, labor leaders, and employers from their own countries during the negotiations, yet had to take into account the multiple layers of interpretation, application, and practical considerations of each detail of the 143 amendments proposed once they returned from Geneva. In the language, rhetorical stances, and debates during negotiations, these ideological differences illuminated both the barriers to regulating domestic worker rights and the potential to reach consensus among the three parties.

In crafting this first formal policy on domestic work, the following key issues captured the most substantive focus within the negotiations—exposing the most serious differences among the social partners. From her oversight role, Manuela Tomei identified three major issues that generated the most debate: conditions of employment, agencies, and the regulation of the private household. Two other key areas caused extensive negotiations: the definition of domestic work and migration. We turn now to an examination of these debates, as a means of understanding the dialogue behind the final policy.

Defining Domestic Work

The term "domestic" raised substantive questions about how to frame the category of workers who would fall under the protections of the ILO. For the Spanish speakers, the equivalent *doméstica* generated a formative debate because its language origins associated the term with a domesticated animal rather than a household employee. Yet efforts to build a wider consensus resulted in the eventual agreement on the term "domestic worker," as Latina activists and Central and South American governments conceded to the wider language usage. In coming to a shared definition of domestic work, negotiators considered the range of responsibilities in this sector to include personal care services, household cleaning, and child/elder caretaking. According to domestic workers, "The definition of domestic work as 'work performed within an employment relationship in or for a household or households' is welcomed as it allows (us) to encompass housekeeping and personal care performed within the house as well as work performed for the house such as gardening or chauffeur services and also addresses the issue of domestic workers performing work for multiple employers."[13] This wider definition embraced the range of country contexts—where in many cases domestic work is sex-specific to "houseboys" or female "maids." Furthermore, it protected men employed by private households as gardeners, thereby recognizing the pervasive gender-labor divides whereby women take care of the interior of the household and men look after the exterior spaces.

In establishing protections for domestic workers, the nature of the employment relationship ultimately determined who counted as a domestic worker. According to labor activist Nalini Nayak, "Even defining someone as a worker in our national context in India has been quite difficult because most look at the employer-employee relationship."[14] Yet in the contemporary context of globalization, household labor includes a range of intimate work—from elder care to disability support to child care to care for the home itself. Thus, discussions on the definition of domestic work had to take into consideration the existence of care agencies that employ women to look after multiple households. The demands of capitalism, particularly the dual-income family structures common to developed countries, have created such specialized care services. Even though the labor takes place in the private home, the agency serves as the ultimate employer, in contrast to the traditional relationship, where a domestic worker's entire obligation has been to one family, often across the lifespan. In a private meeting among NGOs and allies, Luc Demaret, the ILO's lead negotiator in the Workers' Bureau, explained the strong need to establish the working relationship in order to promote the expansion of domestic workers' rights.

Once you have an employment relationship, you have rights. And the employment relationship is not something that is legal or illegal, as soon as it exists, as soon as you have a relationship of employment, you have rights, and the palette of rights that goes with it. So we will really have to get a strong reference to the employment relationship. The second reason is that the employment relationship is the relationship between the workers and anybody else on the other side. So it could be the household, but it could be an agency, it could be anything on the other side. As soon as there is this kind of relationship, you start to have rights, and you can fight for your rights. So that is one thing that our colleagues in the working party are pushing for.[15]

Thus, with the establishment of a working relationship, the ILO's obligation to protections increased. No longer would domestic workers be considered an "adjunct" workforce or an extension of their employers' households. With the legal recognition of a bona fide employment relationship, domestic workers would be eligible for rights and protections, just like any other worker. Simply establishing household labor as a working relationship made the private home a site of formal employment—thereby holding employers accountable to both the individual employee and the binding commitments of the legal relationship.

Counting Work

With the definition of a domestic worker and the domestic-work relationship in place, the tripartite discussions invested a great deal of energy in determining what constitutes fair conditions of work in the private household. In relation to the overall negotiation process, lead US government delegate Robert Shepard identified this portion of the negotiations as the most challenging: "The toughest questions were terms of work and conditions of work."[16] Since many domestic workers are "live-in," policymakers struggled to determine how to "count" the hours of labor, particularly with the common expectations of continual "on call" status. Added to these challenges was the pervasive perception that the terms of domestic work are best sorted out in the private household, rather than determined by the state or international governance. Yet the global market economy demands the migration of domestic workers, often beyond national borders. In many cases, domestic workers are employed by more than one household, making the reliance on regulations even more vital. Thus the tripartite had to engage the collective shifts from colonial-era notions of servitude to regulated "work like any other."

Employers and some governments resisted counting work in ways that placed unrealistic terms on enforcement. They argued that labor in the home could not be easily measured by means of discrete hours. Domestic work often requires live-in responsibilities, night work, and frequent "standby" time. In some cases, domestic workers were expected to "holiday" with their employers—a "perk" some claimed as compensation in kind. Domestic work was understood as nonstandard and therefore outside the realm of "regular" working hours. In this view, domestic work warranted time estimates, with the understanding that some of its requirements would not "count" as real work. "That's just the way it is," claimed one prominent employer. Conceived this way, reproductive labor requires workers to be on call, all the time—be it paid or unpaid. One ILO official revisited a discussion from the interior convention negotiations on this article. A male employer delegate claimed that on-call availability is "just part of what women do." In his assessment, "When the child wets the bed, of course, the maid gets up." These tasks are "natural," he contended, and outside conventional paid working hours.[17] This notion that tending to toddlers at 3:00 a.m. is "just what domestics do" exposes the ideologies underlying the conditions of colonial servitude. Worker activists thus set about dismantling the perceptual foundation that reinforced servitude and subjected domestic laborers to exploitation.

In order to build their case, key advocates had to render domestic work as regular work. Its tasks could be measured; its every demand quantifiable. Louise McDonough, lead Australian representative, called delegates to bring legitimacy to this policy by aligning it with the ILO's protections for all other sectors.

Any text that comes out of this house that suggests we cannot regulate hours, we cannot be proud of. We have a history of conventions that regulate hours. If decent work cannot transfer to regular hours of work, then we have not done our job properly.[18]

Worker advocates challenged the underlying assumption that paid domestic labor could not be regulated in the manner of "real work." Any regulation on domestic work needed to establish a means of quantifying the various features of that work—live-in conditions, standby time, and off-duty periods. This issue generated a wide range of opinions in the negotiations. Halimah Yacob, spokesperson for the workers' group, faced serious resistance to her argument that domestic workers held obligations to the work site. As employers and some governments deeply disputed her claims, she named the escalating tensions' impact on the overall spirit of the negotiations: "It is not winter in here yet, but it is frosty." The question of how domestic work, in all of its dimensions, could be quantified was perhaps the most contentious issue facing policymakers.

Prevailing notions of domestic workers as either "one in the family" or "servants" defined by globalization's caste system spoke to the fluidity of reproductive labor. Most commonly, domestic work demands that women be on call for household needs that extend well beyond regular hours of work. The live-in dimension of this labor generates the expectation that domestic workers are regularly standing by—for crying babies at night, employers' shifting social calendars, and the unpredictable needs of elders often in their care. Ida le Blanc, lead domestic worker organizer from Trinidad and Tobago, described the 24–7 nature of work for live-in domestics.

> We need provisions which make the words "decent employment" mean something for live-in domestic workers. They often have no stipulated hours of work, and must always be on call, especially where they are hired to provide services such as child care, or care for the aged, the sick, or the disabled.[19]

The question of being "on call" posed the biggest policy challenge in the negotiations, according to Martin Oelz, the ILO legal specialist for the convention. In Oelz's assessment, in order to be relevant and meaningful in implementation, the policy had to address the problem of standby time.

> It's not possible just to say because they are caregivers that live in, you cannot separate between free time and working time. This argument is used to protect 24-hour availability for care.

In order to regulate household labor, every task had to count, particularly those occurring outside a regular work schedule. Advocates demanded, for example, that workers be fairly compensated for their "on call" nighttime care duties. Thus, rather than the expectation of continual availability, Convention 189 declared that standby time must be counted as hours of work, worthy of regular compensation. As they contended, any time a worker is tied to the workplace, and not free to engage in the activities of his or her personal life, that worker is fulfilling the expectations of labor and must be compensated.

This labor rights perspective stretched across discussions of night work and holidays, as domestic workers are so often required to contribute during these periods. One of the child domestic workers present at the negotiations through Anti-Slavery International described her existence like this: "Working very long hours, at night, carrying babies alone. It is not good."[20] Advocates claimed that night labor could compromise workers' basic needs, asserting, "We all know that biologically people need to sleep at night."[21] Yet domestic workers' daily conditions change with family transitions—as babies enter the household, family members become sick, and elders lose their independence. Advocates therefore contended, "If we do not provide sufficient measures, then we are not doing them any justice."[22] To create a global policy on domestic work without recognizing the irregularity of labor hours and the heightened demands that fall to this group would be to usher in a set of rather meaningless regulations.

Holiday time also held the attention of 187 governments, employers, and labor leaders throughout both negotiations. How would domestic workers' time be counted when they traveled with their employers on holiday? According to some, these periods represented a vacation for workers as well, who enjoyed the surroundings of the holiday accommodations they could otherwise not access. Yet for workers who had "vacationed" with their employers, care for children consumed most of their time, regardless of the geographic location of their labor. As one domestic worker asserted, "We still dance with a baby in the airplane."[23] In other cases when employers leave for holiday without such a built-in support network, domestic workers are expected to take vacation at the same time, thereby further tying women in this sector to the lives of their individual employers. Yet domestic worker advocates confronted the shadows of this colonial practice and its lingering power imbalance. Regardless of when their employers decide to take a holiday, they contended, the domestic worker "should not have her annual leave affected."[24] These distinct conditions emerge from the reality that so many domestic workers reside at their employers' homes, thereby increasing their dependency and tying their lives more closely to the individuals who employ them. The ILO policy worked to sever these ties in substantive ways—by counting workers' time when they are expected to "holiday" with their employers and providing rights for separate leave time.

Employers put up the largest resistance to the required measurement of *all* contributions made by domestic workers. Their arguments repeatedly centered around the "huge cost implications" of compensating such additional hours for all levels of care labor. In their eyes, these required protections reached far "beyond the practicality of domestic work."[25] Once again, employers turned to the realities of implementation to assert that required enforcement of these protections would turn countries away from ratification. They claimed this complexity would lead to larger tensions between the national and international law because of the substantive challenges in assuring compliance. Furthermore, vehement resisters emphasized the "burdensome and unrealistic" demands such required protections would place on "ill-equipped householders." They contended, "We cannot risk bringing this uncertainty into family homes."[26] Up to that point, employers enjoyed domestic workers' subsidization of the real costs of care labor. With these requirements to count all of the conditions of standby work, employers would bear the real cost of care services, while the global economy would rebalance the subsidies domestic workers provide to assure its continued growth. In the end, the negotiations favored advocates' stance to recognize standby time, and count these hours as real work.

Separation Rights

Throughout its history domestic work normalized "live-in" labor, where employees reside at their employers' homes as a regular aspect of servitude. With this particular configuration came blurred boundaries around working time, and its necessary balance with periods of rest.

Convention 189 protected the right to one rest period per day and one rest day every seven days. In order to emphasize this "crucial" policy point, Halimah Yacob used the committee's own work as a point of comparison. "What about ourselves here? If we continue, we would suffer from depression, or collapse."[27] The need to include such protections speaks to the most abusive contexts, in which household labor takes the form of contemporary slavery. In the worst instances, domestic workers are forced to work nonstop, without rest. More commonly, however, domestic workers' schedules are defined by the needs—and sometimes whims—of their employers. Thus, to achieve protections, not only was time off to be assured, domestic workers were to have a say in their own right to rest.

Convention 189 shifted the terrain of domestic work by regulating the terms of live-in employment. As the original proposed policy draft reveals, the need to assure separate or private rooms—with suitable furnishings, ventilation, sanitation, security, and heating and cooling— reflects existing frequently subpar live-in work conditions. Yet the terms of living that accompany domestic work symbolize the much more pervasive residue of formerly unregulated conditions of employment, where workers so often lost the right to privacy because of their existence within a family home. Under apartheid South Africa, for example, domestic workers who lived in could not receive visitors because of the strict geographic separations that governed contact, even with their own families. Thus, domestic workers not only passed decades of their lives in the same live-in situation, they forwent intimate romantic lives because the state deemed visitation illegal for women who lived at their employment site. In the existing context of globalization, women travel far distances to take domestic work jobs that are subject to extensive employer control—where personal lives and romantic relationships are also heavily scrutinized. Without citizenship, economic means, or a representative organization, women in the contemporary global economy are subject to exploitation and control as a result of their on-site status. The global market, in which cross-border migration can be necessary for workers' survival, creates these conditions of live-in dependency. South African domestic worker Hester Stephens pointed to this dependency as the source of the most severe oppressions associated with this sector. As she stated:

Many domestic workers are scared of joining a union as they depend on living on the premises of their employers. They are working in isolation, which makes it very hard to organize, especially in our country with security such that we are living behind walls and bars.[28]

The traditional terms of live-in domestic work are thus both a vestige of the former colonial era and a reflection of the modern global economy, which can require domestic workers to cross national borders and live at the sites of their employment. In the end, negotiators agreed to an article that requires states to "take measures to ensure that domestic workers: (a) are free to reach agreement with their employer or potential employer on whether to reside in the household."[29] Similarly, domestic workers could not be obligated to remain on their employer's premises during rest periods and personal leave. Furthermore, to redress a pervasive practice whereby employers controlled workers' personal space by means of live-in requirements, these discussions assured that domestic workers' accommodations would include privacy, security, and suitable furnishings, as well as access to sanitation facilities, light, heat, and cooling. In these live-in work contexts, the agreements entitled domestic workers "to keep in their possession their travel and identity documents."[30] An additional gain for the workers issued from discussions of the cultural differences surrounding food customs, which ultimately led to the agreement that meals provided by employers "adapted to the extent reasonable to the cultural and religious requirements, if any, of the domestic worker concerned."[31] These measures worked collectively to assure that the convention addressed the various power imbalances stemming from a worker living under an employer's roof.

The norms of live-in labor traditionally included forms of "payment in kind," often in lieu of cash remuneration. Through this global movement for rights, domestic workers repeatedly avowed, "Leftover food is not payment in kind."[32] In some cases, in a practice stemming from the colonial era, used clothing, toiletries, and even alcohol are given to domestic workers as part of an overall compensation package, often along with room and board. In the worst situations, employers purchased the uniforms they required of domestic workers, yet deducted these costs from their salaries as payment in kind. Halimah Yacob vehemently opposed these practices, which sharply reinforced the pervasive social inequalities between workers and employers. When the employers' group wanted to count payment in kind as partial salary, she reminded the house, "These are poor workers and they need protection," particularly in the highly vulnerable area of salary distribution, when so many "do not even have a bank account."[33] Payment in kind, in Yacob's eyes, "is not a technical amendment," rather, "a material determinant of workers' lives."[34] The US government backed this stance by asserting that the terms of any payment in kind must be "voluntarily agreed upon," such that the domestic worker is part of the decision. In the end, the workers' group acquiesced to the employers' demand to legitimize payment in kind, recognizing the larger ground they had gained on compensation for standby time. The final outcome still assured that only a limited proportion of domestic workers' remuneration could take form as payment in kind, and that such forms of compensation "are agreed to by the worker, are for the personal use and benefit of the worker, and that the monetary value attributed to them is fair and reasonable."

With these first standardized protections, governing live-in work and payment in kind, the ILO process set about dismantling the neocolonial underpinnings of global domestic labor. In regulating the living space and setting restrictions on in-kind compensation, the policy succeeded in penetrating the previously inviolable domain of household labor. Still to be grappled with in formulating Convention 189 were the pervasive gaps between policy and practice, as well as the challenges of meaningful implementation. Addressing the lingering colonial labor practices in transnational households consumed a substantial portion of the negotiations and challenged the ILO to confront the larger global migration patterns inherent in the prolific "maid trade."

Underwriting Migration

We often migrate from our own families and homes to work in homes that are very far away, isolated from the support of our own communities. Many domestic workers see their own families not even once a year, especially those who work outside their own countries.

—Vicky Kanyoka, IDWN speech to the 2010 ILC

To write protections into public policy, Convention 189 had to deal with the global state of migration. At the time of these negotiations, ILO experts estimated that there were 232 million migrants living outside their home countries, 50 percent of whom were women.[35] In the domestic work sector, women comprise over 90 percent of transnational migrants.[36] Thus, while migrants reflect relatively equal gender distributions, domestic work remains one of the most heavily feminized sectors of export labor. As they leave their own countries to pursue work in other households, "women migrants are doubly vulnerable to this lack of legal protection for domestic work, because of their gender and their status as migrants."[37] Peruvian domestic worker activist Ernestina Ochoa contended, "Our migrant sisters are the most exploited; they are the ones who live in the shadows. Their paperwork is withheld, and for them, there are no rights."[38] This staggering "multiplier effect" grounded domestic workers and their allies in a guiding commitment to bringing migrants into the realm of convention protections. While the ILO had to deal with the most relevant interrelated dimensions of migration, reform measures could not be seen as unduly burdening member states, which were not fully prepared to deal with the massive undertaking of transnational labor across borders.

The first proposed draft called for three particular standards in relation to migration: (1) the assurance of a written contract; (2) regulations for entitled repatriation; and (3) cooperation across sending and receiving member states. Thus, the policy handled migration by dealing with the technicalities of transnational employment and state relations. More complex and far outside the scope of the convention were larger questions about how international governance could regulate the scale of migration, as well as the ethical responsibilities owed marginalized workers who leave their own families in pursuit of work in global cities.[39] As the house debated the articles dealing with migration, the very process of coming to clarity on practice exposed the limitations of labor policy in dealing with such larger issues as international border-crossings and massive economic inequality. One activist reflected on the most difficult aspects of her life as a live-in domestic worker, saying, "There is a gap between you and your children."[40] What policy could address this emotional toll, or the lost years of separation from one's children? Yet even given their insufficiency in addressing larger injustice, the negotiated terms reflected the most comprehensive attempt to date to deal with the migrant global workforce. They could be seen as treating the symptoms of globalization, without a larger analysis of its effects.

In the end, the social partners agreed to three original focus areas, on contracts, repatriation, and relations between sending and receiving countries. Yet the final policy draft also included a rather banal blanket protection, 8(3), that read, "Members shall take measures to cooperate with each other to ensure the effective application of the provisions of this Convention to migrant domestic workers." This article granted international migrants the same rights as citizen workers. Yet its placement within an article listing three other technical protections is telling. Furthermore, without naming migration, Article 2(1) stated, "The Convention applies to all domestic workers." Thus the language of the convention reveals the sensitivities surrounding (and at times a strategic avoidance of) larger questions of migration. With reference to related conventions, the final document links to larger, more comprehensive established agreements that place the protection and regulation of migrants in the hands of global governance—at both applied and ideological levels. The preamble of the final document notes "the particular relevance for domestic workers of the Migration for Employment Convention (Revised), 1949 (No. 97), the Migrant Workers (Supplementary Provisions) Convention, 1975 (No. 143), the Workers with Family Responsibilities Convention, 1981 (No. 156), the Private Employment Agencies Convention, 1997 (No. 181), and the Employment Relationship Recommendation, 2006 (No. 198), as well as of the ILO Multilateral Framework on Labour Migration: Non-binding principles and guidelines for a rights-based approach to labour migration (2006)." With these references, the final document reinforces that migrant domestic workers are protected by established instruments that apply to migrant workers more generally. Furthermore, the preamble includes reference to the International Convention on the Protection of the Rights of All Migrant Workers and Members of Their Families, among other related documents that create a protective umbrella for migrants across all sectors. With these wider references established in the preamble, the convention's treatment of migrant domestic workers focused on the practicalities of this specific sector—where the particularities of labor in private households evoke larger concerns about responsibility and rights within these global transnational flows.

As the debates around migration transpired, a pervasive tension arose between recognizing the need for "special protections" for migrant workers and assuring the feasibility of implementation. As migration arose in the 2011 negotiations, the lead French delegate underscored the importance of recognizing the distinct needs and vulnerabilities migrants shared: "After all, they live and work in a country that is not their own."[41] The United States backed this position, claiming "certain classes of migrant domestic workers must receive additional protections" and pointing out the need for "appropriate regulations." Yet many countries resisted policy protections that would lock them into offering migrants the rights to social security frameworks and citizenship benefits. With their core commitment to social democracies, many European countries presented strong resistance to this notion of extending benefits to outsiders. In their eyes, such assurances would require the distribution of tax-based resources for the "masses of migrants" that reach their borders in search of undocumented work. The UK, for example, resisted these requirements, stating, "This will only make the convention non-ratifiable."[42] The Arab country bloc also opposed special protections for migrants, contending that workers' treatment as "one in the family" assured their protections. According to the 2010 Arab country statement:

> All the domestic workers are migrant workers, temporary or provisional workers that live in the Gulf area and most times we deal with those workers as part of our family. We provide to them decent housing and decent meals that we share a family with them as well, taking into consideration the social conditions prevailing in our countries.[43]

Yet within these Arab countries, the only bodies representing domestic workers are the employment agencies that arrange such trade, mainly with Asia. Unionization and collective organization of domestic workers is prohibited in the countries that comprise the Arab bloc. Thus, to date, small faith-based operations, such as Catholic Relief Services, provide the only advocacy for migrants in these countries, advocacy that in some cases must be offered in clandestine forms.

Given this circumstance, rather than relying on the variant systems, laws, and power structures within countries, the ILO set out to assure a global rights scheme as a means to deliver the special protections migrant domestic workers needed. With these standards "from above," domestic workers held out hope of a shift in values and beliefs within the countries that rely on migrant labor. Grace Escaño, a Filipina activist within the Netherlands, spoke of this hope.

> For us, this convention is a big tool. We are trying to prove to them that there is a capacity issue. We want to prove that Dutch women can have a career because the domestic workers are taking their jobs. We are trying to impose the idea that Dutch children must respect the domestic workers. So, for us, we are really working so hard from the Netherlands. Now, it is so hard because of the criminalization of "illegals." We are always telling to them [government officials] that there is a demand for domestic workers . . . Hopefully this convention will be approved and we will go home with a positive outcome.[44]

The domestic-work policy negotiations turned ILO conversations to the notion that "you can have migration with rights."[45] As the hopes of domestic workers like Grace show, these rights must transfer to effective implementation, both in terms of labor practices and societal perceptions of domestic labor and its importance to the global economy.

Throughout the Convention 189 discussions, migration became an expression of the need for multilateral cooperation in recognizing the mutual dependency on domestic work between the world's sending and receiving regions. Domestic workers do not just leave their countries to set out for the promise of economic gain in more developed countries. Their movement is orchestrated through extensive state relations, coordinated structures, and a massive system of interdependency that thrives upon women's care labor as a vital source of national income. Sending and receiving countries build relations around the trade of women's care labor, elevating the need for protections to the level of international governance. No longer can national laws assure fair labor standards when so many migrants work in countries where they have no citizenship rights. Thus, in order for Convention 189 to be effective, it needed to spell out the terms of migration as a vital dimension of policy.

States that send and receive domestic workers depend on work-permit systems and third-party agencies that recruit and place domestic workers in employment sites abroad. Sring Atin, the chairperson of the Indonesian Migrant Workers' Union, attested, "Every migrant worker leaving the country must go through a labor agency. No one can organize their own work abroad."[46] In the best circumstances, these agencies accurately convey the labor expectations in the destination country, offer extensive training, and take responsibility for the longer-term health of the employment relationship. The reliance upon third parties also creates conditions for some of the most egregious forms of human rights violations, including trafficking, misrepresentation of the work, and extreme exploitation. Across this continuum of third-party practices, domestic workers remain completely dependent on two levels. First, their livelihoods are largely determined by the geopolitics of transnational care. Second, their well-being is entirely contingent upon their employer and access to minimal rights as noncitizens. When the work environment assumes the only tie to migrants' rights to live in the destination country, employers hold even greater power. The threat of deportation mixes fluidly with economic and racial oppression in the most exploitative conditions. Thus, systems and people work together to create particular vulnerabilities for migrant domestic workers outside their own countries of origin. As leader of the Hong Kong and international domestic worker movements, Ip Pui Yu described this problem.

> Poor work-permit systems also lead to abuse. Where a migrant domestic worker has a permit that says she can only work for that employer, or indeed that particular diplomatic mission, in her host country, this keeps her in a situation of dependency. She dare not leave that employer, no matter if someone in the household is being abusive, because, if she does, she is rendered "illegal" because she is not allowed to work anywhere else.[47]

Yu centered her public addresses on governments' responsibility to work together within a regulated global set of standards, so that domestic workers would be protected across borders. In one of the designated public addresses to the ILO's entire tripartite, she contended, "Governments of origin and destination countries need to collaborate better to ensure there will be no abuses in the job referral process." She asserted that "member states have obligations to remove all obstacles" to the achievement of decent work for migrant domestic workers.[48]

In negotiating potential migrant protections, the ILO reinforced particular alliances and drew lines among countries based upon their positions and practice. The conversations on a domestic worker global policy became an expression of the larger geopolitics surrounding migration. The range and complexity of these issues posed challenges to the convention's capacity to make a difference given the dominant market-economy forces. In the final document, countries are obligated to ensure that the designated protections are accessible to migrants working within each country. Ultimately, migration's connection to domestic work fortified the case for global standards as the only type of policy that could address the realities of this sector—where protections must travel along the human supply chain. Even though the workers' group felt it had compromised in ways that reduced members' original hope for protections, the extensive focus on migration, as it relates to employment agencies and bilateral relations, increased workers' claim to rights, while bringing greater awareness to the conditions affecting domestic workers.

Ideological Links

Interwoven within these key issues, a series of ideological questions linked the topical to the more philosophical dimensions of rights. These inquiries focused on the constitution of an employment relationship, issues of privacy, and the relevant rights of individual workers and employers. Throughout the negotiations, these larger considerations connected the particulars of many articles to a larger cause and gave fuel to arguments across all sides. These underlying ideological arguments link many of the particular articles together and offer a wider analysis of the meaning of the rights debates that consumed negotiators.

At the foundation of these considerations, the household space became a legitimate site of paid labor, and therefore employment within it would require protections. By making the private domain a public worksite, employers' accountability increased, while domestic work gained substantive ground as a bona fide occupation. As one leader put it, "The point really is that when someone decides to employ a domestic, they become an employer." With this employment relationship in place, the household space became the source of substantive debates between employers' right to privacy and the vital need to regulate labor within this protected domain. The workers' group, and several ally governments, strongly supported the importance of inspections of private homes. To them, it seemed the only way to assure that policies would "have teeth."[49] As Halimah Yacob contended, "Inspection does not mean the invasion of private homes."[50] Yet employers dug in their heels, because this notion violated the constitutional protections of the private home. To them, this principle was unassailable. As their spokesperson vehemently contended, "External people in the home present a matter at the heart of it all. From the employers' perspective, we are 'utterly opposed,' and I use the word utterly again."[51] For workers, the only assurance of effective policy implementation would demand some form of regulation of the household. Yacob responded to this opposition by asserting, "Privacy is very contextual. The main point is to establish effective means of ensuring compliance with national laws and regulation. It is one that is much broader than privacy."[52] This dialectic tension between the terms of labor and the capacity to enforce rights arose repeatedly throughout the debates. In favor of both positions, the Africa bloc captured this complexity. "We agree with the right to privacy. There is also a right to ensure proper labor legislation."[53] As ILO internal officials reflected on this topic at the end of the 2011 negotiations, they surmised that the process placed too much emphasis on an attempt to fit labor inspections into the existing notions of enforcement. The case of household labor demonstrates a concrete need to go beyond such traditional thinking. For example, in the United States, as legal scholar Peggie Smith points out, with adoption, foster care, and even animal ownership, the household is inspected to assure the integrity and capacity of those taking on such a commitment.[54] Given the value and necessity of reproductive labor, such procedural processes could be implemented as a means of investing in this labor contribution. States' willingness to do so would assert a central shift in perceptions about individual rights. When home becomes a workspace, employers must give up some of their rights to privacy in order to assure a wider and more consistent level of shared protections.

For workers, privacy rights very often find expression in the terms of the body, as a site of labor, intimacy, and control. The very nature of domestic employment breaches the boundary of the body because the intimacy of this work is physical, as well as affective. In the colonial period, employers regularly surveilled the physical bodies of their employees.[55] Not uncommon was the practice of employers managing domestic workers' medical needs, food intake, and access to sanitary supplies. Under the most dominant households, women's monthly supply of toilet paper, soap, and menstrual supplies would be doled out by employers. In Asia and Africa, tea, sugar, and rice allotments remain common practice as monthly stipends. This proximity to the management of workers' bodies often violated confidentiality norms, with medical doctors sharing the results of domestic workers' examinations with employers, rather than their own patients. In the contemporary context, HIV/AIDS enters the household working relationship, as employers fear the possibility of disease transmission from women providing intimate care. During the negotiations, employers put forth an amendment that would allow for medical testing to screen potential employees and protect employers from a range of possible transmissions that could take place in the household context. In making their argument they contended, "We must remember that we are dealing with children here, there are certain vulnerabilities. We cannot put employers at risk."[56] The same passion that employers brought to their arguments for the sanctity of the private household, the workers' group brought to their professions of domestic workers' privacy surrounding their bodies. They adamantly opposed any amendments that would require domestic workers to submit to pregnancy and HIV/AIDS testing. While the discussion on the table focused on a particular amendment that would allow for such testing, Halimah Yacob presented employers with an ethical query about the power relations undergirding any such measure.

We always talk about risk to employers. What about risk to employees? Domestic workers work in close proximity; they are also vulnerable to transmission. Why don't we ever talk about this? [laughter from the floor] The risk to the domestic worker is actually greater than the risk to the employer! If she has to care for a family member who is ill, this is risky!

Why is the risk always on the employers? . . . The issue here is about discrimination in testing.[57]

Yacob's contention that employers could transmit undesirable conditions to workers generated a great deal of laughter on the floor, particularly from employers, exposing underlying assumptions with respect to class and social status.

In their own accounts, domestic worker activists repeatedly expressed the risks they faced in the provision of contact care. Ida le Blanc, IDWN leader from Trinidad and Tobago, brought cases from her country to the discussions around this topic.

Domestic workers in Trinidad and [those] who contract diseases from taking care of the sick have no rights to the benefits, Workmen's Compensation, as it is called, that other workers have . . . One of our domestic workers told us how she took care of a sick household member. She was unaware that that person had tuberculosis. Eventually she contracted it herself, though none of the other household members did. She had protected them and became ill in the process, but she received no compensation.[58]

Le Blanc felt so committed to exposing this reality as a central call for domestic worker rights that she included it in her 2011 speech to ILO delegates. To governments and employers, she directed this question: "Who is looking out for the health, as well as safety, of domestic workers? All over the world, this question has so far barely been taken into account."[59] Father Peter O'Neall, director of the Hsinchu Catholic Diocese Migrants and Immigrants Service Center in Taiwan, brought another dimension of this power imbalance to a public forum organized by the Friedrich-Ebert-Stiftung Foundation for Social Democracy during the ILO talks. "Taiwan wants 'healthy' domestic workers. They contribute enormously to the economy. Yet when they become sick, they are put on a plane home."[60] Thus, the body became a site of negotiation of rights. In many cases, discussions of the protections of the body illuminated prevailing neocolonial assumptions at play, even in this very civilized, formal, tripartite discussion of basic human rights.

Another important topic in the negotiations related to the body through discussions of health and occupational safety. How could the private household site protect domestic workers from injury, exposure to toxins, and even psychological harm? According to domestic workers attending the meetings, with household work, "physical, emotional and mental health is impacted."[61] Media coverage of the most horrific dangers of this occupation features stories of women who have fallen from Hong Kong's high-rise apartment buildings while cleaning windows, suffered extreme physical abuse through acid attacks and burnings, and faced ongoing sexual abuse in the isolated private (and often live-in) occupational spaces. Many domestic worker activists reported frequent cases of sexual abuse, which "in some cases led to increased levels of HIV/AIDS, sexually transmitted diseases, and unwanted pregnancies."[62] In one instance, after a member reported the incident to her union, "she was instantly dismissed," yet had "no recourse under law to unfair dismissal."[63] In addition to these extreme violations, everyday risks presented serious needs for policy response. As Ida le Blanc explained:

> Domestic workers also handle many chemicals used for cleaning and laundry. They daily use sharp objects such as knives. They often lift heavy loads, including mattresses and furniture to clean, or indeed household members who are sick, elderly or disabled. But where are the training programs in the safe handling of chemicals, sharp objects or heavy loads that are specifically for work in the home?[64]

One of the child domestic workers accompanying Anti-Slavery International admitted, "Actually my fellow domestic workers are experienced in using toxic chemicals."[65]

Advocates referred to the ILO Occupational Safety and Health Convention (No. 155) to establish the right for information and training on risks, as well as the right to refuse dangerous work. Furthermore, organizations like WIEGO provided extensive research on the heightened levels of risk and danger required of domestic work. When woman are worn out by the hours required of the occupation, their exposure to risk heightens exponentially.[66] As the importance of health and safety measures came into the discussions, advocates also asserted that the inspection of domestic work must extend to labor agencies, who are often the "worst violators of rights."[67] Issues of health and occupational safety spoke to the need to assure education and training systems that can deliver policy protections in the actual contexts of work in private households.

Other key topics of negotiation stemmed from broader questions about the lines of domestic work: Who is a legitimate domestic worker? How can a domestic work relationship appropriately end? And, are there any cases in which the exclusion of domestic workers would be just? At the most ethical level, the discussions relied heavily on larger ILO guidelines to establish boundaries around domestic labor. These distinctions drew some of the clearest lines, and generated least disagreement. Without question, all members of the tripartite agreed that child labor would not be acceptable in any form. One Guatemalan sister brought to the public floor the contention that "little girls are still earning 300 quesales" while "our children are left at our grandmothers' houses."[68] Connected to these shifts in the family systems that accompany domestic work, forced labor and trafficking marked the most egregious violations of human rights. These conditions fortified the larger aspirations of the ILO: to impact these global human rights concerns by bringing rights into the household, the space that allows these larger networks to exist as illicit industries. Thus, with the substantive focus on contracts and conditions of work, the ILO also had to deal with relevant questions about termination of employment. Most commonly, domestic workers recounted repeated stories of their sisters' job dismissals in the absence of due process. In some of the worst situations, employees are fired when they "fall pregnant" and "suffer from morning sickness," in ways that compromise their daily productivity.[69] Related to these violations of basic labor rights, domestic workers and their advocates emphasized the importance of trade unions and collective bargaining to protect unfair dismissal and build in appropriate grievance systems for dispute resolution.

The ongoing tensions about "hybrid work" surfaced throughout these conversations on the appropriate lines surrounding domestic work. While the ILO and its advocates repeatedly emphasized that domestic work is "just like any other work," the special nature of this employment relationship became central to these discussions. Some governments have relied upon its placement in the private household, along with a particular history of racialized labor relations, to develop exclusions in the law. For instance, the 1936 US National Labor Relations Act excludes domestic workers and farm workers from basic employment rights, including collective bargaining. Such legal exclusions protect governments from requirements to establish effective systems of monitoring and compliance within the private household. Furthermore, the constitutional protections of the private sphere justify such exclusions in many cases. Yet this ILO decision to finally recognize domestic work as legitimate labor called for a reexamination of these frequent justifications. As one activist summarized:

> We strongly caution against any broad exclusions of domestic workers in the proposed convention, as that would defeat one of the primary goals of this instrument, which is to finally ensure protections for a group of workers repeatedly marginalized and repeatedly left out.[70]

To develop a global instrument that then allowed governments to get out of applying its terms and recommendations through this use of exclusions would render the entire international governance policy process as mostly performative rhetorical theatrics. Notably, around all of these questions on the boundaries of work, with domestic workers themselves in the room, the importance of addressing the vital concerns in the everyday experiences of household work became that much more pressing. Furthermore, these negotiations for domestic workers' rights set standards for conditions that would not only affect women in this industry, but a much wider network impacted by this transnational chain of care labor.

Regulating "Harmony in the House"

Throughout these public dialogues, the debates on each article rendered domestic work "conventional." By regulating terms and building standards for domestic work "like any other work," the process of policymaking normalized household labor to make it fit within the demands of the global economy. Rather than a radical movement to question who does the dirty work around the world, or a serious critique of the advances of global capitalism's demands, the ILO process promoted paid domestic work, as long as it is "decent." Furthermore, by making domestic work regular work, the ILO fit this feminized, racialized industry into the needs of the growing global economy, thereby supporting the supply of this service. This campaign strategy read "domestic work is inevitable, so we might as well make it regular and fair." In doing so, domestic workers would be assured certain basic rights and those with privilege would be able to continue to outsource household labor, with a UN institution of global governance sanctioning this feminized, racialized industry. Yet in this process of normalizing domestic work by defining each of its terms, many of the regenerative aspects of this human exchange fell far from policy's reach.

Chilean domestic worker activist and poet Aida Moreno captured the rare value of contributing to the lives of others in their homes.

> It is wonderful. It is one of the most beautiful things that we can sensitize the world about the work. It is such a noble type of work. This service, it is impossible to compare, yet it is not yet valorized, it is not seen, but now you can see it. It is like recompensation. This great step, I believe that this is just the beginning.[71]

In Moreno's eyes, this "great step" of getting to the ILO symbolized the beginning of a larger journey to recognize domestic work as not just "decent work" but noble work to be celebrated. Many organizations proclaimed, "Domestic workers care for the most valuable aspects of their employers' lives." They contribute to employers' "sacred space" to assure the "smooth functioning and harmony of the home."[72] One Uruguayan employer at the ILO, Maria Lorenzo de Sanchez of the Housewives League, distinguished domestic work from other forms of labor on the basis of its location in the intimate confines of the home.

> A person comes into our home because this is the setting of our labor relationship; it's not a company, it's our actual lives that a person is coming into and we should be able to trust this person to handle all of our things, so we need to know that she is going to behave well.[73]

In her view, while policy would support "good relationships," it could not take into account the particular dimensions of intimacy and reciprocal trust at the absolute foundation of this work. With a contract in place, de

Sanchez went on to say, "our homes would be more peaceful, more calm," with "fewer misunderstandings." Yet, as others emphasized, any formal policy or procedure is enacted based upon the foundational relationship between the domestic worker and employer. Without this relationship, no convention or national law will assure "peace in the home."[74]

While domestic workers uniformly supported Convention 189 as a "huge victory," in personal conversations they spoke of their field in language that transcended policy concerns and centered on intimacy, aesthetics, and morality. Eunice Dhladhla, a union activist who fought for women's rights under apartheid, connected domestic workers to the "breath" of life in the home.

> When the employer comes back from work, she will find the house spotless. So who cleans the house? A domestic worker. So this person is a very important person. Without her in the house, the house has got no oxygen. There's no *oxygen*. So once that worker enters the door, as soon as she enters the door, everything comes to life—even flowers. If flowers were dying, because she will come in and give them water and give them love and clean the house, because she's got love. She will give everything, love in this house. And then when the employer comes in, everything is alive because of a domestic worker.[75]

After 35 years of activism, this national union leader went on to call domestic workers the real VIPs. "I would like to tell workers that workers walk tall. Be free. You are a human being and you are a very important person. You know, VIPs!" This description bestows a measure of intimate agency, whereby domestic workers take charge of formative aspects of the private household through their own initiative and autonomy— harmonizing relationships, adding "life" to the physical environment, and, indeed, providing love to the "sacred space" of the home and to its occupants. Going far beyond the terms of a contract or policy requirements, this sense of accentuating forms of human existence elevated domestic work to a noble profession in which workers could take pride and to which they could bring their individual vision.

Shirley Pryce, the leader of the Jamaican domestic workers' movement, articulated this autonomous leadership so central to peak performance in this work.

If you are working in the house, you must be rounded. You have to look outside and see a few flowers and pick [them], and set [them] in a vase, so the house is, when the bosses come in, they feel good, because it is not about you only, it is about the family you are working with. Everybody must feel good about what you are doing. And when they come in the house, they must feel good, feel like they want you there. And you must take pride in your job, basically. You must take pride in whatever you do. Even if you work with limitation, you must find ways and means of letting it work for you.[76]

This advice—delivered by a woman who managed the Jamaican prime minister's home—speaks to the value of domestic workers' capacity to foresee the emotional, operational, and relational aspects of the entire household. Beyond the cleanliness of the space, assuring that the people who reside in it feel safe, comfortable, respected, and protected in their privacy is a vital emotional-intelligence resource. Ida le Blanc spoke of labor policy as secondary to the consciousness for care that comes from human connections. In conversations about night work, le Blanc balked at the notion of policy determining whether or not a domestic worker would step in.

They say it [regulation] is needed in case a sick or elderly person falls out of bed in the middle of the night, for example. But I doubt that many domestic workers would turn away and do nothing—it is not just about our duties as an employee but about us as human beings, with a conscience, just like anyone else. Why would we need to legislate for such a situation?[77]

In her mind, legislation actually undermined the moral value domestic workers express in their commitment to care. Even though le Blanc and all members of the IDWN supported this global policy, they resisted a level of regulation that would take away from the value of the work they perform by putting it in such "regular" terms. In other words, care could not be commodified in all of its expressions. These intangible yet critical dimensions of household labor set it apart from any other profession. Yet the policy achievement required a certain uniformity of domestic work. A convention left no room for these intangible articulators of the real value of domestic labor. While lead officials within the ILO empha-sized that in order to build the case for protections, they avoided any notion of domestic work as special, for the workers themselves, these dimensions fulfilled a core aspect of their identity. Moreover, as domes-tic workers' testimonials reflect, these intimate and moral expressions of labor often enabled their own emotional survival in many of the most difficult circumstances.

Summary: "No Longer Invisible"

The path to putting rights on paper marked a monumental turn in the recognition of domestic workers' contributions to households and econ-omies, as well as their legitimate claim to protections. Most of the work of getting to the formal policy proposal involved defining domestic work in ways that allowed for the diversity of contexts, while providing a serious policy instrument that could be applied across locations. With two years of review on the initial draft policy, governments, employers, and workers weighed in on the details of over 100 amendments, focus-ing the work of 187 governments and over 900 representatives for 25 days of negotiations. Throughout this process, domestic work moved from a position of servitude to one of standard labor exchange, at least on paper. At the same time, this policy became a way of confronting the global migration proliferation, albeit often in covert terms. With Con-vention 189 ironed out to such fine detail, individual employers became responsible parties and the household shifted to a site of public labor.

Convention 189's closing discussions generated celebration across parties. Workers' group representative Toni Moore acknowledged the committee's capacity to develop a "robust" policy, "addressing the speci-ficities of domestic work and its heterogeneity." She closed the final policy sessions by acknowledging, "Today, as a result of constructive dialogue, we are all winners. We are winners because we have reached a very significant milestone."[78] This statement reverberated with domestic worker representatives in the room, who fed into the dialogue strategi-cally as activist experts. As Carmen Cruz, a lead Costa Rican domestic worker organizer proclaimed, "We're no longer invisible. Now we're vis-ible, and our rights are being recognized."[79] Through these discussions, María Luisa Escorel de Moraes, government delegate from Brazil, emphasized domestic workers' capacity to "enjoy rights to health, education, and housing, and respect for their working conditions." Alongside these accomplishments, she emphasized her hope that both employers and domestic workers "may enjoy a full life."[80]

Given the level of policy specificity, many of the larger values and distinct contributions of domestic work got lost in efforts to make this labor "just like any other." The existential dimensions of beautifying a house, harmonizing relationships, and tending to the emotional needs of employers could not be articulated in even the most refined policy. Yet with so many details on paper, domestic workers earned recognition that allowed their greater contributions to become evident. They gained a global public stage where the value of care love labor came into the discussions in ways that amplified and strengthened domestic workers' place in the conversation. In the view of many domestic workers, once they got to the ILO, they knew they were "on the map." From here, the vital work of changing attitudes ideally accompanies changes in the law. No policy polished to such refinement can be effective if it lives alone in the libraries of the ILO. Yet, as Manuela Tomei repeatedly contended, "This is not the end, this is the beginning."[81]

5

"My Mother Was a Kitchen Girl"

Mobilizing Strategies Among Domestic Workers

If somebody would have said to me 45 years ago that I would have sat here today and really get to the end of slavery, I would not have believed them. But 45 years ago, I was sitting in my employer's garage and I was organizing domestic workers. Today I'm here. And I'm here because of the cause of so many domestic workers. And if you did not believe in us, if you were not so passionate, we would not have been able to win this fight. But because all of you believe, you believe there's a better life for domestic workers, you believe that the time of repayment has come now for all of us. We want to be free. We don't want to be called slaves anymore. We want to get what every other worker has in this world.
—Myrtle Witbooi, Closing Statement, 2011 ILC

Sunita works in Saudi Arabia as a live-in domestic worker.[1] With the encouragement of employment agents who promised riches in return, she left her Indian village at the age of eight to support her family. Sunita arrived in Riyadh to meet her employer—a family of six with very strict cleanliness, food, and ritual practices that soon defined her daily life. Her employers held Sunita's passport, controlled her movements beyond the household, and relegated her to sleep in the kitchen. She had no means of reaching other domestic workers, until her passport was about to expire. Her employers took her to the Indian Embassy, where she waited for some time in a holding room that captured the complexities of women's social locations—as employers or workers. In this one space, awaiting the embassy's attention, Sunita asked to use the public restroom—a space Saudi women refuse to enter because it is perceived as "filthy." Here Sunita finally met other domestic workers. She exchanged numbers on the cell phone that comprised her only means of outside communication, in a country where unions are banned, women are severely oppressed, and domestic workers carry the added burden of gender, migrant, and labor status. Later, Sunita texted her sister comrades, asking if they knew of a means to report abuse, a way she could eventually return home. This is the extent of domestic activism in the country that had come to contain Sunita's life. She could not travel to the ILO, for no organization represented her, her employer would not release her, and her minimal salary would never cover the cost of her participation in global activism. For Sunita, agency emerges from within, in her commitment to a better life, a larger purpose, and her eventual escape from the oppressive circumstances of her employment. Even in this most severe case of isolation, Sunita feels an affinity with other domestic workers, women like her, in distant parts of the world. Her internalized expectation of an eventual release from her present struggle is a thread of hope that runs through her daily existence. Lucille Clifton's poem "Study the Masters" reflects the dialectic of resilience and oppression that connect women through their daily lives as domestic workers, across the world's contexts.

> study the masters
> like my aunt timmie.
> it was her iron,
> or one like hers,
> that smoothed the sheets
> the master poet slept on.
> home or hotel, what matters is
> he lay himself down on her handiwork
> and dreamed. she dreamed too, words:
> some Cherokee, some masai and some
> huge and particular as hope.
> if you had heard her
> chanting as she ironed
> you would understand form and line
> and discipline and order and
> america.[2]

This chapter looks at the central strategies domestic workers employed to reach the Convention 189 victory. By learning the ILO system, working with allies, building unified claims, drawing on activist techniques, and relying upon affective appeals, domestic workers made it impossible for ILO delegates to deny them in their quest for rights. Yet the path to recognition was not easy: the IDWN faced power politics, competing priorities, and its own growing pains along the way. These challenges form a central part of this larger policy-activist story. The newly formed network had to iron out its own process and working structure as it interacted within the new ILO terrain. But IDWN members persevered, mindful of the larger collective of workers they represented, whose attainment of rights were at stake.

Throughout their work both within and at the perimeters of the ILO, IDWN activists embodied domestic workers' historical struggle and contemporary realities, persuading the policymaking community that they had a moral responsibility to address these workers' concerns. The direct involvement of domestic worker representatives within the ILO decision-making processes merited frequent recognition by leaders of labor, employer, and executive bodies. In his 2010 ILC opening remarks, chair of the overarching ILO workers' group, Sir Leroy Trotman, stated that because domestic workers were "present in the room" the deliberations would assuredly reflect a certain "reality on the ground."[3] Secretary of the workers' group, Raquel Gonzales, welcomed the experiences of domestic workers as a "very lively dynamic"[4] in the negotiations. ILO Director-General Juan Somavía endorsed domestic workers' inclusion in the convention negotiations by stating that "in different ways, domestic workers' activities are in fact present here in the room," allowing for "an important capacity to come down to the reality of what you are discussing today."[5] These public endorsements by key leaders reinforced the acceptance of a new form of participation in the tripartite process. IDWN representatives expressed their enthusiasm about the opportunity to take part in the dialogue, noting that domestic workers had waited a very long time for labor protections. Within the confines of a heavily tradition-bound organization, however, domestic workers remained largely on the sidelines of the formal tripartite process, while holding a distinct moral position of power as those who experienced the very oppressions that international conventions are intended to prevent. This tension pervaded every phase of the ILC negotiations over the course of two years.

Domestic Worker Standpoints

Domestic workers chartered new forms of activism, as they engaged with the ILO structure in strategic and often unconventional ways. While the IDWN brought a history of social protest and public demonstration, the heavily bureaucratic ILO institutional practices upheld strict rules about procedures, order, and authorization to speak. The tripartite social dialogue structure allows only one formal delegate from the labor and employer groups to speak during convention negotiations. Government representatives from each of the 187 states may participate in the social dialogue, yet the labor and employer groups must rely on one official spokesperson. As NGO observers, domestic workers could not formerly participate in this tripartite dialogue within the Committee on Domestic Work. Yet they employed new forms of voice, resistance, and representation even as they played by the ILO rules. IDWN leaders took three innovative approaches: (1) infusing domestic work experiences and national data into government and worker representatives' testimonials; (2) creating new forms of voice through nonverbal means; and (3) utilizing the physical spaces where delegates gathered to make their presence known. IDWN leaders skillfully navigated the ILO bureaucracy, optimizing their efforts to shake the institution to its very foundations.

IDWN leaders worked behind the scenes with key networks to influence formal statements on behalf of labor and the interventions of key governments. They fed national statistical data, personal testimonials, and rhetorical frameworks to the labor vice chair, Halimah Yacob, who served as a muse for the voices of domestic workers. This continual injection of "real life" experiences of domestic workers profoundly affected the formation of global policy. When delegates heard the story of Shirley Pryce, for example, who was forced to sleep in a doghouse for years while caring for her employer's home, the need for global standards sharpened in scope, application, and urgency. Furthermore, the presence of workers who had lived through the struggles of unregulated household labor rendered opposition to the convention a cold denial of human rights. In essence, domestic workers like Shirley Pryce became

living symbolic representations of the costs accrued in the historical failure to provide standards for this group of workers. Yet it often required
the voice of officials within the system to legitimate domestic workers'
experiences in the policymaking process.

As activists with a history of public demonstration, IDWN leaders
found ways to amplify domestic workers' collective voice. Each day of
the ILC negotiations, both domestic workers and many of their NGO
affiliates wore clothing, buttons, symbolic cooking aprons, sticker messages, and campaign colors that readily identified the presence of "actual
workers" in the negotiation chambers. In this sense, the physical bodies
of domestic workers became a rhetorical tool to strengthen the position
of labor on ILC terrain. By using their bodies as visual placards to END
SLAVERY NOW and assure JUSTICE FOR ALL, workers brought new
forms of influence to civil society organizations working within the formal structures of ILO policymaking.

Such physical messaging underscored the sheer volume of civil society representatives present within the negotiations. Indeed, the number
of IDWN members and allies that came to Geneva to support domestic
workers posed serious challenges in terms of accommodation. At the
opening ILC in 2010, the first official workers' group meeting for the
Committee on Domestic Work took place at the UN Palais des Nations,
one of the most imposing venues in the UN infrastructure. Domestic
worker representatives made history as the first group to force the relocation of ILC discussions in order to include the large number of civil
society representatives. In moments like these, the IDWN interrupted
the flow of the deliberations by posing logistical and procedural challenges stemming from the strength of the domestic worker coalition.
The overflow crowds exposed the ILO's inexperience in engaging "actual
workers" in its formal process, while building momentum for domestic
workers as a social movement.

Beside these original strategies of expanding the wider presence of
IDWN and its allies, a sophisticated NGO policy-expert team coached
these representatives of "actual workers" in the few designated spaces
that allowed their voices to get to the wider delegations, as well as the
formal record of the proceedings. As civil society observers, IDWN
members could engage in two key proceedings: (1) the workers' group
meetings, where all representatives of labor met with the vice chair and

executive committee to build strategies for the tripartite discussion; and (2) the formal ILC opening and closing plenaries, where select delegates from all working groups report out to the larger conference and form official content for the ILC proceedings. In these public occasions, the IDWN selected key delegates to speak on behalf of domestic workers. As they engaged verbally in these sanctioned forums, providing perspectives and data to government delegates and the workers' group chair, the IDWN maximized their platforms for influence, while defining a new strategy of public rhetoric.

Building a Common Campaign

I think strength is the same everywhere. Today, our faces may be a little different, but we're the same workers scattered throughout the universe. We've all suffered in some way through the same humiliating situations, like feeling small, and feeling invisible.
—Aida Moreno

The struggle of one woman is the struggle of all women.
—Marcelina Bautista

Once they "got in" to the largest and most historic labor institution, domestic workers strategically constructed a common identity to maximize their demands for rights and recognition. To make policy, they told stories. The use of personal narratives became one of the most effective tools in increasing the likelihood of passing a convention. These testimonials positioned domestic workers as "the backbone" of the global economy, keeping the ILO accountable to the women workers and migrants who hold up the international service sector. Even though domestic workers came from five continents with distinct work contexts, the IDWN demanded a global umbrella policy for *all* domestics. The public testimonials of shared personal experiences of oppression brought the realities of women workers into the highly procedural policy forum. By putting a human face on their appeal for global standards, domestic workers made it impossible for government leaders to overlook those who have lived without standardized protections since the earliest establishment of relations of servitude. Their ability to speak as "one voice" for domestic workers ultimately mirrored the legitimacy of the universal rights claims that ILO conventions and other UN human rights policies seek to establish. In the public dialogue, domestic workers built a collective appeal by emphasizing three common themes: (1) the historic nature of the institution of domestic work; (2) individual stories of oppression as a result of exclusion from labor standards; (3) a common experience of vulnerability. Their request to ILO voting delegates: "Listen with your hearts" as you consider the domestic workers in the room.[6]

Historic Nature of Domestic Work

As a representative body of a larger historic struggle, domestic workers drew from their own stories to represent a legacy of workers who suffered in the absence of labor protections. In public platforms, domestic workers consistently referred to their long-standing exclusion from national labor protections in positing a central moral obligation for the ILO to establish meaningful standards of work. This historic exclusion became a central point in the collective call for convention protections, in both individual stories and the IDWN's organizational statements. Narbada Chhetri, of the National Domestic Workers Alliance in the US, called the ILO to attention by drawing on the symbolism of 100 years of meetings to emphasize domestic work as a final frontier for policy inclusion. "This is the 100th Labor Organization Conference, and within the 100th year, our sisters are not recognized as workers." The IDWN collective statement echoed this demand for accountability for this historic imbalance with a call to write a new script:

> If adopted, these international instruments will truly break new ground. They will take a huge step forward in human history to combat the exploitation, abuse, and lack of respect endured by many of the world's domestic workers. Some of us work in conditions of forced labour or slavery, with no respect for our rights as fellow human beings . . . It is an injustice that has lasted too long.[7]

By emphasizing the historic absence of standards, these domestic workers appealed to policymakers' capacities to address historic injustice by formulating what would not only be an international law, but a moral marker in the course of human rights.

Their demands called for protective ILO policies "with teeth."[8] As Ernestina Ochoa, IDWN vice chair from Peru, expressed in her report to the media immediately following the Convention 189 vote:

> I am a domestic worker. I *work*. Up to this day, I have worked. I am here because I want to be re-vindicated of all of the mistreatment of our ancestors. We are asking you governments. We do not want nice speeches; we want *actions*. We want you to hear us. We need your support . . . We don't want you to say, "This is what we have done for women." We want you to open the doors, sit down with us, and listen to our voices.[9]

In her statement, Ernestina references historical suffering to gain universal rights that go beyond gender-sensitive rhetoric alone. As she later proclaimed in her reflections on the convention victory, "It is not free, it is what society owed to us." Just as domestic workers asked for democratic relations of respect with employers, at a larger scale, the IDWN demanded that the ILO recognize domestic workers through global rights.

When domestic workers referred to both their ancestors and the hundreds of thousands of "poor migrant women" who have been excluded from protections, they drew upon a large body of workers to strengthen their demands for institutional reparations. In her opening public statement at the 2010 ILC, IDWN President Myrtle Witbooi professed:

> We want to say to you, the ILO delegates: We have been waiting for 65 *years* for this to happen and we cannot lose this opportunity to appeal to you to please secure the minimum labor standards for the millions of domestic workers that are still unprotected in their respective countries, in order to create an international instrument that will not only protect domestic workers, but will also give us back our dignity and allow us to walk tall as workers, just as any other worker in the world![10]

The repeated allusion to historical struggles to attain "dignity" and "respect" in the household became an extremely effective tool of moral and collective persuasion. As H.E.M. Christian Guillermet-Fernandez said to the child domestic workers who brought their struggles to the ILO special forums, "You may not be an expert, but you speak from the heart.[11] At the same time, by asking the ILO to "set right a historic record of injustice" at the 100th meeting of the ILO, activists placed a great deal of confidence in the potential for international policy to address centuries of historic marginalization. For domestic workers, this use of story comprised one of the most important tactics in ensuring that the lives of their sisters earned a central stage in the debates around the terms of their protections.

Story Platforms: Narratives of Oppression and Exclusion

In the telling of these stories, domestic workers used their personal experiences of suffering in making their emotional appeals, as Shirley Pryce exemplified in the following statement.

> I am very happy just to see where we are now, because I have been abused, I have been through it all. So now, if I can help to make domestic workers' lives better, then I will continue fighting for that.

From stories of her abuse at the hands of cruel employers and the history of suffering among domestic workers worldwide, Shirley Pryce vindicated her position as a leading national labor activist and the first domestic worker to be granted voting rights for the convention. In a nuanced strategy, like Shirley, IDWN leaders took advantage of traditional constructions of gender to enact an affective shared domestic worker narrative within the traditionally masculine space of the ILO. Feminized testimonials, stories of women's struggles, and highly personalized histories brought the presence of "actual workers" into the negotiations in ways that amplified a wider empathy for the life experiences of the domestic workers. As they spoke, domestic worker leaders positioned themselves as representatives of a much wider experience of labor oppression.

> My name is Guillermina Castellanos. I've worked ever since I was five years old as a domestic worker. I immigrated to the United States when I was fifteen, and I immediately began working as a nanny. I was abused as

a domestic worker, in Mexico as well as in the United States. I'm not the only one to have this experience. This is the shared experience of millions of domestic workers.

In this formal address to the ILC, this very public domestic worker activist in the US highlights her experience as a child laborer, migrant, and survivor of abuse to convey the realities of domestic workers worldwide.

Hester Stephens brought memories of her childhood experience to the public forum to show how women and girls suffer in the gendered family constructions that send them into domestic work at a very early age:

> While we are here, it just runs through my mind, where did I come from and where am I today? I mean if you really think about the domestic workers as a whole, because we don't have proper education, there was no time for us to go to school, because we had to leave school and to try to provide and help our fathers put bread on the table.

This positioning of shared historical suffering across diverse geographic divides widened the legitimacy domestic workers brought to the negotiations. As other social movements for justice reveal, the demonstration of bodily harm and collective pain strengthens the use of story as a symbolic political tactic for transnational activist networks.[12] Within the ILO policymaking landscape, no other group could offer the depth and rhetorical influence of real-life stories as domestic workers themselves. Their testimonials of prolonged hardship imposed serious challenges to decision makers' abilities to ignore these public statements of private trauma.

These narratives of domestic workers interwove emotional, psychological, and economic hardships, as the story of Marissa Begonia, a Filipina domestic worker activist in the United Kingdom, illustrates in her public ILO speech:

> Years ago I took a decision to leave my children behind. It is my responsibility to keep my children alive. Through domestic work, that is how my children grew up, it is how I educated my children. This has made me strong. It has given me the courage to continue.

Marissa's experience locates her as both a victim of the harsh requirements of physical separation central to domestic work and a strong
advocate who became a labor activist as a result of her circumstances.
This dual positioning of domestic workers as both victims of suffering and resourceful survivors contributed to a persuasive standpoint
throughout the policy negotiations. As they presented their personal
histories of suffering, domestic workers simultaneously demanded that
they be taken seriously as central stakeholders in the policy process. US
activist Juana Flores captures this sufferer-survivor stance in an interview with the Latin news agency Agencia Efe during the 2011 conference.

> Honestly, there are those of us who have gone through those types of
> abuses, and we've remained silent. Or if we've talked, we've had the ex-
> perience of what happens at those times when we say: "That's enough for
> me. No. Enough already. Today, today, it's enough. I'm going to risk it."

Flores's capacity to "risk it" placed her on the official US labor delegation, as one of the most prominent experts on domestic labor in the
country. Her colleague in the National Domestic Workers Alliance,
Guillermina Castellanos, embodied this "enough is enough" stance
to expose her shared experience of abuse as a measure of the importance of changing these realities through a strong and widely applicable
convention.

> I represent 100 trade unions and organizations in all parts of the world. A
> weak convention will only reinforce the reality that we are experiencing.
> We have been living this way for centuries and we have the opportunity
> to correct this . . . This convention will create a better world for all. On
> behalf of all of my sisters, I would like to say thank you very much for
> listening to us.[13]

By placing individual stories of oppression in the formal record, the
IDWN put a human rights framework on the negotiations. According
to global union experts, the domestic worker convention negotiations
included the most directly personal content from workers themselves in
the history of ILO policymaking.[14] While other movements such as the
Anti-Sweatshop campaign and national suffrage events utilized workers'

testimonials as rhetorical tools of persuasion, no other movement has used personal storytelling to this extent within the ILO.[15] When testimonials across a range of national contexts came to the ILO in such frequency, and within the rules of the organization, The impact of these testimonials, across a range of national contexts, had a dramatic impact on the policy process.

Storytelling brought power and legitimacy to domestic workers as they took to the public stage. Yet, affective testimonials also link women to the emotional domain, while reconstructing domestic labor as feminized through the "heart strings" these stories intended to pull. Even though this technique worked as a distinct strategy in the case of this policy, these narratives of struggle also fed into a subtext of domestic workers in need of charity, which allows the ILO to come in as a paternalistic rescuer to the "millions of abused women out there in this field." Thus, this strategy teaches us that the trade-offs between "selling suffering" for a greater good and risking further essentialized constructions of "vulnerable" domestic workers is constantly negotiated in the larger purpose of a movement and its immediate goals. In this case, constructing vulnerability and suffering more often won over the risks of reconstructing traditional associations to race, national status, gender, class/caste, sexuality, and religion in the process of presenting a collective transnational domestic worker story.

Crafting Vulnerability

As the stories of domestic workers moved into the spotlight of policy discussions, advocates frequently drew upon constructions of "vulnerability" as a persuasive strategy. Their call to protect "those who have suffered" as "poor domestic workers" held a strong affective power within the negotiations.[16] During the debates, Vice Chair Halimah Yacob would remind delegates that they were constructing policy to emancipate the "millions of poor women" worldwide, "many of whom are migrant women." As resistance to protections grew in the negotiations, she appealed, "Please remember that these are young girls, very vulnerable."[17] NGOs upheld this notion of vulnerability throughout their reports and discourse on domestic workers, as they lobbied for protections. To expose severe exploitation, their promotional material often positioned domestic workers primarily as victims of some of the more dire human conditions—trafficking, physical abuse, and sexual violation. For example, one NGO campaign poster depicted a heavily fatigued young woman, with a caption that read, SHE DESERVES A DAY OFF TOO.[18] Many called this institution "modern slavery," conveying stories of women locked in households at the hands of their employers. This construction of vulnerability often conflated domestic work with popularized notions of abuse, much like the media accounts that rely upon sensationalized imagery. With this added affective appeal, the ILO discussion set up the need for global protections by universalizing domestic workers as vulnerable victims in need of legal protections.

Sociologist Shireen Ally problematizes this use of vulnerability as a central rationale for state protections. She draws upon the South African case to show how a newly democratic government rooted its attention to domestic workers in assumptions about women's victimhood that ultimately bolstered the state as a paternalistic protector. "'Vulnerability' as a mode of entry into citizenship rights for domestic workers presumed a victimized subject with compromised capacity. It presumed the protection of a more capacitated actor, to act on behalf of, and for the empowerment of, the 'vulnerable' category."[19] In the realm of international governance, the ILO assumed the role of the global protector of domestic workers, which necessitated the construction of very particular forms of vulnerability among the benefactors of policy protection. This approach is woven into the ILO's framing of "decent work for domestic workers." Its summary report on the 99th session emphasized an awareness of "the ethical consequences of leaving this isolated and vulnerable category of workers outside effective regulation and social protection."[20] Thus, the ILO's reliance upon construction of domestic workers' vulnerability reproduced notions of "poor, migrant women" in order to build the foundational justifications for these policy protections. While domestic workers got into a widely publicized global arena through these policy negotiations, the ILO's construction of their need for its protections ultimately amplified its own capacity to serve as the benevolent policy father, with the capacity to dole out protections to those who fit within this framework. This use of vulnerability reflects that in some ways, domestic workers became the charitable giving dimension of the overarching ILO machine.

By proposing standards for this "formerly invisible" population, the ILO assumed a role that attempted to regulate international human capital and labor flows through policies that would parallel the regulations in place for the flows of goods and monetary resources set forth by the World Trade Organization and global finance institutions, including the World Bank and the International Monetary Fund. The capacity to reach into this new terrain, however, hinged upon constructing the workers who needed ILO protections as extremely vulnerable. In this sense, as an international governance institution, the ILO falls into Ally's analysis of the dialectical relationship between subjects' vulnerability and the expansion of state powers. As she contends, "The state imagined workers as lacking the capacity to effect change themselves, and constructed itself as the agent to act on their behalf, thereby extending the state's responsibility and, with it, its powers and reach."[21] In this case, the ILO extended its power by constructing its own role as the only institution set up to respond to this global migration crisis and increased informality of work. To prove its capacity to do so, domestic workers would come under its newly expanded reach, while the ILO would provide policy as a means to rescue the world's most vulnerable.

The ILO expansion to the informal sector prompted a series of images and rhetoric that crystallized this vulnerability around migrant, abused, young, and trafficked women from the Global South. In some cases, domestic worker organizations bought into this construction and reproduced it to position their appeals more powerfully. In her public statement at the 2011 ILC, IDWN leader Narbada Chhetri pronounced, "This convention is for vulnerable domestic workers, not for the privileged workers. If this makes law, then our sisters are protected, socially, economically." As a representative of domestic worker organizations, Chhetri positioned her "sisters" as predominantly vulnerable, and in need of a convention to change their living circumstances. Furthermore, even when they did not use the term "vulnerability," domestic workers played into notions of victimhood through stories that highlighted severe suffering, historical injustices, and the traumas of unregulated work within such unequal power positions in the household. This image of a poor, vulnerable domestic worker recalls the scholarship of postcolonial feminist theorist Chandra Mohanty, who critiqued the "typical Third World woman" so pervasive in development discourse. By creating an

"Other" in binary opposition to "Western women," the Global North is perpetually reinforced in its capacity to rescue the Global South.[22] In a parallel form, as an agent of development and international standards, the ILO embodies this notion of Western advancement. Its power at this level, however, relied upon domestic workers' position as the marginalized "Third World Other" in need of development. At the heart of these assumptions: with the ILO protections in place, domestic workers would move out of their Third World conditions and step closer to the standards of the so-called First World.

In many instances, domestic workers resisted this framing of vulnerability as central to their identity and collective cause. South African domestic worker union leader Monica Phumzile Ntuli contested the use of the term "vulnerable" in relation to domestic work.

> It makes that vulnerable name a word. It makes a worker feel so small and unconfident. And she feels like she is nothing, and she loses the hope of herself or himself, that she is also a human being. She's got a right to stay in this world. She always feels not happy about herself—thinking that I'm nothing. Nobody's recognizing me as a human being, because, I'm *vulnerable*. I also don't like it. Yes it is there, but I don't know how can we change this vulnerable sector.[23]

In her assessment, the "vulnerable" label reinforced individual workers' sense of self and position within the social hierarchy. Among her peers, at a union workshop, she called for a reconsideration of this term in both the national government and ILO discourse, resisting the idea that domestic workers are necessarily vulnerable and calling upon her "sister comrades" to reframe this sector's image.

Within the ILO policy negotiations, domestic workers both resisted this construction and also played into its appeal as a persuasive tool to build emotional and moral support. Certainly, the individual and collective power of the domestic worker leaders in the ILC negotiations refutes such assumptions of victimized women. Yet in their public statements, they demanded ILO protections for women "trapped in households throughout the world." As they spoke directly about the experiences of "poor migrant women," they reinforced essentialized imagery in order to advocate for global protections within their own sector. This notion of vulnerability stands in sharp contradistinction to the models of domestic worker leadership we see throughout the ILO process, namely in the pioneers who launched national movements in the face of the most severe forms of domestic workers' exclusion and abuse. Leaders like Aida Moreno, Myrtle Witbooi, and Shirley Pryce ushered in the first national labor policies, risked their own lives to establish unions, built schools for their *compañeros*, and received recognition from national presidents for their vast contributions as labor leaders—achievements far beyond the capacities of "vulnerable" women. Throughout the negotiations, the collective IDWN leadership embodied activism, dignity, and strength, as women who entered the ILO with a vast collection of experiences leading movements in their own countries. Thus, these global policy negotiations created a new space where domestic workers could draw from notions of vulnerability within a wider sector, as prominent activists who disrupted this construction in their very presence within the ILO.

Activist Policy Strategies
Coalition Building

The network has played a very important role. So, if we had not have had this organization, I am not sure how we would have sustained the intensity of this conference. I don't mean to diminish the power of workers, because we are freedom fighters.
—Leddy Mozombite Linares, General Secretary, Domestic Workers Union, Peru

Domestic workers attended the ILO negotiations as part of an established coalition led by widely recognized organizations in the labor, policy, and gender arenas. With their historical support and most active agenda on domestic work, WIEGO and the IUF served as the IDWN's two complementary allies. The inclusion of domestic work on the ILO agenda, however, engaged an entire network of NGO and faith-based organizational allies, who employed common activist strategies to bolster the presence of the domestic worker cause within the negotiations. For the IDWN's membership organizations, their capacity to draw support from these larger NGOs and prominent organizations bolstered their political capital. At the same time, this wide network fortified the labor position and to a certain extent tipped the balance of power within the tripartite dialogue. The expansion of the representation and participation of civil-society "observers" within the tripartite system ultimately served as a means of increasing the impact of social movements within the ILO system because more powerful NGOs took on the plight of domestic workers and presented a united front that linked actual workers with civil society and international NGOs.

This wider NGO network underscored the strong "political will" that distinguished this convention process and, to a large extent, strengthened its ultimate victory. These ally organizations provided important political support by expanding the presence of civil society representatives and demonstrating consistent solidarity with domestic workers throughout the meetings. By showing to represent such wider causes, NGOs framed domestic work as a vital concern for migrant rights, faith-based organizations, and antitrafficking child-slavery networks. This coalition of invested NGOs served three vital purposes: (1) they strengthened the voice of civil society, (2) their publicity efforts vastly widened awareness of domestic-labor rights; and (3) their participation mainstreamed domestic labor as a larger human rights cause. The key activist strategies in operation throughout the ILC debates, however, came from the WIEGO/IUF organizations, which were largely responsible for organizing domestic workers in the decades prior to the conferences. These two organizations—a women's informal-labor policy network and a global union—provided training, substantial resources, organizational strategizing, and expert links that mobilized the IDWF as pioneers in using the policy arena as a site of transnational domestic worker activism. This WIEGO-IDWN-IUF relationship served as a feminist-activist-labor triumverate that fostered new civil society access; it was as if the bandwidth on policymaking multiplied to make room for the voices of "actual workers."

The support of these organizations worked along a continuum flanked by expertise in applied practice and pivotal sociopolitical capital. Working together, both organizations provided numerous direct strategies that formed the domestic worker identity and presence within the ILO negotiations. Beyond the policy discussions, the tangible resource bases

Figure 5.1. Human rights activists align at the IUF Headquarters in Geneva.

and sociopolitical backing of these organizations positioned domestic work as both a labor and women's movement priority. Through the IUF global union structure, domestic workers gained vital support from a wider labor movement. This partnership allowed domestic worker organizations to circumvent their recurring exclusion from national union structures that so often labeled their cause as "nonviable."[24] This affiliation echoes historical organizational strategies, whereby domestic workers aligned with other labor sectors in order to strengthen their base and increase the potential for instituting change.[25] On the women's movement side, the support of WIEGO prioritized domestic work within a larger gender labor policy arena. Rather than positioning household labor as an isolated sector, WIEGO linked domestic workers with other largely feminized sectors of the informal economy, including home-based workers, street vendors, and waste pickers. At the same time, the prominence of this organization placed domestic work on the radar of larger funding institutions, such as the Bill & Melinda Gates Foundation and the Ford Foundation. With the backing of WIEGO, domestic workers joined the largest initiative to address the global circumstance of women workers in the informal economy. Through these two pillar organizations, domestic workers gained a solid stance in the dual worlds of labor and gender, and the associated frameworks of unions' collective standards and development's focus on human rights.

The WIEGO-IUF alliance provided a team of policy experts, labor lobbyists, and technical assistants to carry out the organizational campaign strategies within the complex ILO system and build the IDWN as an aligned transnational network. Domestic leaders relied on this team of *técnicas, aliadas, hermanas,* and academicians to provide training in the ILO system, coordinate communication and media campaigns, link to larger civil society organizations, provide research information, interpret meetings in Spanish, French, and English, develop public statements, and promote the widest reach of awareness on the domestic workers' cause. At the helm, a feminist trio of WIEGO leaders fought tirelessly to get domestic workers to the table and assure their capacity to be a forceful presence within the negotiations. European labor expert Karin Pape worked across both organizations as the point person for the organization of domestic workers within the ILO system. From the IUF, Barbro Budin took on domestic worker protections as a core priority in her role as a gender specialist. WIEGO organizational strategist Chris Bonner brought her long-standing efforts to support domestic worker mobilization in Africa to the global network's first policy undertaking. With the resources available through these women experts and the wider IUF-WIEGO technical team, domestic workers could focus on their own role within the ILC negotiations and the concerns most relevant to each leader's national context.

Domestic workers' transnational network within the ILO emerged largely through the crafting of a collective identity and cause—by domestic workers themselves, professional representatives of domestic workers within the IDWN, and the WIEGO-IUF technical team. This tri-representative approach achieved five strategic interventions that maximized domestic worker activists' influence within the policymaking ILO machinery. First, the IDWN developed a *Platform of Demands* that expressed shared conditions of labor injustice across a range of sectors, thereby building a common set of policy expectations throughout both years' negotiations.[26] Second, domestic workers accessed key players within the ILO, presented a unified front to the entire tripartite (by literally scattering copies of their *Platform of Demands* throughout the negotiation venues), and established common leverage points for their conversations with government and employer representatives. For example, by drawing upon her long-standing relations, WIEGO director Marty Chen facilitated an IDWN meeting with Juan Somavía—a conversation that launched the 2010 ILC policy process and made tangible the new organizational commitment to opening the ILO to "grassroots organizations." With the ally organizations, domestic workers' reach stretched far beyond their own capacity as leaders within their own national contexts. This collective professionalization of domestic work proved extremely beneficial for the IDWN's exposure and perceived legitimacy.

Third, the WIEGO-IUF support partnership played a vital role in exporting the global domestic worker story to the media and related activist causes. Aida Moreno emphasized the importance of activist efforts in shaping the workers' narrative, bringing to the global stage the stories of those who suffer under globalization.

> Yes, the fact that, seeing so many workers, and not only from one continent but all over the world, this is creating a great impact. The press must be informed. If that would have the same diffusion as everything else, like football and violence, but this does not have the same diffusion. It is ignored . . . If this movement were spread, that would give more energy, more strength to the workers.[27]

Throughout the course of three years, WIEGO media specialists designed central talking points for all members of the IDWN, to assure a unified stance much like that outlined in the *Platform of Demands*. "This victory marks the end of slavery for 100 million domestic workers," they stated. At strategic moments throughout the process, the media technical team positioned trained representatives outside the official ILO press release room (reserved for ILO delegate briefings) to bring media attention to the stories of domestic worker union leaders and activists. Reporters from around the world were asked, "Would you like to talk with an actual domestic worker?" This initiative landed the movement a cover story in the Swiss newspaper *Le Temps*, in which a photographer posed domestic workers as ILO delegates in a feature entitled "La longue marche vers la dignité" (The long march to dignity). The only male member of the IDWN, Fataou Raimi, from Benin, was positioned to resemble an official delegate; the headline to his story reads, "Ne m'appelez pas: boy!" (Don't call me boy!).

Figure 5.2. Narbada Chhetri at the ILO. Photo by Alan Humerose. Source: *Le Temps*, June 13, 2011.

Alongside Fataou, Narbada Chhertri appears as a global human rights activist, under a headline excerpted from her interview that reads, "Les chiens dorment dans un lit, pas nous" (Dogs can sleep in a bed, not us).

The juxtaposition of iconic elements of the ILO and everyday instances of domestic worker exploitation proved effective in bringing domestic workers' campaign for labor protections to the wider public. WIEGO-IUF technical resources also enabled the creation of a compelling website, with a daily blog bringing the IDWN activities to a much wider global community.

The fourth core contribution of the WIEGO-IUF technical team stemmed from the extensive coordination of their joint efforts to build the IDWN's capacities and impact during the ILC meetings. Both prior to and following long days of negotiations, the team organized extensive workshops for IDWN leaders to advance their organizational objectives and functions. Within the ILC meetings, IDWN members participated in daily morning briefing sessions that interpreted the state of the negotiations, strategized the maximum impact of the network within the process, and facilitated upcoming events. These sessions proved to be vital for sharing information among the wide IDWN membership and coordinating best use of resources within the extremely demanding meeting sessions. Furthermore, by meeting each day and aligning in strategy, the IDWN built a stronger solidarity among workers through their co-investment in the strategy process.

Lastly, this coalition approach provided a framework for the advancement of a domestic worker movement beyond the ILO. While the Convention 189 process marked a core victory, the cross-national alignment and active engagement demanded by the policy-making efforts grew a domestic workers' movement far beyond the attainment of the convention victory. With this shared policy, the experience of establishing a common platform, and the extensive relationship building that took place through the ILO, domestic workers were well-positioned to advance their movement as an emergent organization with continued aspirations and purposes beyond the policy victory seeded in the ILO process. In her analysis of this distinct coalition strategy, social movements scholar Helen Schwenken noted:

> Strategic cross-movement relation-building therefore made it possible for domestic workers to reach something that appeared impossible: namely, for a group of female workers in precarious jobs in the informal sector to sit at the negotiating table in Geneva and gain moral, political and legal recognition.[28]

In many respects, the convention victory served as a public relations and movement-building tool, which ultimately may be more important for the recognition of domestic workers than the attainment of a formal set of international standards. As Dan Gallin observed, "The struggle to obtain these conventions is an opportunity for propaganda and agitation."[29] In any case, this policy celebration, and the strong organizational ties it achieved, can be traced directly to the investment of this professional team, and its building of a savvy global marketing campaign around the experiences, collective identity, and activist leadership of the domestic workers who founded the first transnational network.

Framing a Human Rights Argument

They [domestic workers] are challenging the tripartite sectors in the ILO, who are considered instruments of change, to prove our value for freedom and human rights.
—Florencia P. Cabatingan, executive board member, Trade Union Congress of the Philippines (TUCP-ITUC)

Once they got in to the negotiations and established a strong coalition presence, IDWN representatives centered their position around persuasive interlocking arguments that spoke to human rights and the ethical obligations of global institutions like the ILO.[30] They utilized moral considerations, personal stories, emotional content, and historical conditions of injustice as compelling evidence to build central frameworks that linked domestic labor to three larger values: human rights, gender equity and economic justice. By placing this sector within a much wider context of shared priorities and ethical commitments within the international community, domestic work became a conduit for the ILO to demonstrate its emphasis on human rights, as well as the UN's established gender priorities. These vital ties provided fluid conduits for allies in government and labor representatives to take up support for the convention in a number of contexts. Their aligned approach gave domestic workers amplified credibility and social-political capital, as they held the ILO to its own ethical ethos.

Domestic workers staked their claim as human beings with "universal and inalienable rights" to social and legal protections.[31] According to the UN doctrine adopted in 2003, human rights must be indivisible, interrelated, equality-based, inclusive, and accountable to the rule of law. Extension of such rights to domestic workers is complicated by the distinct nature of work within the private household, as well as the complexities of migrant, gender, and class-based location. Marcelina Bautista, IDWN's Latin American regional coordinator, contended, "As domestic workers, human rights in the workplace are particularly important, as they are the least respected."[32] While they spoke of the discrimination they faced in their everyday work contexts, domestic workers called upon the ILO to uphold its commitment to the UN Common Understanding of Rights. Marissa Begonia, of Justice for Domestic Workers, shared this narrative on her own life experience as a Filipina migrant working in the UK.

> Alone in the wilderness, inside a beautiful house, behind the closed door, I work from 6 o'clock in the morning to 4 o'clock in the morning. Are two hours enough sleep for a human being? Are domestic workers not human beings?

In Begonia's public statement, the daily conditions of her work reflect core values about her worth as a human being. While the ILC negotiations hammered out the very particular details of work contracts, payments and recruitment time, domestic workers continually reminded the house of the larger impact of the 148 clauses they debated within the legal framework. In this sense, each of these technical dimensions reflected core labor standards placed into a larger context of human rights.

Just as the ILO conventions require states to uphold labor policy agreements, within the negotiations domestic workers held the ILO itself accountable to aspirational UN standards, where human rights are esteemed in the highest light. In her public address at the closing of the 2010 ILC, Vicky Kanyoka, the African regional coordinator for IDWN, pointed to governments' responsibility to uphold these standards, even in the face of wider global circumstances that may preclude human rights priorities and their implementation in labor practice.

> Facing the economic crisis, some governments—including those from the rich countries—are afraid of taking on further commitments. They feel they do not have the resources to organize such things as social security, maternity benefits, occupational health and safety, and regulation of employment agencies. But these are key human rights as well as labor issues.[33]

By bringing in this human rights framework, domestic workers held a trump card in their ability to demand that the ILO honor UN standards.

This larger ideal reverberated throughout even the most technical discussions. Furthermore, the ally training machinery behind the IDWN instilled "UN-speak" language as a tool for domestic workers to hold power by placing their demands within the core values of the very institution that would determine their access to such rights. One IDWN activist surmised the purpose of domestic workers' participation in the negotiations, "Like all people, we're reclaiming our human rights."[34] This capacity bolstered domestic workers' credibility, while rendering the denial of their rights unethical through the use of UN values as a litmus test of allegiance to international standards.

Feminist Investments in Domestic Worker Rights

Ida le Blanc hoped the whole world would see that "when women stop, everything stops."[35] She held this idea as her "dream" for the future following passage of Convention 189. The strategic interventions of the IDWN reflect core feminist concerns on several levels. By framing domestic work as a gender issue, activists gained that much more traction in their demands for fair work in the household. Their gender rights strategy took three forms. First, they equated domestic work with historic conditions of marginalized women's work in the private sphere. Second, activists and allies framed domestic labor as a crystallization of existing global race, class and gender injustices. In doing so, they repeatedly interjected descriptors that identified the institution as one that relies upon "poor women," with the least access to social power on the intersecting continuums of gender, race and citizenship. Third, domestic workers turned their demands for protection back on the ILO, using its adherence to UN gender equity standards as a means to promote the importance of uplifting this sector for the sake of larger global human rights and universal "decent work." Collectively, these three feminist foundations constructed a context that made opposition to Convention 189 an affront to the wider plight for gender justice, girls' rights and feminized poverty reduction.

Key governments worked directly with domestic workers to amplify the case for standardized protections, thereby redressing the historic exclusion of this quintessentially feminized, racialized and class-based sector of "private" labor, held in such a devalued relationship to "public" productivity. The bifurcation of these spheres holds deep roots in a core feminist movement to recognize the value of reproductive labor, traditionally performed by women. In her public address at an NGO forum during the 2010 ILC meetings, Elizabeth Prügl situated the importance of Convention 189 in a much larger struggle to recognize the value of household reproduction. As she pointed out among activists, advocates, and academics:

> With industrialization, with development, more work moved from homes, from farms into factories and the work in factories was the work that got regulated, that got recognized and that got social security protections, and all of those things. In contrast, the work that was done in homes, the work of reproduction, the care work that today domestic workers are doing, got devalued, and people that did that work received no minimum wage, no social security protections, all the things that you are talking about today. There is of course in these relationships, a deep message of gender. It was women who stayed in the homes to do the work, and it was men who moved outside of the homes to do the other kind of work.[36]

Prügl's succinct summary of the history of reproductive labor shows how the devaluing of unpaid household labor sets up the conditions for exploitation of this work when it becomes a paid profession. In a similar vein, as one member of the workers' group put it, "If anyone paid their wife, it would be good, but nobody does that."[37] In the spirit of these arguments, one of the guiding frameworks for the domestic worker movement has been to contrast this enduring virtual dismissal of the value of women's work with its vital importance in the literal regenerations of society—from birth, to formation, to socialization, to aging, to death.

Hester Stephens's life story embodies this contradiction between intimate dependency and devalued recognition. Over the course of 23 years of work in the same household, she raised the family's only child and cared for her male employer throughout his last stages of life. As he battled cancer, Hester tended to his extensive needs and treatments, while maintaining the everyday routines of household reproduction, including ironing, cooking, cleaning, meal production and locking her employers into their bedroom each night as part of her responsibility to manage the complex security system of their six-bedroom home. In her recollections, she held memories of pram walks with the family's toddler, whom she affectionately called "my Andrew," alongside the experience of tending to her employer's most basic bodily needs. Yet even as Hester cared intimately for this family throughout its most difficult seasons, her work remained deeply undervalued in the larger system, where domestic work is still among the very least paid and "most vulnerable" sectors. Her retirement will depend upon her employer's level of generosity after decades of interdependency.

Given the focal link between household labor and "women's work," the IDWN and its pro-convention allies often framed domestic work as central to women's wider liberation. As one domestic worker activist contended, "All that you are talking about, discrimination, social security, pay equality, isn't that what we are here for as domestic workers? We feel we should not separate and make it a domestic worker issue. It is a *woman's issue*." The South African domestic worker union has long carried the slogan, "Women won't be free until domestic workers are free." This statement upholds the notion that all women suffer when less privileged women are relegated to substandard work conditions and exploitation in the female household domain. As many scholars of domestic labor point out, as long as women with resources pay "other women" to do their "dirty work," men are left free of the obligations of household labor, and its added 20–60 hours of work each week, depending on the demands of daily tasks, such as supplying water, cooking meals, doing laundry, and accessing care products.[38]

While domestic workers did not name these arguments as "feminist" per se, their grounding perspectives capture the earliest concerns about household labor central to women's movements throughout the world.[39] Beyond a "woman's issue" scholars of domestic labor have repeatedly placed this institution at the apex of race, class and gender inequalities.[40] In the ILO public negotiations, however, only the Brazilian government specifically named race in their rationale for the convention. First they described domestic workers as "women, the majority of them, 93 percent majority of whom are black."[41] Throughout their public statements, the Brazilian government representatives continually integrated race and gender as core factors in the larger levels of discrimination that exist in domestic work. As the lead national spokesperson for Brazil put forth:

> The ILO conventions speak about lack of equality and gender. In the case of domestic work, there is discrimination on the basis of gender, race and class. We do not have the same rights as other workers. It is not just a matter of workers rights; it is trade union rights. We don't have the right to form unions as workers. There is still a great deal to be done.

This statement includes race in the analysis of domestic workers' exploitation, while exposing the larger gender struggles in national unions, where class struggles are so often bartered at the expense of gender justice.[42]

With this overarching emphasis on domestic work as a larger gender rights consideration, the IDWN and its ally spokespersons often painted more vivid pictures of the women who bore the brunt of unregulated household labor, in attempts to evoke empathy in the wider audience of voting delegates, namely employers. In doing so, they wove the complexities of the gender into their references to domestic workers themselves, deeming the recipients of policy more real, "vulnerable," and in need of protective regulations. Halimah Yacob often interjected descriptors of domestic workers, such as "young," "poor," and "vulnerable," in the tripartite dialogue to clarify the particular demographics of this sector. When the debates turned to domestic workers more generally, she appealed, "We want to include that this sector is often performed by girls, who often travel across borders."[43] By pointing to the disproportionate representation of young women, girls and migrants in this "unprotected yet prolific" sector, domestic workers and their allies held the ILO more closely accountable to its protection promises.

These embedded feminist arguments in the policy negotiations imposed critical philosophical questions about the central necessity of sustaining human life in the private sphere. Domestic worker representatives' interventions passionately queried the collective responsibility of privileged populations to assure that the world's caretakers are respected, able to provide for their own families, and valued as critical contributors to the global economy. As she delivered a public address to the Gender Commission in 2010, Marcelina Bautista turned the predominant "woman's issue" argument by calling for a larger ideological shift in the collective value of domestic work. "Some say that this is a 'woman's issue,' but domestic work is not a 'woman's issue,' it is an issue for *everyone* and it should be recognized as important and productive work." As a leading domestic worker activist, Bautista's public input repeatedly promoted the normalizing of this work as central to all human beings, not just women.

Caring for the Global Economy

If they could pay us what they owe us from our girlhood, the
entire economy would be in debt.
—Juana Flores, NDWA[44]

The IDWN approach accepted the ILO's invitation to fair globalization, with an activist edge. Rather than advocating for the complete alleviation of paid household work—with its origins in a history of servitude, slavery and sharp socio-economic divides—the IDWN demanded "decent work" and "all the benefits of the formal economy." Again and again, domestic workers asked the ILO to see "domestic work as *work*, just like any other."[45] To the international media, IDWN representatives reinforced their demands for equal recognition, "Domestic workers are a representative sector of the global economy, and we deserve full labor and social protections."[46] In many ways, their stances aligned with the mainstream model of economic development—where capitalism's expansion necessitates a greater need for specialized intimate care labor. In her book, *Servants of Globalization*, scholar Rhacel Parreñas shows how domestic workers supply massive amounts of human capital across national borders to assure the productivity and constant growth of our larger system of economic globalization.[47] Given this reality, domestic workers' demands for the ILO's transnational labor protections and the assurance of "decent work for domestic workers" normalized service labor as a private commodity exchange, rather than the state's responsibility. As Barbro Budin posited, "Domestic workers play the role that public service should do."[48] Even though most domestic worker activists ideally aligned with this state responsibility for child and elder care, they also recognized an existing context that assures the growth of domestic work as vital to the service economy and transnational exchange relations. As one advocate put it, "to exclude domestic workers is to turn our backs on the realities of the global economy."[49] Rather than fighting a revolution that holds states accountable to support the labor that regenerates society and allows nations, governments, capital and the global relations to flourish, the ILO's Decent Work agenda strives to elevate the quality of this service commodity and bring it into the existing neoliberal capitalist development frameworks.

Domestic worker activists walked a fine line to balance revolutionary aspirations, collective resistance to dominant forces and recognition of the ILO agenda as a pivotal turn toward realizing rights. As they strategized on how to maximize protections within this overarching global ethos, domestic workers maintained core activist practices by pushing the limits of the ILO in their tactics and nuanced persuasions. To balance these perspectives, the IDWN held a trump card that elevated their position within the negotiations. Through their embodiment of lifetimes of direct service within this "hidden" sector, domestic workers asked for "decent work" as a retribution for the suffering they endured. Their shared requests for equal rights amped up the legitimacy, urgency and ethical grounding of the IDWN position by continually referencing the price domestic workers paid for their lifetimes of labor in unregulated private households.

This dual position domestic workers assumed—as both accepting the ILO's "decent work" agenda in the existing economic system and demanding their access to fair labor because of the distinct history of oppression in this sector—echoes Eileen Boris's notion of the "hybrid domestic worker." In her assessment of rights claims and policy history, Boris demonstrates a prevailing tension between framing 'domestic work as work' and recognizing the distinct conditions that arise through the very nature of private household employment. This hybrid standpoint is evident throughout the ILO negotiations, as domestic workers positioned themselves as both worthy of standard labor regulations and at the same time in need of "special protections" because of their distinct vulnerability in unregulated household work contexts.[50] Thus, domestic workers leveraged persuasive capital from their own life histories, as they asked for rights within this prescribed ILO framework of "decent work in the context of fair globalization." Rather than demanding Juana Flores' proposed repayment of the full debt of their collective lost girlhoods, or staking a revolution to hold states and men more widely accountable to the costs of social reproduction, the IDWN sought tangible rights, recognition and a larger portion of the resources generated in the existing global economy. With this framework, the IDWN positioned domestic work as a necessary and unwavering labor resource that would only grow with the direction of the global economy.

From this perspective, they strived to elevate the conditions of household labor by expanding the notion of domestic work to that of "care labor" to address the prevailing "compassion deficit"[51] in the existing global economy. In the United States, this shift takes expression in the National Domestic Workers Alliance's pioneering leadership in "building a movement of love" to support "Caring Across Generations."[52] This shift to care work positioned the women who perform paid "labors of love" as benevolent, noble, and often "angelic" pillars for the most needy portions of the global population. Rather than devaluing traditionally feminized domestic work, or linking it to "illegal immigrants," the care movement reenvisioned the women who perform this labor as empathetic, conscientious human beings who "assure the long-term wellness of our elders." This call to recognize domestic workers as human beings who "care for our most precious resources" reflects a central aspect of the larger IDWN strategy to elevate the status of domestic work beyond "maids" and "bed pan changers"[53] to vital care contributors. Furthermore, by demonstrating the crucial role domestic workers play along the lifespan continuum, employers' dependency on this sector is evident, as is the often long-term nature of the employment relationship itself. Their call to consider the household as a space of life-affirming care, versus a reflection of the demands of "dirty work," shifted the terrain of the policy discussions, while personalizing the sector for delegates, all of whom face care demands at some point in their lifespan.

With these unavoidable needs to reproduce daily life and care for loved ones within the household, domestic workers supply critical resources in a global economy where these demands cut across social strata. Their strategy emphasized the specialized care labor necessity that allows more privileged portions of the population to participate in the formal economy. As one domestic worker delegate from Brazil expressed in the 2010 committee meetings, "We are the enablers for others who are then free to go out and work."[54] The National Domestic Workers Alliance in the United States has branded this concept as its central campaign slogan, with MacArthur Genius Awardee Ai-jen Poo at the forefront, celebrating domestic work as "the work that makes all other work possible." On public platforms and throughout her book, *The Age of Dignity*, Poo tributes the sacred work of care and calls for a shift in our collective responsibility to assure that care labor is woven into the fabric of society.[55] This framework posits that better protections for domestic workers uplift all. By treating domestic workers with dignity and respect, and assuring rights, advocates continually emphasized a multiplier effect where the implementation of Convention 189 would ripple into better lives for employers, the families of domestic workers, and the wider societies in which they work. Vicky Kanyoka, IDWN African Regional Coordinator, focused her two speeches at the opening and closing of the 2010 ILC on these multiple benefits of increasing the quality of work for domestic workers.

> Providing more protection for women through this convention will impact on the well-being of so many families throughout the world—those that these workers care for, and also their own.[56]

In her second public address, Kanyoka spoke the ILO language by contending, "Decent work for domestic workers is an effective way of reducing poverty, and increasing the quality of the work provided to millions of households."[57] This poverty reduction promise holds ground in the UN system. By demonstrating such wider impacts, domestic workers held the ILO to its own UN-binding commitments. Such values are echoed in the ILO's report on the 2010 discussions on domestic work, where it claims that decent work protections ". . . can contribute to a greater welfare for the citizens, to the wellbeing of employees and to greater gender equality."[58] With these assurances, who could say no to domestic workers' requests for fair working conditions?

By emphasizing the increased capacities of "all other work" through their care for employers and their loved ones, domestic workers leveraged wider support for the crucial role they played in the larger global social, political, and economic arenas. As lead domestic worker activist Ernestina Ochoa from Peru proclaimed, "Las trabajadoras del hogar somos el motor, el aceite, la espina dorsal de la sociedad."[59] By claiming that domestic workers are the "motor, grease and backbone" of society, Ochoa contends that without them, society cannot operate. So, domestic workers' asked the ILO to pay attention to the "cogs in the wheel" of global labor. By caring for "other workers" in the international economy, migrant women allow for the optimized performance of that economy, by regulating capitalism's new domain—the global household.

Drawing on Emotion

We ask you to bear with us when we became *emotional* the first day of the conference. But, as you all say, this was a *historical moment* for the ILO as well as for domestic workers worldwide.
—Myrtle Witbooi, 2010 Opening Speech[60]

In advocating for policy protections, the IDWN repeatedly posed direct emotional appeals, challenging delegates to *see* the women who "face abuse every day" and "are left alone in the backyards of their employers."[61] Their representative voice, Halimah Yacob, encouraged delegates to listen to the stories of domestic workers and look "deep in your heart and your conscience" when voting on the convention. This strategy of eliciting empathy, as in Witbooi's opening speech above, made the convention-setting process "a bit special." Throughout the process, domestic workers used emotion as a lobbying tool while abiding by the rules of the organization and the overarching codes of conduct that have characterized the ILO since its inception. Thus they built legitimacy by adapting their distinctive voices to the tripartite process.

Their emotional appeals centered on three key dimensions of domestic work. First, the historic exclusion of domestic workers separated families, normalized servitude, and enslaved people of color throughout the world. Second, domestic workers were highly vulnerable to abuse and exploitation by virtue of the sharp power imbalance between employers and domestic workers and the unregulated nature of the private household. In their statements and input in the process, they demonstrated how such abuse takes physical, emotional, and sexual forms. By highlighting the bodily and emotional layers of oppression in their own experience, domestic workers repeatedly evidenced the painful realities of abuse to sensitize delegates' understandings of the impact of protections. For instance, domestic worker statements often referenced severe psychological suffering as a result of the frequent familial separation required to perform domestic work, sharpened by the demands for migration embedded in the work. As one domestic worker activist from Guatemala asserted, "Our children are left at our grandmothers' houses."[62] As they drew upon the power differentials between employers and domestic workers, representatives highlighted the emotional hardship of facing the sharp inequalities between their own lives and those of the families they served. For instance, daily tasks like walking employers' dogs—while leaving their own children to the care of aunts and grandmothers who often reside far away in the most basic living standards—caused extreme psychological hardship for women. As Hester Stephens recollected, "There is a gap between you and your children."[63] Their cris de cœur created a social dialogue process that demanded a certain level of respect and empathy for the workers in the room, who had lived through experiences of severe suffering and emerged as activist leaders.

Domestic workers developed a very particular policy-activist strategy in their appeals. In their arguments and public statements, IDWN leaders aspired to "reach the hearts of employers." The technical training sessions that prepared domestic workers for their public delivery emphasized that speeches should "leave the audience in tears."[64] In doing so, to a certain extent, leaders of the IDWN drew upon traditional constructions of gender by enacting an emotional "women's story" within the predominantly masculine space of the ILO. This approach feminized the wider appeal for domestic worker rights, which held a particular moral power within the heavily masculinized organization. By making the image of domestic work concrete through strong affective appeals, domestic workers notably increased the legitimacy and impact of their claims. At the same time, however, this frequent use of emotion linked domestic work to traditional constructions of womanhood centered in the affective realm, most often seen in opposition to the rational/intellectual male qualities. As domestic workers asked for the "hearts" and "tears" of delegates, they positioned the predominantly male representatives of employer and government bodies as their protectors—able to assure rights through their power locations. Their plea to bring emotion into the negotiations recognized the normalized value of the rational, male-centered global governance institution. In many ways, the IDWN's affective strategy served to utilize guilt as persuasion by making it look as if policy makers were heartless (as well as immoral) if they ignored domestic workers.

In the 2010 negotiations, three members of the National Domestic Workers Alliance met Kamran Rahman, vice chair of the employers delegation and the strongest public opponent of the convention and the regulation of service labor. Rather than recognizing the value of domestic work, Rahman positioned it as a special case not relevant to international law. On behalf of the employers, Rahman led a series of maneuvers that attempted to stall the negotiations and even prevent consideration of a convention. The three IDWN leaders hoped to disarm Rahman via a personal encounter, greeting him with the statement, "We know you have a heart."[65] To this, Rahman laughed and concurred that his heart was in tact, then smiled for a photo with these three domestic workers. This exchange captures a certain ironic quality within the convention interactions, where parties who stood in ideological opposition could jest and engage over the idea of breaking through these divides with emotion or "heart" agency. Such micro exchanges accomplished one of the most impactful strategies domestic workers employed throughout the policy-making process—they made public spaces personal.

IDWN leaders often represented delegates' own use of domestic workers, and at times played upon this in their interpersonal encounters with governments and employer representatives. "How would you feel if your domestic worker were not protected?," they would ask. Through these exchanges, delegates in each of the tripartite bodies had to look at their own lives when confronted with the affective strategies of domestic workers. In some instances, however, male delegates responded to these public confrontations with humor, and a touch of dismissal of the cause. In one instance, a prominent employer delegate closed the second ILC by stating his general support for the convention yet his relief that his own "babysitter" would be 18 before the policy went into effect, freeing him from any binding regulation in his current life. In other instances, male delegates joked about "owing a beer" to their counterparts for supporting the convention. The tone and context of these statements reflects an undertone of mockery and performance among some delegates that placed particular associations on domestic workers, and the impracticality of implementation. Here, such individual scripts reflect the broader power dynamics played out on the very public ILO floor, as the standpoints of domestic workers encompassed the negotiations.

This integration of domestic workers' stories, and the emphasis on the moral obligation of those in power to redress the experiences of suffering on the floor, functioned in two ironic ways. On the one hand, it assured that domestic workers' narratives remained central considerations in policy-making—a maneuver that played a key role in the overall negotiations. At the same time, this collapsing of women's emotional stories with domestic work re-produced vulnerable gendered subjects—placed in visual and narrative forms as poor, migrant, women of color from the Global South, dependent upon the state and transnational institutions to protect their rights. In essence, the IDWN played with this dialectic of dependency as a pragmatic feminist activist maneuver through the use of emotion. This affective rhetoric became a vital strength in domestic workers' strategy, however, it also played directly into Shireen Ally's analysis of how the construction of the benevolent state is made possible through women's disempowered status. To a certain extent, domestic workers recognized and played upon this evident mutual dependency. In doing so, they both reinforced the power of traditional male institutions, and subverted it by performing as *well-behaved activists*.

Testing Delegates' Decency

They have relatives, they have kids, they have wives, they have husbands, they should be as concerned as we are. I think first of all that, and secondly, it would be very bad if at the end of the process, the employers are not capable of putting their signature on the convention. It will destroy their reputation and they will be effected in the ILO for many years to come.
—Luc Demaret

The domestic work delegation worked with the structure of the ILO to turn the negotiations into a more intimate performance of tripartite relations. In front of over 600 participants, IDWN activists interrogated ILO delegates on their own reliance upon domestic workers. The private households of labor, government, employer, and ILO officials came into the discussions as domestic workers pressed delegates to measure their own decent work practices and dependencies. To government officials, Myrtle Witbooi asserted, "You would not be here today if it were not for the domestic worker in your household." She went on to ask, "who ironed your shirt?" to point to the inherent contradiction in delegates who opposed standard setting, yet benefitted extensively from domestic service in their everyday lives. As others put forth, domestic work makes the whole world go round.

By making all voting delegates accountable to their own household environments, this strategy built common grounds across the social partners. In her early statements, Halimah Yacob reminded the House, "we are all employers of domestic workers." Even labor delegates held privileged social positions that allowed them to outsource household reproduction to the global care supply. By putting these personal practices on the table, the IDWN repeatedly gained moral and ethical ground to hold policy makers accountable to their own decisions. Unlike any other sector, domestic workers could bring the private lives of delegates into the public policy arena, and point to their collective reliance on outsourced household labor to garner convention support.

In their public discourse, domestic workers spoke directly to delegates to bring intimate labor directly into the private worlds of those seated in the negotiations. In her 2010 address to the entire ILC, Vicky Kanyoka exemplified this embedded accountability when she asked delegates to look at the core contributions of domestic workers, and the women in that very chamber who perform this work each day.

> It is us who take care of your precious children and your sick and elderly; we cook your food to keep you healthy and we look after your property when you are away.[66]

Through her use of the second person "you," Kanyoka made delegates' own lives material for the negotiations. This tactic imposed a moral obligation to redress historic inequalities by "taking domestic work seriously" and "thinking about the women in your household" to take the higher ground position for decent work protections. With domestic workers themselves in the room, the IDWN held the house to a heightened level of accountability. Through their very presence, even when they were not authorized to speak, domestic workers made this particular policy process highly personal to all voting delegates. By asking the House to establish protections with a heightened accountability to the actual workers in the room, the IDWN gave those with power an opportunity to enact benevolence publicly. Support for Convention 189, particularly among employers, became a means of showing how "compassionate capitalism" may operate to protect the world's caretakers. Furthermore, as employers and governments turned toward support, they upheld a wider recognition of their inherent reliance on intimate care work to allow their own social status to flourish, as members of the most elite sectors of society.

"Solidarity Forever": Strategies of Song

Among their most strategic and influential maneuvers, domestic worker activists refined one of their most powerful persuasion tools: solidarity songs. When the chair's gavel called the negotiations to a close, domestic workers immediately broke into song and danced in large public displays of their unity. Delegates could not exit without hearing and seeing the domestic worker activists singing, "Are you listening, *governments*? Domestic Workers need a convention . . ." As they performed these songs, the IDWN leaders moved into the physical spaces occupied by government and labor delegates, while dancing and gesturing in harmony, in many cases until the last voting delegate left the chambers. Delegates and officials often lingered to watch these performances at the end of each session. One prominent member of the ILO administration later revealed "We were happy and we wanted to sing but we could not because . . . we're supposed to be mutual."[67] As domestic workers sang historic struggle renditions, like "Solidarity Forever," and enacted radical resistance chants, like "Si Se Puede" (Yes, it is possible) and "Amandla! Awethu!" (the power is ours) they connected a history of social justice movements to their own contemporary activist cause, while fortifying global unity throughout the process.

Shirley Pryce went from sleeping in the doghouse to working for Jamaica's prime minister to spearheading Jamaica's domestic worker movement. After her IDWN experience in Geneva, she enrolled in Penn State University's graduate program in labor studies. During her first semester, Pryce developed a paper on Convention 189, based upon her own experience inside the ILO. In her reflections on the most influential aspects of the IDWN, she wrote:

> We would make sure we sang songs with every given opportunity, singing "Domestic workers, need a convention, domestic workers, need a convention, domestic workers in the ILO" and "My mother was a kitchen girl, my father was a garden boy, that's why we are unionist, we are unionist, we are unionist," and "Solidarity forever, for the union makes us strong," among many others. These songs made it difficult for employers and governments to ignore our existence, and they invigorated the strength of the network . . . Sharing songs also gave us spirit and motivation to keep going through the long, formal sessions.

Through song, she found individual strength that connected her to a larger cause and centered her purpose at the ILO. Shirley's experience echoes an underlying message in one of the historic union songs adapted by the domestic workers. Rather than "the union is behind us," in the ILO, activists chanted:

> IDWN's behind us
> We shall not be moved.
> Just like a tree that's planted by the waters,
> We shall not be moved.

Through songs like this, domestic workers also carried the IDWN collective voice into the streets and back to their countries as they taught these lyrics to their own union sisters and connected the struggle from global to the local levels.

The public performance of song most powerfully exhibited the IDWN's force, determination and activist spirit. Through song activism, domestic workers realized three distinct accomplishments. First, song became a means of working at the borders of ILO formality. The moments when domestic workers broke into song blurred the lines between the formal and informal sessions—while maximizing a key opportunity to be heard. Second, through song, the IDWN gained strength as it represented larger social justice movements with a history of persuasive power. As the chamber filled with the echoes of "La Lucha Continua" (the struggle continues), domestic workers garnered credibility through their direct connection to the moral high ground of historic revolutions. Lastly, the ability to adapt song to the most relevant ILC conditions strengthened domestic workers' transnational solidarity, while allowing them to access agency through the power of performing their own messages publicly. Women from Asia, Europe, Africa and North America sang, clapped and danced in unity as their Latina sisters performed the following original song for the IDWN and Convention 189.

> *Vamos vamos companeras no debemos de parar,*
> *nuestra lucha sigue y sigue va por todo organizar,*
> *se ha formado una alianza, una alianza nacional,*
> *vamos a organizar.*

> Let's go, let's go, companions, we should not stop,
> our work continues over and over, it's important to get organized.
> An alliance amongst nations has been formed,
> let's work together.

The full version of this song recognizes the first transnational movement of domestic workers, and its potential to shift the global conditions of household labor. Its debut at the ILO created new testimonial expressions, where local material takes original form as it is performed by the larger international network.

Domestic workers from across the globe bonded through song over the six weeks they spent together at the 2010 and 2011 ILC conferences. As they waited for buses, opened their own early-morning briefings, strategized in planning workshops, and took to the streets of Geneva, song aligned their cause. At the same time, as song infused the IDWN working culture, it supported the global domestic workers' identity and allowed activists to bring their own forms of self-expression to the procedural formalities of the ILO system, and its demands for strict "discipline." At one of their final planning workshops, Vicky Kanyoka held a paper report in her hand, as if it were the approved legal convention, as she taught the IDWN her new song.

To whom to whom does this belong to?
It belongs to *us*!

Each verse quickened in pace, as Vicky danced in sync, asking the entire network to join her with enthusiasm, as if they had already won their dream of international rights. When they seemed not exuberant enough, she exclaimed, "You are not shaking!"[68] Song conveyed domestic workers' messages not only through lyrics, but physical movement. Domestic workers could express their energy, creativity, and activist foundations through song. While they sang about "kitchen girls," they claimed a powerful and original stance as global activists. For the IDWN network, song became one of the few venues to convey their true spirit of expression, while accessing the strength of the social movements before them. At the same time, through the process of writing, practicing, and performing song, the IDWN strengthened its group solidarity across lines of difference.

Summary

As activists working within the ILO, IDWN leaders developed a parallel capacity to operate both by the rules of the house and by resisting those rules. Through their acquired knowledge of the system and the support of a wide civil-society coalition, the IDWN developed a particular *resistance compliance* that disrupted the system to an extent which allowed "the subaltern to speak."[69] This ability to "know the rules well enough to break them"[70] gave WIEGO and IUF, which shared years of historical familiarity with the ILO internal and formal operations, a core advantage in achieving their aims. Only by understanding the ILO map of players and procedures could the IDWN push the boundaries of the standard-setting process, thereby demanding that this global institution rethink the place of "actual workers" in the policymaking process. As they participated "by the rules" of the formal process, they consistently pushed up against those rules, seeking new opportunities for individual and collective influence. In doing so, they enacted pioneer US domestic labor scholar Judith Rollins's notion of modes of deference at the institutional level—demonstrating a level of compliance with the governing system as a means of overcoming the restraints posed by that system.[71]

This deference to the ILO rules of order mirrored the covert strategies domestic workers throughout the world have employed to find agency and shift the power relations within the private household. Since they operate in two specific social locations—that of their own communities and that of their employers'—they demonstrate a capacity to navigate multiple social, cultural, political, and economic contexts. In many countries, domestic workers speak more languages than their employers and transgress various physical and socioeconomic locations in their daily lives. As a South African domestic worker stated, "When I leave my kitchen, I leave the Third World and go to my employer's kitchen in the First World. Every day, I return to the Third World."[72] Their capacity to daily navigate these material and psychological divides gave domestic workers a distinct insight into the multiple cultural, political, and socioeconomic realms they inhabit. Because policymakers generally do not cross the socioeconomic divides that domestic workers traverse each day, their points of reference were relatively limited. In contrast, IDWN activists drew upon their knowledge of the social worlds voting delegates occupied in making their case for, and ultimately winning, Convention 189.

6

"Put Yourself in Her Shoes"

NGO, Union, and Feminist Allies

I think the ILO convention has united the world, not just the governments, not just the employers, but the NGOs, all sectors came together. It is already (finally) the right time to really recognize domestic workers as workers.
—Marissa Begonia, Justice for Domestic Workers, UK

Elizabeth Tang and Ip Pui Yu are professional domestic worker organizers. Based in Hong Kong, Elizabeth formed the first migrant-trade union, the Asian Domestic Workers Union. Her political awareness stemmed from the teachings of Paulo Freire, whose liberation theology she'd absorbed in her university education.[1] In this activist training, she recollected, "you don't just learn about democracy and freedom, you internalize them. You have to live them yourself." For her, to live Freire's teaching meant seeing the world from the perspective of those most marginalized and oppressed. In Hong Kong, domestic workers and migrants engaged the political consciousness she had developed in her student days with the Catholic Student Federation. Elizabeth devoted her life to organizing workers, from Coca-Cola to hotel and food workers, to those underrepresented in the informal economy. This focus connected her to the IUF, where she began to look at the potential to organize domestic workers. She described this move as one that "came very naturally, because I organize all the time." In 1990 she formed the first migrant domestic workers union, comprising workers from Thailand, the Philippines, Nepal, India, and Indonesia. She became a core advocate in the IUF for the inclusion of domestic worker representation, while continually pushing her national labor movement to consider household workers as part of their larger struggle. Among migrant domestic workers, Tang sees household workers as having the greatest potential to reap the benefits of social change. In her view, "society's attitude to domestic workers is starting to improve."[2]

Ip Pui Yu, "Little Fish," as she is known, earned her degree in labor organizing, and graduated with the intention of focusing her efforts on domestic workers. She is a one-woman public relations campaign—building websites, translating meeting transcripts, and assuring that Asian domestic workers receive the support they need in their nearly three weeks of participation in the ILO meetings. She brings spices and noodles from Hong Kong to Geneva, and cooks for the Asian contingency into the late evening most nights. She writes songs of solidarity for the network. At the first ILO meetings, she carries the symbolic apron quilt containing 3,500 domestic worker handprints, and coordinates the public demonstrations that took to the streets of Geneva. Little Fish works to ensure that her Asian sisters can get to the Geneva meetings and draw the most meaningful experience from the policy dialogues. After the global gatherings, she tells the world about the victories shared, managing all of the social media communication for a burgeoning network among domestic worker leaders working across six continents. As her sister comrades describe, "Fish never stops." Like Elizabeth, her mentor, Little Fish lives out her progressive political stance through her solidarity with domestic workers. Together, these two professional activists head the largest national representations of domestic workers worldwide. While their advocacy focuses on the household, their own lives are consumed by the representational demands of both reaching domestic workers throughout Asia, and reflecting their stances in the international arena, as they comprise a centerpiece in this global movement. As Fish contends, "The many domestic workers who are losing their lives daily depend on us to keep this network strong." In many respects, the opportunity to align domestic worker organizations with a larger transnational movement may be equally, if not more, important than the actual achievement of an international policy. Convention 189 anchored larger struggles for labor, gender, and migrant justice in the pursuit of human rights for domestic workers. At the same time, the possibility of a convention provided a concrete platform to express the visions of the two complementary founding investors in this movement, with a balance in attention to the IUF's focus on labor struggles in the global economy and WIEGO's foundational purpose of building awareness and

Figure 6.1. Elizabeth Tang (front row, far left) and Ip Pui Yu (second row, far left) with domestic worker delegates from Nepal, China, and Indonesia.

attaining rights for women workers in the informal economy. The ILO arena allowed these invested ally organizations to gain substantive publicity by staging domestic worker rights as an embodiment of their larger organizational causes—on human rights, migrant justice, gender equality, global labor, and protections against contemporary slavery, child labor, and trafficking. The involvement of such a wide range of NGOs transformed international policymaking, while breathing new life into national and local justice and rights movements. Alongside this band of organizations in solidarity with domestic workers, key government representatives stood as strong supporters of the convention, often voicing aspects of the platforms of NGOs in the public negotiations. This wide investment in a "domestic worker cause" played a central role in the ultimate convention win.

At the same time, the investment of these key allies challenged core considerations of representation, particularly given the power dynamics that have placed domestic workers at the periphery of state policies, national labor unions, and, often, women's rights organizations. Furthermore, as such a wide range of organizations took ownership of domestic workers' rights, their representation at times reproduced persistent standpoint concerns of domestic workers themselves. Myrtle Witbooi pointed out that former power struggles created circumstances whereby "those who are so far from us are speaking for us."[3] In the ILC discussions, domestic workers gained strength and legitimacy in their self-representation as the largest group of actual workers at the table. At the same time, while the political and financial representational capacity of larger NGOs bolstered the domestic work cause, these organizations also risked "speaking for" domestic workers in ways that might objectify them within this power-laden traditional system of international governance. This chapter explores the tapestry of alliances and political processes that formed around domestic worker rights—from the NGO-ization of rights claims, to state allies, to the original support of the global union-policy partnership of WIEGO and the IUF. Collectively, the original way in which this policymaking process brought together a range of ally organizations, as well as sympathetic governments, makes Convention 189 an emblem of a distinct transformative social justice movement, as much as a landmark victory in the global policy realm of human rights.

Building a Movement Through the ILO

They have a goal and they insist to reach that goal . . . and they are warm for each other. They are like brothers and sisters. They believe in what they want . . . It is very important to believe in what you want.
—Maysoon Qara, Jordanian National Commission for Women[4]

International policy anchored what became a domestic worker operation. The IDWN emphasized its larger political support to bolster its stance and maximize the benefits of the new spaces Convention 189 carved for civil society participation in policymaking. Myrtle Witbooi's public statement echoes this strengthened stance through the collective backing of allies. "With the help of many supporters, friends and allies, we have managed to bring domestic workers to the ILO and I am sure you feel the spirit and see the hope and expression on our faces."[5] This reference to a united stance included the wider trans-alliance network that stood with domestic workers to call for this group's protections as a matter of universal human rights and the imperative need to extend policy protections to this predominant sector of the informal economy. In this sense, the leader of the domestic workers' cause presents as if the range of transnational NGOs and unions is nodding along with her.

The galvanizing global policy goal brought together a series of 'causes' that could hang their claims for justice on the domestic work hook. This trans-issue apex became a symbol of a loftier call for human rights. Lead ILO legal specialist Martin Oelz pointed to this overarching link as a core feature of the effectiveness of this international policy.

> One of the strengths of the instrument is its relevance for our organization and its connection and relevance for the promotion of human rights, which makes it really a good instrument that's also being promoted by other organizations.

With the prominence of the ILO, other NGOs could easily align with the many issue concerns for human rights, gender justice, and labor protections. As Nalini Nayak, leading advocate of India's SEWA, proclaimed, "The issue of migration links us!"[6] For others, domestic work represented the call to end child labor, modern slavery, human trafficking, and even hunger. Throughout the halls of the ILO, one NGO developed a promotional tote bag that linked three messages in one: "Don't Globalize Hunger, End Violence Against Women!, Recognize Domestic Work as Work!"[7] In a sense, domestic work served as a broad brush stroke for so many of these interconnected human rights concerns. For domestic workers' transnational organization, this investment heightened their political and social capital by placing this sector within a much larger transnational civil society movement. Jill Shenker, the US representative to the IDWN, surmised that "alliances will be critical to this movement."[8] By building ties with these larger claims—in the wider social justice, labor and women's rights movements, domestic workers gained a nearly irrefutable moral grounding, while drawing from the social, political and economic capital of these established organizations to bolster the capacity of those who perform globalization's love labor.

Branding Rights Claims: The NGO-ization of Domestic Work

All of the abuses that you see on the posters around us are all
true. We don't show them because we want to make pretty
posters. We show them because this is the reality domestic
workers are facing.
—Guillermina Castellanos, outside the Broken Chair of the
United Nations

Convention 189 carved a new space for civil society in policy making
through human rights, justice and moral claims captured in domestic
work. These expressions appeared consistently within the negotiations
through the presence of the very workers who would be directly
impacted by the outcomes of this debated policy. The IDWN representatives became persuasive, living examples of the need to build a global
policy—to reflect the imperative gap between the realities of the world's
populations and the substantive policy gaps in their protection. Through
domestic work, NGOs could address these shortcomings and advance
their various agendas in shared efforts to "build a better world."

With this elevated role for NGOs came wider concerns about their
potential to "take over" the process. The ILO's deeply embedded allegiance to the tripartite manifesto fueled notions of NGOs as inappropri-
ate disrupters of the abiding government-labor-employer trio. Yet as the
publicity surrounding these negotiations expanded, NGOs amped up
their place in the process. Their heavy investment of resources, existing
agendas and political positions at times also blurred the lines around
who actually represented these "workers in the backyards."[9] Each organization choreographed domestic worker rights in accordance with their
own priorities—to end child labor, protect migrants, reduce trafficking,
assure human rights for all, or draw attention to the plight of informal
women workers. These larger, more influential NGOs built a campaign
that drew the largest global attention to domestic work ever seen in the
history of social activism. Their investment put domestic workers in the
spotlight, as representatives of so many of the world's larger struggles for
justice. Yet with the funding and political backing of these major players in the human rights world, complicated questions arose about who
sets the agenda for this rights-through-policy movement and how the

plight of domestic workers would best be framed. Would a human rights theme prevail over an end to "modern slavery" as the tagline for this movement? Or would global unions and policy organizations' central demand that the ILO meet the realities of the contemporary informal economy make the strongest case for the assurance of protections for the women workers who supply the lion's share of globalization's expansion? NGOs' central role as allies and key players in this policy negotiation interrogated all of these ideological and applied questions, while posing important considerations about solidarity networks in the context of such power and resource differentials surrounding domestic work.

The multiple vantage points NGOs offered widened the scope of concern and relevance for this formerly excluded force in the global economy. Their ability to publicize so many plights staked a claim on domestic work that placed policy in perspective. The larger moral grounds to protect the world's most precarious populations from suffering in their daily livelihoods framed resistance to Convention 189 as a vote against human rights and social justice. With their persuasive case on domestic work's encapsulation of so many of the world's wider justice and rights imbalances, NGOs ultimately strengthened this policy movement and played a critical role in achieving Convention 189.

The elevation of the plight for fair household labor standards— from local mobilization to national governments to international institutions—provided a wide audience for the ILO and domestic workers' rights negotiations. This stage-setting social movement that emerged through policy-making built upon the strength of NGOs' capacity to call for social change. By making the lofty ILO values accessible in evident human form, NGOs assured that real people stood at the heart of policy. Their sophisticated campaigns for domestic worker rights housed undeniable injustices in the images and narratives of domestic workers themselves.

Because NGOs exist as "survivalists" in a world with massive human needs and an array of worthy causes, they must make their claims to funders and supporters in ways that justify their existence. In the case of Convention 189, this larger circumstance inclined NGOs to promote the "tragedy of domestic work"[10] as grounds to call for universal rights. In order to maximize their reach and impact, this NGO operation collectively constructed a symbolic global figure of domestic work to articulate suffering, oppression and the impact of the absence of global protections for the "100 million domestic workers who toil everyday." In many cases, such awareness building efforts branded servitude, vulnerability and essentialized constructions of domestic workers as a recurring theme in the call for rights. Namely, the use of a familiar face of women's oppression served as an affective technique to brand a universal domestic worker image. Depictions of poor, women of color—most often Asian, African or Latin—became iconic images for domestic worker rights. In many cases, portrayals of young women carried a particular message about the exploitation of migrants in this global industry. Such campaigns used victimhood, modern slavery, migrant exploitation and the oppression of women of color from the Global South as central moral and emotional grounds to make the most compelling cases for policy protections.

In the business of human rights, suffering sells. Thus, NGOs relied upon affective campaign structures, asking decision makers and governments to extend empathy to the women "who make the whole world possible." To bring personal experiences into the political realm, Human Rights Watch posed a series of questions in one of their central campaigns for domestic worker rights.

Have you ever worked for months without pay?
Have you ever been forced to sleep in the kitchen?
Have you ever been denied food when you are hungry?
Have you considered a Sunday spent with your boss a day off?
Have you ever been called a "donkey" at work?
Have you ever been locked up in your workplace?

The end of this messaging reads, "Put yourself in her shoes." While such human rights PR pulled on the emotional strings of decision makers, at times NGOs' branding of the lives of "invisible women" bartered political strength with the reproduction of the very imagery domestic workers sought to dissolve.

In many respects, the ILO process made domestic labor the cause of the day. As organizations aligned around the promotion of the convention, their collective messages branded imagery of domestic work through race, migrant status, age and class. Notions of vulnerability and dependency held substantive persuasive power in the larger NGO movement to assure protections. In a similar vein, NGOs symbolized domestic workers through the use of hands—worn hands, disembodied hands, and colorful hands in unison. These image associations to the labor movement reflected larger historic struggles for justice, while injecting a stronger class-based rhetoric within the policy conversations of this formal organization.

Along with the hands of domestic workers, their bodies carried powerful imagery in NGO branding—often as uniformed, aproned, and adorned with a *duk* to symbolize the iconic status of servitude.[11] This designing of a "typical domestic worker" within the global movement surrounding Convention 189 reinforces power-laden West/Other binary imagery reminiscent of Chandra Mohanty's postcolonial feminist analysis of the "typical Third World woman."[12] Although these dynamics of representation served as powerful emotional and moral rhetorical tools, we must be cautious about how NGOs' construction of domestic work also reinforced a hierarchy within the social justice, women's rights and labor movements. When the Save the Children campaign featured a young, uniformed, brown-skinned girl making a bed in a very feminized, well-appointed pink bedroom, with a tagline that read, "Domestic Work Isn't Child's Play," it painted domestic workers as extremely vulnerable, morally exploited and ultimately in need of the protection of the larger Western NGO voice to assure their rights. Furthermore, NGO campaign material spoke directly to an imagined community positioned as rescuers for those who could not speak because of their entrapment in the household. For instance, the faith-based Caritas Campaign to Protect Domestic Workers poster featured an oversized red ticking alarm clock with a challenger to employers: "Would you tolerate being exploited around the clock? Treat foreign workers as you'd like to be treated. Human regardless of race and status." Such messaging constructed an 'us/them' binary that linked fair labor to employers' willingness to humanize the profession—across lines of difference.

Such advocacy campaigns built upon the same dimensions of colonial servitude that arose as the central inequalities within the domestic work labor relationship: race/class/gender divides, social status differentials and migration. The predominant visual and narrative discourse that emerged in the convention proceedings reveals how such social constructions became a central part of the international policy making on domestic work. With the extreme marginalization of domestic workers came distinct opportunities for NGOs to build campaigns that bolstered their political strength by highlighting the voicelessness of domestic workers themselves. This imagery stands in sharp contradistinction to the models of domestic worker leadership we see throughout the ILO process—as Hester Stephens built a union in her employer's garage, Shirley Pryce moved from Jamaica's Prime Minister's home to the founding of a domestic workers' school, and Aida Moreno wrote an autobiography and poetry collection based upon her life work. Rather than domestic workers' stories of strength and survival, NGO imagery painted pictures of exploitation, as tragedy trumps agency in the business of human rights lobbying.

Yet within the proceedings, domestic workers aligned with force, unity, and the persuasive political strategies of this larger NGO alliance. When domestic worker organizations developed their own campaign material, the messaging made bold statements that reflected a new wave of liberation for the 'masses' of the world's most marginalized. For example, domestic workers in the African Regional Network of the IDWF wore worker bold t-shirts that read, "Decent work is our right! I am not your servant. I am a domestic worker!" Alongside them, the Federation of South African Unions created carrying bags for domestic worker that read, "Harass me! I know my rights!" Such statements represent a clear resistance to the founding arrangements of servitude central to the historical configurations of this institution. The messaging that stemmed directly from domestic workers emphasized empowerment, education and freedom from the "master's rules." Thus, the presentation of domestic workers within the negotiations took two forms: those of the poster children in need of protection by the larger NGO rescue projects and the persuasive pillar of domestic worker activists who demanded their own rights, called decision makers to task and "took the ILO by storm."[13]

Suffering, Silence, and Solidarity

The ILO process made domestic work a "sexy topic"[14] for NGOs. In evaluating the meaning and impact of this wider ownership of the global movement for household rights, we must ask key feminist political questions about how allied organizations with increased access to social, political and economic capital represented domestic workers in their campaigns for policy change. The process of setting international standards for domestic worker rights continuously walked a tightrope balance of representation. The larger trans-alliance organizational efforts to take on this particular policy built a collective, highly visible international campaign in ways that domestic worker organizations alone could not have realized with limited funding and no previous experience in building international awareness. Such organizations used their own power to figuratively—and in some cases literally— speak for domestic workers. For instance, Transient Workers Count Too, a Singaporean-based international migration organization created a campaign that depicted a young, Asian, supposedly migrant domestic worker who stands in front of two sets of children, one with parents, a dog and a double-story white, well-appointed house. The other children sit alone on the back of a bike with a backdrop of shacks representing their home. The text for this campaign poster reads, "She is not just your maid, her name is Lita. She works for her family as well as yours."[15] This personalization built empathy for an imagined migrant "Lita," whose life circumstances are so far from the message's audience of employers and policy makers. Indeed, Lita cares for her own family under very different circumstances than her employer's well-resourced existence. Campaigns like this emphasize NGOs' capacity to build awareness of Lita's life, and shift the larger conditions for women like her. With domestic workers as the centerpiece of larger rights struggles, their demands gained much wider attention and strength. Yet NGO ownership of this cause risked the appropriation of domestic workers' lives to amplify the agendas of already established civil society organizations. In this larger NGO movement, efforts to universalize the violations and risks of the domestic work occupation reduced a much more complex kaleidoscope of this industry into stories of suffering, exploitation, entrapment and voicelessness—a maneuver IDWN representatives questioned at times throughout the ILC meetings. Although these dynamics of representation built political will and capital, they also inscribed new terms of representation in this coalition ownership of domestic work.

The ILO structure of policy negotiations shaped the relationships of representation because it so strictly defined who could speak on behalf

of domestic workers, at very particular moments. While the actual negotiations allowed only the worker and employer Vice Chairs to speak
alongside government delegates, the ILC rules designated certain formal
moments where civil society representatives could make public statements that would be captured in the official proceedings. These limited
moments required an orchestration among the NGO delegations, alongside the IDWN, which held NGO status, like WIEGO and the IUF. Vice
Chair Halimah Yacob instructed the workers' group and the civil society
organizations that NGOs would only be allowed 20 minutes to speak
at these specific moments. She emphasized that international organizations would be more representative, and therefore more appropriate
choices for these limited moments of public persuasion. Yet the workers' group left the actual decisions on representation to the civil society organizations. "I hope this is something that you can settle among
yourselves," Yacob requested of NGOs and the IDWN. In each of these
designated opportunities for domestic workers to speak, those closest to
the cause, as domestic worker representatives of the IDWF, joined the
lineup as the most direct spokeswomen for this specific sector. Alongside the "actual workers" in the chambers, a range of related NGOs
made persuasive public statements in support of Convention 189. As
they spoke on the larger dilemmas of migration, child labor and human
trafficking, their ability to reference the domestic workers in the room
emboldened their stances, while strengthening the network of solidarity
behind the IDWN.

The very processes of speaking molded the relationship between
NGOs and domestic workers. The convention negotiations provided a
forum that not only discussed policy; it served as a barometer of the
larger value placed on those who care for families and private households across the world. As policy discussions reflect a microcosm of
larger societal relations, the ways in which NGOs and domestic workers
existed in relation to one another carved new relationships among workers, NGO advocates—and ultimately labor unions and the state. Convention 189 revealed an existence of mutual benefit between domestic
workers and NGOs. At times, this existence favored workers themselves,
while in other instances, the power of a global civil society representation held more power. Yet, in their overall dance, domestic workers and
NGOs created a distinct form of alliance through the particular space

available when so many representatives of a global constituency came together to determine how the world would value those who, as Nisha Varia of Human Rights Watch put it, "provide essential care to the most precious parts of many, many employers' lives—their children, their elderly parents, and their homes."[16]

Domestic workers and NGOs leaned on each other to bolster their own statements and stances. The lived experience of domestic workers gave them a most persuasive political platform, as the direct recipients of any policy passed through the ILO. When Myrtle Witbooi spoke of drying her tears with her mandated white apron uniform, her testimonial carried a political persuasion in a form distinct only to these personalized statements from domestic workers themselves. Or, as Shirley Pryce took to the podium of the Palais des Nations to state, "I am a former domestic worker myself. There cannot be many of us here today. I feel very proud," the very impact of the journey of this one individual woman's existence weighted her formal speech with volumes of accreditation. These testimonials of domestic workers held a resounding strength because they emerged from the highly personalized experiences of individual women's stories—placed on the stage of such a formal transnational institution. Yet, the NGO-IDWN alliance brought a distinctly commanding force to the narratives of individual domestic worker representatives. Indeed, the solidarity support of such a wide lineup of global society representatives created an original form of silent body rhetoric.[17] While domestic worker representatives' most powerful tool came from their ability to speak from a history of direct experience, and the multiple layers of sufferings they faced in this isolated profession, the collective nodding of so many NGOs and solidarity supporters amplified their voices tremendously. This silent bodily rhetoric took form when the entire network of civil society participants metaphorically locked arms in support of domestic workers' statements. When the political and material backup of central organizations like Human Rights Watch, WIEGO, Migrant Forum in Asia and Anti-Slavery International stood behind domestic workers, the IDWN strengthened its presence and gained a collective authority through such a wide support alliance. Thus, in this distinct policy process, the largest collection of "actual workers" at the policy table gained tremendous credibility when such a wide cascade of NGOs visually and verbally upheld a banner of united force. Domestic workers became vessels of the irrefutable impact of their historical exclusion from any form of global policy protection. Their presence alone carried tremendous weight. Yet without the NGO network's central engagement with the protection of domestic worker rights, the IDWN would have remained at the fringes of the debates, as a special interest group, making personal and emotional claims. With this aligned NGO solidarity, however, domestic workers positioned themselves at the center of this wide tapestry of civil society priorities across the globe.

In a reciprocal fashion, NGOs bolstered their stances when they could reference the direct experiences of domestic workers as part of their platform. Whether they emphasized migration, child labor, domestic violence, or informal labor, domestic workers became a powerful conduit of persuasive evidence for NGOs' input in the policy-making process. With their expertise in the rhetoric of rights, NGOs also trained domestic workers to make powerful statements on behalf of their causes. Here, Anti-Slavery International positions a 10-year old child from Mali to speak at a special forum that took place alongside the 2011 negotiations.[18]

> I am one of the hundreds of child domestic workers that Anti-Slavery International has been working with over the past years . . . We are being given an opportunity this week to take action. We support Article 4[19] of the current version. We are children. On behalf of my fellow domestic workers, please take into consideration that domestic work is not a suitable profession for young domestic workers. Much of our vulnerability and our work comes from our isolation . . . We are totally dependent upon our employers to treat us well . . . We have been employed and live in the margins of society for so long, and now, this is the time to protect us.

How could a group of NGO professionals compete with the power of this child domestic worker's plea for protections? When NGOs brought in such living portrayals of their causes, each domestic worker represented the masses of the exploited, thereby bolstering the moral and ethical claims of NGOs that much further. Here, Angelina Joseph, one of Anti-Slavery's child worker representatives, embodies this standpoint.

"I am very glad to be here in this meeting because I am not talking on *my* behalf, but representing the children on *our* behalf." With actual representatives of the domestic work sector in their wider policy-making space, NGOs gained substantive credibility, power and persuasion. Such close alliances stood as an affront to the predominant critiques of those who resisted standards, as detached from the "real life stories" of domestic workers themselves. Thus, NGOs carved a longer trench into the ILO tripartite process when their presence included those on the front lines of exploitation.

While this sophisticated art proved an eloquent rhetorical and political device, NGOs' staging of domestic workers' lives also fringed core questions of standpoint. With their savvy NGO speak, larger organizations sometimes scripted domestic workers' public voices. This process created forms of co-speak where NGOs became the ventriloquists for domestic workers, who could potentially be seen as puppets for such larger organizations. For example, a domestic worker representative of Migrant Forum in Asia made this statement in the larger plenary. "I thank my employer for giving me time so that I could address you today. It is fitting that in the 100th session, we return to our social justice roots." Here, we see how a domestic worker "character" spoke strategically to an audience by evoking notions of a benevolent employer, and emphasizing a core NGO accountability call for the ILO to return to its social justice roots by enacting the core principles of its founding. In a similar fashion, the WIEGO team often emphasized the importance of domestic workers asking for "the same rights as all other workers" in their public speeches.[20] Such accountability placed a consistent charge on the ILO to respond to the conditions of work as they now exist in the informal global economy. While NGOs could bring these core arguments to the tripartite discussions by making maximum use of their civil society observer roles, when domestic workers themselves spoke on behalf of NGOs, these larger organizations gained a moral, emotional and applied influence available only through these strategic alignments between the "subjects" of this policy and their advocates. At the same time, because NGOs like WIEGO taught domestic workers to speak in the language of the ILO, they afforded a much more legitimate claim, and a more likely policy protection when domestic workers could talk in the policy language so formative to this global institution.

In the end, these relationships proved to be mutual in their impact—domestic workers gained substantive force with NGOs standing in silent bodily support. At the same time, they absorbed a range of skills from NGOs, who had been in the business of human rights much longer. With the presence of so many actual domestic workers in the negotiations, NGOs could stage their claims through the voices of those who suffer directly, thereby creating an impermeable moral grounds for rights. Indeed, opponents could reject support for transnational NGOs much more easily than they could deny an individual domestic worker who brought her life story of suffering in the absence of policy protections. In this mutual relationship, the "voice of" domestic workers expanded to a larger network, that both relied upon individual stories and built a much more encompassing script. Just as the IDWN diminished the specificities of particular countries to demand universal rights, NGOs placed individual stories into a larger narrative that demanded a global set of standards, regardless of place. This original configuration of representation between domestic workers and NGOs founded an original form of activism within the ILO that defined this historic rights moment. With domestic workers themselves in the room, alongside this wide configuration of allied NGOs, the collective stance that emerged from such aligned statements and political influence embedded a *lived capital* of connection that permeated a higher moral claim throughout the negotiations. This domestic worker-civil society solidarity ultimately rendered support for Convention 189 the only logical move in this existing state of human rights and globalization.

NGOs in the ILO Landscape

Luc Demaret, one of the lead ILO ushers of the domestic worker rights, claimed that the convention negotiations became a "beauty contest for the NGOs." Among some, a fear that NGOs would "take over" the negotiations persisted. With their moral claims, direct link to domestic workers, and "overenthusiasm" for the cause, NGOs forced the ILO to take the role of civil society more seriously. US lead government delegate Robert Shepard characterized the ILO prior to Convention 189 as "a monopoly for labor and business, and they covet that monopoly."[21] When NGOs showed up in force, they held the ILO accountable to the recipients of policy from both an ideological and a practical perspective. Their rhetoric continually called the ILO to the realities of the world's migrant informal economy. From a practical ground, NGOs challenged the ILO procedures—the hallmark of this historic institution's tripartite manifesto. As they did so, their own strategies shifted from 2010 to 2011. In the first year, NGOs' expressed their "enthusiasm" more boldly, with frequent interruptions in the ILO process. While these activist techniques drew attention to the wider role civil society demanded, they also risked a discrediting within the larger tripartite system.

Some ILO leaders, governments and employers labeled NGOs as "disruptive" and at times disrespectful to the formalities of policy making. In his personal reflections on the process at the end of the 2011 ILC, Robert Shepard captured the wider mixed association about NGOs' growing presence.

> . . . The employer intransience last year, was actually a result I think of the NGOs being there. The NGOs last year were active, they were cheering and clapping, they were heckling on. Some of it was energizing and some of it was destructive, frankly . . . Remember it is a worker-employer organization. So you had this other grouping. This year, clearly, their approach changed a lot. So I felt much more positive. I understand; they were very enthusiastic. They were the people for whom the law bowed. I mean you can't get angry. But in terms of the process, the fact that, I think a lot of the employers saw themselves as almost being on trial did not help at all. I think it created sort of a barrier in a way. It made them feel very defensive and hostile. Whereas this year, there was a much better relationship between the two.[22]

Just as domestic workers noted their decision to curb their emotion and "behave" in the second year of negotiations, Shepard attributed part of the increased success of the second year's negotiations to "the fact that the domestic workers and the NGOs saved the celebration and the singing and all of that till after sessions ended."[23] For their willingness to be obedient, NGOs earned their prize. Yet their curbing of the activist techniques and expressions reflects a clear power dynamic whereby NGOs were respected by fitting into the dominant—historically male, tradition-bound—ILO system.

Shepard's reference to NGOs is reflective of a nuanced association to this new presence of such an active and vocal civil society group. In many cases, the term "NGO" served as a code for domestic workers. The collapsing of these two groups reflects the reciprocity of standpoint crafted between these allies, in their efforts to persuade policy. Because so many NGOs propped domestic workers as their voice, while domestic workers continually referenced their larger NGO allies, in the eyes of employers and governments, the lines between "actual workers" and the wider machinery in solidarity with them easily blurred. For governments, NGOs provided a distinct frame of reference to speak to the domestic worker cause. Without appearing to be biased or overly influenced by the emotional standpoint of domestic workers themselves, governments could refer to NGOs as a means of giving credit to the role of civil society in global policy making. The government of Namibia captured this recognition of the importance of civil society's role in bringing such core issues to the attention of national and international representatives. As the country's lead government delegate pronounced, "we pay tribute to the NGOs . . . we will carry your message in our hearts as we work for you and with you."[24] The Australian government's 2011 closing statement credits NGOs for taking the ILO process beyond Geneva to bring "the plight of domestic workers to the world's attention."[25] As governments responded to civil society support for domestic workers, they presented as closely in tune with the needs of populations "on the ground," thereby increasing their own credibility and engagement with populations in need of rights protections.

Of all the NGOs involved, governments named Human Rights Watch as an exemplar in the civil society–policy process. As the largest international NGO at the ILC meetings, Human Rights Watch brought clout and a history of successful campaigning across some of the world's most difficult locations. Its involvement in domestic work began 10 years prior to the first policy negotiations, through a series of reports that investigated abuses of domestic workers in areas where they were particularly vulnerable to exploitation. This advocacy by a well-recognized organization gave the domestic worker cause moral and political clout. Because it remained invested in assuring that domestic workers themselves would be heard, Human Rights Watch presented as a strong transnational ally, working in solidarity with the groups most directly related

to the experiences of those "on the ground." The organization acknowledged a moral obligation to recognize and prioritize this overlooked and
underprotected workforce.

Human Rights Watch developed an advocacy approach that governments repeatedly named in their recognition of civil society partners'
role in building a global policy on domestic work. Three components
made this strategy particularly impactful. First, Human Rights Watch
gave domestic work a face by focusing on children and migrants. Second, they delivered governments with "model responses" within the
ILO's request for documentation—a maneuver that made the work of
signing on to domestic worker rights so tangible for countries across
a wide range of conditions. Third, Human Rights Watch assured that
Convention 189 reached beyond the two meetings in Geneva with substantive advocacy work investment and relationship building that began
before the first 2010 meetings. In preparation for each stage of the process, they wrote letters to Ministers of Labor, calling each country to
protect human rights through their support of domestic workers. Thus,
rather than attempting to lobby during the haste of the ILC meetings,
Human Rights Watch had already established a strong presence among
governments and employers. Representatives used the time between
meetings to provide persuasive input on the amendments and provisions within the instrument and thank key representatives for their investment in a longer-term dialogue on the importance of human rights
in the decisions surrounding the domestic work convention. With this
notion of building relationships, Human Rights Watch established a
complementary form of social dialogue for civil society to engage in the
process of policy negotiations. Not only did they build relationships,
they actually fed governments with evidence-based arguments in favor
of the convention. Jo Becker, the lead Human Rights Watch strategist
recalled, "In several cases, governments put forward amendments based
on the language that had been provided by NGOs."[26] When asked about
the influence of civil society organizations on the Convention process,
Robert Shepard stated, "we listened to Human Rights Watch" and lauded
their "very helpful" suggestions for government positions. In a sense,
Human Rights Watch made governments' work a bit easier, on both
pragmatic and public relations sides. While they scripted some government responses in support of Convention 189, Human Rights Watch also

helped many countries 'look good' in their overall support for domestic worker rights.

The negotiation of domestic worker policy allowed Human Rights Watch to reach beyond governments to garner the widest possible support for Convention 189. One of the most important maneuvers Human Rights Watch representatives employed involved the strategic linkages they built with employers. While this group began the negotiations with a strong resistance to a convention, Human Rights Watch drew upon an established body of research to point to the extreme abuses within this sector and emphasize employers' gain in supporting decent work. In the final negotiations, Human Rights Watch briefed the entire employer group on its findings on the severe abuses in employment agencies—an area that generated employer interest and some accountability.[27] Unlike any other civil society representative, employers named Human Rights Watch as a significant source of their own process of moving from resistance to support for the convention. In his closing statement at the 2011 ILC, leader of the employer group, Paul Mackay spoke to this shift in employers' perspectives as a direct result of the input of Human Rights Watch and the time its leaders invested in relationship-building.

> One of the things that we talked about in their [workers'] opening statement was the word invisibility and how we have trouble with it. But one of the things we have come to appreciate is that previously closed doors are now open to us and we would like to in fact thank, amongst others, the Human Rights, who came and spent time with the employers' group, helping us to open those doors and to find some of the realities that aren't always apparent.

For employers to recognize an NGO in their final statement, a substantive transformation in the ILO process occurred with the negotiations on domestic work. With the wide participation of so many representatives of civil society, coupled with the ideological engagement of larger human rights concerns within this sector, employers gradually let go of their coveted portion of the monopoly in the tripartite process.

Alongside Human Rights Watch, these NGO alliances carved a new path for civil society to engage with the ILO policy process. With groups working across divides, on behalf of domestic workers, this global governance space became a place to advance larger social justice movements while striving for a collective goal around policy implementation. Even though it served as a template for a more egalitarian and inclusive social dialogue, this civil society-global governance integration did not always materialize seamlessly. In some instances, ILO leaders expressed concern that NGOs had taken up too much space in the negotiations. At the onset, the ILO made a deal with NGO leaders to assure that the goals of their participation centered on policy attainment and ratification promotion, rather than their own public relations campaigns. One ILO official critiqued the NGO competition over advocacy and affective appeals. After the policy is in place, he contended, "they can get their liberty later." Rather than "branding tragedy," social dialogue in the ILO was to focus on attaining rights that could be ratified across all Member States. Thus, much like domestic workers, NGOs walked a fine line to push for a more people-centered presence in the ILO, while respecting the rules of order as a mandatory requirement for any radical nudge within this historically rule and process centered international institution.

NGO-Union Cleavages

As NGOs took a prominent representational role, they assumed the main advocacy position for domestic workers. These established organizations brought years of invested focus on the issues surrounding Convention 189, as well as dedicated resources and a strong motivation to enter the ILO through the domestic worker campaign. At the center of this alliance, WIEGO and the IUF supplied the public relations, network mobilization, and training machinery to bolster the presence and voices of domestic workers. Their political savvy and experience with informal workers, as well as with the ILO, allowed domestic workers to translate their activism into aligned actions focused on the attainment of this first policy. With their focus on labor and global policy, this duo brought a workers' movement front to the negotiations, unlike any other group within the negotiations. Yet, the representational dynamics that emerged through the ILO surfaced larger political questions about domestic workers' affiliations with unions. Critics suggested that NGOs "submerged" unions and therefore compromised the central role of labor in the tripartite. Through its inclusion of a formerly orphaned group of workers, Convention 189 exposed a larger set of complexities about the relationships between unions and NGOs, while carving a distinct role for global unions as domestic workers' main solidarity partner in the labor movement.

The central differences between NGOs and unions played out concretely through their relationship to domestic workers within the ILO negotiations. Historically, NGOs have been seen as the "do-gooders," while trade unions take on a more politicized role.[28] The composition of these respective organizations also inscribes central associations to their histories and identities. NGOs are led mainly by middle class people who work "for a cause" often out of ideological commitments, rather than their own daily circumstances. Trade unions, alternatively, are often comprised of people who experience the injustices of labor in their own lives and pay dues directly as the overarching structure of a member-based organization. They are registered and recognized by the state, and therefore carry a more formal role in the negotiation of policy. Trade unions hold democracy as a guiding value, with processes for participation embedded in the overarching system of operation. NGOs, on the other hand, rely on donors for daily operations, and may be less consistently democratic. Yet both forms of organizations rely on hierarchies, even though they work for values of justice and equality. As both NGOs and unions supported a domestic work policy, the ILO arena pronounced the differences in their structures and overarching allegiances.

Given the distinct funding structures and ideological loyalties, in one way or another, NGOs and unions asked each other "who is buttering your bread?"[29] In the case of domestic work, global NGOs received funding and vital liaisons to represent domestic workers, as part of their larger project profiles that justified their existence. By taking part in the widely publicized ILO stage, these organizations also earned substantive political and social capital for their protection of precarious workers. Thus, the ILO policy work gave a clear and purposive reason for NGOs to build coalitions with domestic workers through Convention 189. For trade unions, support for domestic workers cost, without increased revenue or the same potential public relations boost. Given the predominantly female, informal and heavily migrant composition of domestic work, national unions have rarely taken on this sector, nor have they been willing to subsidize the cost of representation, given the

nature of this "scattered workforce."[30] Many domestic worker organizations are not recognized by national governments because they often
do not meet membership numbers, and are therefore not considered
legitimate bodies. Historical conditions pose serious barriers to inclusion in national unions. In the United States, domestic workers are not
covered by collective bargaining agreements and excluded from the 1935
National Labor Relations Act. By excluding agricultural and household staff members, employers remained protected from the potential
for unionization and high cost increases for labor rights. In the context
of globalization, with outsourced labor and rapid spikes in migration,
many countries continue to legislate domestic worker rights based upon
these historical legal frameworks that keep the household outside of any
obligation for standardized protections.

The absence of foundational rights, such as the ILO's guiding freedom of association protection that assures that workers are allowed to
form unions, creates conditions that allow the underlying gender politics of unions to reproduces sharp gender divides within national movements fighting for labor justice. Shirley Pryce, founder of the national
Jamaican domestic workers' union, captured a predominant position
among labor movement leadership. "Most trade unions are male dominated. They said they knew domestic work was important, but it was
not really their 'issue' or 'priority.'"[31] Domestic worker front line activists in South Africa faced exclusions from the same national union that
fought against apartheid. Even as the country built a new democracy,
male union leaders deemed domestic workers' affiliation to the national
labor organization "non-viable."[32] Across the world, household workers have paid an extraordinary tax because their labor is not deemed
legitimate and therefore they are not able to assure the protections that
accompany union membership, not to mention in many cases, the foundational benefits of citizenship.

At the ILO, unions' historical exclusion of domestic workers came
into the international spotlight. As momentum built for this global domestic labor policy, national unions faced greater expectations to extend
solidarity to their sisters in struggle. In the Geneva forums, domestic
workers voiced the underbelly of representational politics by naming
the inherent contradictions of national unions' exclusion of domestic
workers. Ida le Blanc, leader of the Trinidad and Tobago domestic work-

ers' union, called her union brothers to task by pointing to their own reliance upon domestic workers to support their lives as leaders in the labor movement.

> . . . we need to work harder to bring a greater awareness amongst trade unions and seek to break traditions and mentalities towards domestic work. Trade unions everywhere must support the effort of the domestic workers. Most trade union leaders use the services of domestic workers and some have been cared and nurtured into what they have become today *by* domestic workers. So we are calling for all to give back by supporting domestic workers and allowing them to speak for themselves and to gain some measure of visibility so that we can be victorious.

As le Blanc points out, gendered labor norms in the household transfer to union structures, where women's work is far less valued and severely under-recognized. Leidi, a domestic worker leader from Paraguay, named the exclusion of domestic workers from national trade unions as centrally connected to prevailing masculinized attitudes that take form in organizational structures.

> We are workers like any other, and we have the right to be in unions. We have the right in every country . . . even through the women's department, it has been a very large issue for me to get into our trade union. There is machismo. We have to gain the same struggle.

As these domestic worker activists pointed out, exclusion from national unions persists and takes a particular toll on their capacities to claim the core tenets of Convention 189: access to rights, recognitions and protections "just like any other worker."

These union gender politics travelled to the structures of international governance, leaving domestic workers outside of most official labor delegations and placing traditional male leaders in positions that allowed them to represent women workers in the formal labor structures. Even though their own unions excluded domestic workers, the ILO process allowed official national labor delegates to vote on behalf of women and informal workers—two classifications that drew the sharpest divides in the histories of union gender politics. Marcelina Bautista, leader of CONLACTRAHO, demanded domestic workers' rights as legitimate workers and recognized delegates to the ILO.

> . . . in order to participate in this function we need to be delegates. In labor unions in our countries, the issue of domestic work hasn't been taken into consideration. So in order to participate and to be part of the central unions, gain support and play a role in this conference, we must be seen as delegates and recognized before this conference as being in positions of authority.[33]

Even with this expansive public attention, national labor structures could not catch up to these gender demands fast enough to include domestic workers in their formal delegations.[34] In order to have an actual vote in the policy process, domestic workers needed a formal seat in their national labor delegations. A few countries shifted their representation, with a notable increase in the second year of negotiations when 25 domestic workers attained the formal T-badge as voting members of national labor representatives. While some national unions made their delegations more inclusive, the disproportionate level of domestic workers' exclusion from these formal labor bodies remained a source of ongoing struggle.

As a leader of the IDWN, Ip Pui Yu repeatedly demanded inclusion in the wider union movement. "I call upon the trade union brothers and sisters. We really need to bring more domestic workers here to the ILC."[35] Not only would domestic workers' inclusion in national unions rebalance the historical gender struggles, such access would allow domestic workers closer relations to the state. As Marissa Begonia, a Hong-Kong native domestic worker in the UK movement, asserted:

> I believe it is vital that we understand that every day we are fighting our governments. We do not have access to trade unions or governments. Trade unions here must help us to influence our governments because they are closer to governments than we are. We are sitting here to legitimize the rights that we are denied.

These statements exposed male union power structures publically as a first step in shifting the terms of labor representation. Throughout this process, domestic workers made promising inroads as the international attention to Convention 189 piqued national unions' interest and softened some of the edges of historic exclusion.

While the international policy arena gradually shifted the grounds of union politics, domestic workers found their much more solid and assured support from their ally-ship with NGOs and global unions. As one domestic worker activist described, "As it was recognized, trade unions were very weak, because they did not understand. We thank the NGOs and other partners, which means that we need to alliance with other groups, which means that domestic workers [still] need to be accepted as workers." Thus, their exclusion from national unions rerouted domestic workers into the ILO arena, and allowed them to set new precedents for activism and policy change. As the role of NGOs strengthened through the domestic-work deliberations, rather than relying on national unions to change, domestic worker organizations worked from their established relations and strong ideological alignments with NGOs like WIEGO and Human Rights Watch. At the helm of this support, the IUF bridged the labor-civil society divide through its long-standing commitment to the inclusion of domestic workers as centrally important to the global labor movement.

Domestic Work and the State

The ILO process altered states' relationships with domestic labor. As government delegates took to the policy floor, states' multilateral relations, regional affiliations, and broader reliance on the migrant maid trade rose to public attention. Not only did governments have to take a position on domestic worker rights, in doing so they faced their own employer and labor constituents, as well as the representatives of the women whose lives would be most affected by the negotiation's outcome. For some states, such as the Philippines and the United Arab Emirates, approving domestic workers' rights meant maintaining smooth relations between sending and receiving countries in their reliance on women workers. For others, like the United Kingdom, Belgium, and France, a policy on domestic workers' rights raised questions of social-security protections. Domestic workers' migrant status forced those countries with generous support systems to examine their practices of restricting rights to naturalized citizens. While some embraced an expansion of protections for the migrants who provided reproductive labor, others deemed domestic work incompatible with state-level social and economic protections. These diverse ideologies, practices, and dependencies brought the larger struggle for rights into realistic focus.

At the ILO, domestic worker representatives could observe their own governments' positions, with NGO and global union support. In their own countries, many domestic worker organizations could not gain recognition from their governments. Some did not have a sufficient membership base to be officially recognized, while many others faced overarching gender, race, and class discrimination. Yet in the ILO, domestic workers merited attention. As a domestic worker representative from Singapore said in the 2011 meetings, "Even though I cannot raise my voice in Singapore, it is a privilege to raise my voice here."[36]

When government representatives spoke, the wide network of domestic workers in the room listened. Strengthened by alliance support, IDWN leaders could hold their own governments accountable in the face of state testimonials on working conditions. In some situations, the domestic worker representatives themselves provided research for states to advocate on their behalf. In other instances, domestic workers engaged with their own governments, and in many cases gave input on the real working conditions in their respective countries. As Dan Gallin pointed out, the terms of representation made it virtually impossible for governments to deny human rights for domestic workers. "What government is going to say that they're in favor of domestic workers continuing to be mistreated?"[37] This public interplay widened the moral grounds for rights, while setting news terms for negotiations between domestic workers and governments.

As the negotiations unfolded, key state advocates emerged to stand in solidarity with domestic workers' cause. While they spoke from their own national platforms, these government allies referenced the broader transnational conditions for the women who deserve protections as they care for the global economy. Those states with particular histories of social movements for justice, or distinct connections to domestic work, held especially persuasive positions within the negotiations. Legal specialist Martin Oelz attributed much of the support for the convention to the persuasive power of what he called "the Big Five."

> Some countries are what you'd call the friends of the convention, you know. As countries and ILO members . . . they have to move it along, because if you wouldn't have had these countries—like Brazil and South Africa and the United States, Australia, Argentina, Uruguay—putting their foot on the ground and countering the arguments, politically [the negotiations] wouldn't have happened like that.

By getting five of the consistently strongest allies of the convention to back each article in the negotiations, the domestic worker cause gained considerable momentum and collective political strength. These lead support countries influenced the dialogue through various combinations of three factors: (1) they were states with strong political influence and standing within the UN system; (2) they had a national history of domestic work; and (3) they worked in blocs to build stronger government support for the convention. Australia repeatedly took to the floor with powerful arguments that positioned the country as a leading advocate for domestic worker rights. As her country's spokesperson throughout both conventions, Louise McDonough situated an ILO convention in the context of a larger movement for rights, particularly among those most marginalized workers. McDonough's statements repeatedly called for a global shift to "recognize domestic work for the profession that it is."[38] Even though Australia did not rely on migrant domestic labor, its position as a G20 economic power with a history of peace and stability gave it a particularly persuasive voice throughout the negotiations.

Among the "Big Five," Brazil distinguished itself as one of the heaviest hitters in the lineup of domestic worker allies. As they drew upon the nation's history of social struggle for race, class, and gender equity, the Brazilian delegates acknowledged Brazil's long-standing history of reliance upon domestic work and emphasized the importance of charting a new course for care labor at a global level. María Luisa Escorel de Moraes, government delegate from Brazil, acknowledged her country's close relationship to domestic work: "Above all, certain countries are very important with domestic workers because they're a part of our culture, they're part of our lives, our daily lives, and we know how much we depend on them." Along with this recognition, Escorel de Moraes went on to emphasize "the awareness of [domestic workers] being parts of our families, but not parts of our families because they have their own families and their own lives."[39] This statement echoes feminist scholars' long-standing critique of the "one in the family" notion that denies domestic workers' core responsibility for their own families.[40] Given this particular history of imbalance, exclusion from protections, and labor exploitation, Escorel de Moraes surmised, "I think there was a common sense of wanting to give them the recognition and respect that they deserve." Along with this delegate's strong statements of alliance with domestic workers, the Brazilian labor minister brought his own personal history into the public discussions to advocate for global protections, stating that his own mother worked as a domestic worker.

Another of the "Big Five," South Africa, also drew from its distinct history of racial governance to take one of the strongest stances on domestic workers' rights. Its rhetorical strength stemmed from the position it shared with Brazil, as the top two countries with the most developed legislative frameworks in place for domestic workers. These lead advocates brought the historical impact of their social struggles to the floor. Such national "struggle credentials" legitimized the IDWN cause, backed up by the strong presence of domestic worker organizers from Brazil and South Africa. Unlike any other country, South Africa could stand on the merits of its expansive legislation, established throughout the 15 years prior to the first ILC meeting, as human rights ideologies took form through the establishment of social and labor policies. Proudly in support of a global convention, South Africa proclaimed its strategy as "to treat domestic workers as any other workers."[41] With the most developed legal framework in place, this relatively new democracy stood as a powerful source of evidence to employer and other government critics, who suggested that with more legislative protections, unemployment would rise. Department of Labour officials from South Africa refuted such claims by drawing upon the "sectoral determination" minimum wage standards they had established in 1999. South African government leader Virgil Seafield confidently recounted that in the 10 years since minimum-wage standards had been implemented, domestic worker employment rates had not decreased. "People did not go out and buy larger washing machines and brooms"[42] because of the state regulations, he insisted. Rather, they saw the sector grow in ways that aligned it more closely with the recognitions that came out of these first legislative protections for domestic workers. These concrete examples held a particular ground in the negotiations because they came from South Africa—a country that models a "forward to freedom"[43] potential for social change.

This history fortified South Africa's position within negotiations, as the representative speaker for the Africa group. In his opening statement, Seafield articulated the region's position, while also making a bold statement about the larger meaning of the convention. "Africa . . . believes that we stand on the threshold of change for domestic workers," he said.[44] While representing the African position, South Africa also had strong linkages with NGOs and the IDWN, and a distinct legal support network. Its public statements dovetailed with NGO strategies that linked domestic work to other critical areas of concern for the ILO, as well as to larger UN commitments, treaties, and priorities. Rather than speaking to domestic work as an isolated sector, South Africa opened its 2010 statement by asserting that both child labor and human trafficking have, to some degree, their "roots in domestic work."[45] Throughout the negotiations, South African delegates repeatedly positioned the convention as a vehicle by which the ILO could address a range of global crises, as a leader in the UN system. Their statements reflected both an analytic capacity to link the convention to wider global circumstances, and a concrete ability to put tangible legal instruments on the table, based upon the successes realized in South Africa's new democracy.

To strengthen South Africa's position during the ILC, experts from the Social Law Project in Cape Town gained civil-society observer status and consulted government representatives during both years of negotiations. Darcy du Toit, an established anti-apartheid activist, labor lawyer, and professor, and Fairuz Mullagee, social development expert at the University of the Western Cape, supplied South African government leaders with tangible data, perspectives, and arguments linking the country's established legislation with this first international instrument for domestic workers. With this team in place, and the high public profile of IDWN president Myrtle Witbooi, South Africa went further than any other country in terms of its ties to civil society representatives. South Africa's history of transformative politics thus infused the domestic worker negotiations.

In its advocacy for domestic worker rights, South Africa embodied the visionary ideals and human rights values central to the ILO's mission. Government representatives' public support for domestic workers highlighted South Africa's leading role in the establishment of legislative standards, while their human rights aims echoed the ILO's overarching social justice ideals. Yet throughout the negotiations, the South African government did not have to account for the challenges it faced in enforcement and employer compliance with its impressive labor legislation. Recent data suggest that the country's national laws affected only 20 percent, or 30 percent at best, of its domestic workers.[46] At the same time, the Commission for Conciliation, Mediation and Arbitration, the state body charged with labor-dispute resolution, is most effective when domestic workers are accompanied by union representation. Yet, even with its lauded victories, less than 5 percent of South Africa's domestic workers join the national union.[47] These realities would water down the power of South Africa's stance, and the wide acclaim it held for such impressive rights "on paper." The nation's relative fledgling democracy allowed for some leeway, thereby effectively sanctioning the silence of discussions of practice in its model legislative framework. Much more persuasive was South Africa's signature rhetoric that held to the potential for a modest revolution in the policy world. By standing with domestic workers, the South African government did find ways to emphasize the need for any international instrument to have a direct impact on domestic workers' lives. As South Africa took the floor on behalf of the Africa Group, its leaders asserted, "This seminal event for the ILO must be as significant for domestic workers."[48] They demanded that domestic workers be seen as more than an "adjunct" workforce. Any policy that emerged from the ILO, they asserted, "must go beyond just using gender-sensitive language and make a real difference for domestic workers."[49] By referencing this policy-impact consideration, South Africa stood "in firm support of the proposed convention," while acknowledging the realities of implementation as a core measure of success—a stance strikingly familiar to its own governance challenge to make policy meaningful.

Femocrats Speak

Among the state allies, key women delegates voiced larger feminist considerations within the domestic worker rights debates. As central proponents of the convention, these leaders used their positions to voice ideologies consistent with the IDWN's *Platform of Demands*. Their statements focused on three main rationales for the convention: (1) the world's dependency on domestic labor; (2) the injustice of denying protections to this legitimate group of workers; and (3) the gender and racial underpinnings of domestic workers' precarious labor conditions. Louise McDonough, one of the most outspoken state advocates for domestic workers, infused a central feminist demand to bring policy up to date with the existing structure of the world's economy. In her speech just before the final vote at the 2011 ILC, she spoke of delegates' moral obligation to protect domestic workers through policy—a route she saw as the only assurance of real change.

> I would like to encourage all those charged with formally voting on the convention and recommendation concerning domestic workers tomorrow to recognize this as a vote on an international standard for a group of up to 100 million workers who have been confined to the informal economy for hundreds of years . . . To give a no vote or an abstention risks denying the opportunity for many countries to legitimize formally their domestic workers in line with a recognized international standard. To not support this convention and recommendation is to confine domestic workers to the unregulated, invisible, and vulnerable circumstances they are currently in. To say, as some employers have here today, that change for the domestic workers will happen regardless of the outcome of the vote, is folly, in the Australian government's view. A lack of support for this convention would send a strong message to the world that domestic workers do not deserve the protection otherwise provided by this House to other workers, and take us right back to the 1950s.[50]

The 1950s model conjures images of the oppressed housewife, women's return to household labor in the post–World War II era, and the feminization of domestic work. McDonough thus links resistance to support for domestic workers with a return to women's oppression in the home.

Alongside McDonough's, Brazil's bold public positions aligned women government leaders with a larger gender struggle for their sisters' protections. One of the iconic moments in the story of Convention 189 took place when the Brazilian government delegate brought a domestic worker to the floor to stand beside her, as she delivered a statement of solidarity for the convention. While the domestic worker could not speak during this address, she conveyed a powerful message about the terms of women's solidarity within the negotiations, as well as the larger issues of gender justice contained within this policy. With a national union of domestic workers in the room, Brazil used its delegation to model larger values of inclusivity and alliance support. As government delegate María Luisa Escorel de Moraes conveyed, Brazil's delegation reflected the state's vested interest in domestic work.

> I think that Brazil is committed to assimilating domestic workers with other workers, right, and they still have a long-standing tradition with their legislation that comes from the 70s . . . Therefore, the composition of the Brazilian delegation, I think, reflects the interests and the common feeling that exists amongst the various powers that be in this Republic, which are the executive, the judicial, and the legislative branches, regarding the importance of this convention and this topic . . . As the one hundredth conference, it's very historic, and that's very interesting to us as well. We had, in fact, a group of domestic workers that was with the workers, and we also had the government representatives from the three branches . . . and within the executive, we also had the Minister of Labor and the work inspector, and also the Secretary for the Promotion of Women's Interests.

This Brazilian alliance presented a model of unity that both reflected the country's larger political value system and placed domestic workers squarely at the table. By bringing a domestic worker to the floor with a government delegate, Brazil modeled a feminist notion of recognition for women who earn a livelihood in the quintessentially feminized household space. Furthermore, by injecting race and gender into the discussions, the Brazilian government positioned domestic work as an iconic social struggle, worthy of the attention of the international governing community.

The women in government who stepped in as domestic workers' core advocates used their public positions to exemplify feminist values while playing by the rules of international governance. By promoting domestic worker rights within the ILO they carved out a distinct position for state feminists—as *femocrats* who are able to push feminist values within larger systems, in this case within the context of a mainstream institution.[51] Their strategic influence translated gender (and often race and class) awareness into policymaking practices, while their public positions made support for domestic workers unquestionably an obligation for women's rights advocates worldwide. Women in government positions could speak on behalf of domestic workers in the formal negotiations in ways no other member of the civil-society group could.

One of their most persuasive arguments centered on their close personal connections to domestic work within their own families, as they acknowledged that "we would not be here without the women working in our own homes."[52] Women leaders' advocacy efforts outside the ILO also referenced personal ties to domestic workers. For example, at the National Domestic Workers Alliance Care Congress in 2011, Hilda Solis, then US secretary of labor, spoke about her mother's migration from Nicaragua through domestic work. She drew upon these legacies of suffering to support an ILO convention and promote decent work for all. Like Solis, at the ILO, *feminists on the floor* assured the promotion of domestic workers' interests in gaining legitimacy and making inroads toward government recognition. As powerful women spoke for the women who "work in a hidden way,"[53] they reinforced the lines of privilege running along race, class, geographical, and citizenship lines. At the same time, femocrats worked within the confines of the ILO's traditional structure, arguing that "women won't be free until domestic workers are free."

With respect to femocrats' representation of domestic workers' demands, the behind-the-scenes processes are vital to analysis of larger questions of standpoint. During the ILC meetings, they spoke directly with IDWN leaders and held strategic planning sessions with other governments to develop bloc alliances in support of the convention. In their position as proxies for domestic workers, femocrats drew from their conversations with domestic workers, the data research that placed the personal in a larger geopolitical context. While they held influential government seats, when they spoke on behalf of domestic workers, they often deferred to IDWN representatives in emphasizing the impact of the policy outcome. The Brazilian government representative asserted, "Domestic workers are to be commended for standing up against all odds."[54] Statements like this strategically critiqued the silencing of the women in this profession, who sat among policymakers during the negotiations. This approach repeatedly placed domestic workers next to women in positions of state power, thereby asking central questions about the relative reach of a global women's movement, given the profound disparities reflected between these two representative groups and the severe policy gaps that leave migrant household workers unprotected from global human rights accomplishments.

The femocrats who brought their voices to the ILO made a powerful mark on the long-standing struggle to bring women's voices, rights and perspectives into this global labor institution. This representational strategy, while promoting a "Women's ILO,"[55] also reinforces lines of privilege and power. To mediate this inherent divide, progressive feminist delegates proposed notions of reciprocity between women employers and domestic workers. Brazilian government delegate María Luisa Escorel de Moraes described her ideal notion of relations between women in this distinct work context, in the feminized private household domain.

> May it be a relationship based on mutual respect. I've always said that, on trust and mutual respect, reciprocal, that's how it needs to be. A person works in a home, she needs to respect the home also, the home needs to respect the worker and have respect and trust on both sides. That's the only way it can work.[56]

With the law in place, such relations of mutual respect and reciprocity gain footing in a system that protects workers beyond the traditional relations of power that afforded decent work only through the assurance of "good employers." The femocrats who played such a powerful role in the Convention 189 discussions illustrate the potential to change an iconic patriarchal system through the alignment of a relatively small group, with outreach across the tripartite. The voices of government delegates aligned easily with NGOs' innovative techniques, along with the IDWN's persuasive strategies to carve out moments where their voices could be heard, even when the system allowed only their silent rhetorical techniques. At the same time, the input of women in government aligned fluently with Halimah Yacob, who led the workers' group as a member of Parliament in her own country. While the NGOs and the IDWN stood in numbers representing the "masses" of workers, the femocrats on the floor stood as revolutionaries in their use of their acquired state power to give voice to larger injustices that played out in this formerly overlooked labor space. By politicizing the household, state representatives shifted the policy conversation, while bringing larger feminist ideals into practical analysis.

Diplomats and Domestic Workers Summary

If walk out of there on Thursday night with the vote in our
pockets, and the victory is ours, it is thanks to all of our great
friends all over the world.
—Myrtle Witbooi, Closing Speech

The "great friends" of domestic workers took many forms. For NGOs, domestic work encapsulates a range of injustices—from trafficking to child labor to contemporary slavery. With domestic workers themselves present in the room, these transnational networks gained a level of authenticity that created unprecedented leverage in their shared human rights platforms. When Anti-Slavery International brought in child domestic workers, they symbolically and literally revealed their scars to render the denial of the first public policy virtually inconceivable. At the same time, domestic workers' ties to NGOs bolstered their own voices, allowing them to speak from a much stronger platform, with the support of some of the most powerful international organizations behind their cause. This NGO-domestic worker alignment developed reciprocal relations that amplified both voices and presented a united front for rights. In this way, beyond policy formation, the ILO served as the formative site to build a movement for women's, migrants' and informal workers' rights that stretched far beyond Convention 189.

The ILO's agenda formed new friendships for domestic workers through the act of placing them in proximity with both state and labor negotiations of the new terms of the global economy. The acknowledgement domestic workers received in the global union movement placed pressure on nation unions to get on board with labor's ideological responsibility to embrace the informal economy as a critical component of the larger class struggle. While domestic workers had previously been considered a financial burden to national unions, the global attention they drew led some national labor movements to reconsider the political assets gained through some investment in solidarity.

Among these newfound friends-in-policy, key government representatives also stepped in as domestic workers' allies. In some cases, the timing of the Convention 189 discussions fell closely in line with state political priorities, such as the Obama administration's emphasis on human rights and international standards for protections.[57] In other cases, the gender labor dimensions of this sector allowed women in government positions to voice support as advocates of a larger struggle for justice. The historic significance of this debate brought together a state feminist response to domestic work, unlike any former global or national conversation. While the Home Work Convention focused on a predominantly female sector, Convention 189 provided the widest platform to discuss the critical intersections of gender, class, race, migration and citizenship within the ILO. With "actual workers" at the table, unlike any other policy discussions, state allies could build ties to the women who held the deepest pool of experience and earned authenticity in the room. As they looked to their "sisters," key women government representatives challenged the ILO's longstanding gender inequalities through the very direct focus on domestic work, and the impact of the extensive history of policy exclusions. Feminist state delegates—femocrats—got behind the powerful rhetoric of NGOs to embolden the larger plight for rights, and underscore the moral responsibility to use this official house of international governance to set higher standards for this "formerly forgotten" sector. As these femocrats carried the privilege of speaking publicly, their ally input engraved a trail of signatures that wove national histories of labor struggles and domestic workers' voices into the dialogue.

With the backing of global unions, key government allies, influential femocrats, and the original IUF-WIEGO parents of this movement, the IDWN's statements reflected a much wider movement that bolstered their strength and served as one of their most persuasive activist techniques. The broad support for domestic workers displayed a virtual banner of collective investment in the symbolic and moral impact of this global rights movement. As this trans-alliance network of supporters latched on to this timely and highly publicized cause, the voice of domestic workers at times melded into larger rhetorical strategies, raising a continual need to negotiate standpoint in the interest of the larger politics of building a global movement. The public stage acquired in this formal house of international governance solidified a blueprint of global activism that extended far beyond Geneva. With the strength of this landmark policy, domestic workers launched an innovative movement made possible only through the relationships formed within the ILO. In the end, the depth and demands of the policy process itself solidified domestic workers' ability to emerge as a burgeoning force with tentacles in civil society movements, national and global unions, and the politics of state responsibility for care labor.

"A Little Bit of Liberation"

Moving Beyond Rights

The entire ILO process was a lesson to me in the importance
of movements—movements that create progressive governments, movements of women and workers that demand
change, and the great acts of leadership that movements create. Paying tribute to the leadership of women in movements
in particular as I leave Geneva today.
—Ai-jen Poo, 2011 International Labor Conference

After two years of tripartite negotiations, the ILO's government, labor,
and employer delegates voted on the world's first Decent Work for
Domestic Workers Convention on June 16, 2011.[1] Hester Stephens sat in
the observation section of one the largest venues on the United Nations
grounds as the vote read out: "Votes in Favor, 434; Votes Opposed, 8;
Abstentions, 42; the Majority [gavel strike] *Approved*."[2] With these
words, the formal rules of order gave way as domestic workers exploded
in cheers, activist songs, and tears. Their demonstration generated
a wave of applause throughout the Palais des Nations, the room that
workers had overtaken during the 2010 meetings. From the third story
of that great hall, activists dropped an enormous banner reading C189
CONGRATULATIONS, NOW THE DOMESTIC WORK FOR GOVERN-
MENTS, RATIFY, IMPLEMENT. In this moment of victory, activist
practices held sway over the formal procedures of international governance. When security personnel asked the workers and their allies to
remove the banner and cease their cheering, they simply relocated to
the lobby outside the General Assembly and began chanting, "Up, up
domestic workers! Down, down with sla-ver-y!" followed by their signature song, "My mother was a *kitchen girl*, my father was a *garden boy*,
that's why I'm a unionist, I'm a unionist, I'm a unionist!" Just as one ILO

Figure 7.1. Victory activism. Photo by Sofia Trevino.

Figure 7.2. ILO victory moment, June 16, 2011. Photo by Sofia Trevino.

official interrupted the boisterous celebration, telling IDWN leaders to "be quiet, we are not finished yet," the director-general stepped in behind her to offer congratulations, with wide embraces and the shared chant of "Viva!" among all. With the vote solidified, domestic workers gave voice to the intense emotions they had held in check during the long hours of formal negotiations. The international media took the opportunity to document a rare global human rights victory. As she reflected on the past 50 years of her life's work, Hester's first statement to the press captured a wider domestic worker story of personal struggle and collective strength. "I feel it is like a baby was born that I give birth to. For me, it is such an emotional moment. It is just to think today, the 16th of June 2011, that freedom at last came for domestic workers around the world."

With the adoption of Convention 189, the IDWN's influence on the world stage was affirmed. Every national member could take credit for the victory, reinforcing common bonds. IDWN President Myrtle Witbooi claimed this moment on behalf of domestic workers worldwide:

> Today we celebrate a great victory for domestic workers. Until now we have been treated as "invisible," not respected for the huge contribution we make in society and the economy and denied our rights as workers. It is an injustice that has lasted too long. After three years of organizing domestic workers throughout the world, the International Domestic Workers Network became the driving force behind this massive campaign to finally recognize domestic work as real work, worthy of the recognition and protection of all other sectors.[3]

Not only did domestic workers celebrate the rights and protections codified in the convention, they recognized their enormous achievement in having attained this historic policy. In their public statements, they asserted that their victory had been made possible only through the years of struggle they had invested in their local and national contexts. Hester Stephens captured this history in her reflections on the day Convention 189 passed.

> I must say that while we are here, it just went through my mind, where did I come from and where am I today? Myself, I come from a very poor background. This conference, it is such a history, it will be a history

worldwide . . . Through the years, I empower myself as a woman. I never thought that I have to sit like this, like a parrot in a cage. I want to get out of the cage.

Hester went on to explain that her capacity to move "out of the cage" stemmed from the national domestic workers' union in South Africa, and later her work as a leader in the global movement. She equated Convention 189 with "a baby that I gave birth to" and a moment when "freedom at last came for domestic workers around the world."[4] Every woman in this pioneer collection of domestic worker activists carried her own story of personal and national struggle.

These stories all contained a larger motivation for justice and rights. As Aida Moreno captured in her poem for her local sisters:

> Joy at this new task and in all of us working united
> In order for this agreement to be passed in 2011
> So that we can gain more social justice for domestic workers
> And so they are appreciated as workers and people

In this poem, she refers to "some of the wonderful gifts that we have achieved" in mobilizing domestic workers from the national to the global scale. Thus, as domestic workers celebrated their victory, they recalled their own histories of struggle, and the moments when their activism seemed a drop in an ocean of systemic injustice.

Meaning of the Movement

I fought my way in getting to the ILO in Geneva to fight for laws to be put in place to protect domestic workers so they will be able to work, live and die in dignity.
—Shirley Pryce[5]

In the next 10 years I see domestic workers continuing to stand tall and to reach out to those who aren't so that this circle that we have here will go around the globe.
—Margo Legault, Association des Aides Familiales du Québec

The recognition of the value of domestic work became as important as the tangible set of standards that emerged from Convention 189. In this sense, domestic workers won three victories. First, the adoption of an international convention and accompanying recommendations affirmed their fundamental rights to regular work hours, maternity leave, collective bargaining, and access to dispute-resolution systems. Yet the second victory realized a moral high ground that finally legitimized "domestic worker rights as human rights."[6] Based on the global activism that surrounded this two-year campaign, this second victory fortified a unified movement beyond the recognition of rights ascribed within the legal convention. As IDWN leaders confirmed, the alignment of domestic worker organizations, unions, and allied networks during the collective organizing for Convention 189 became as important as the actual achievement of a global policy on domestic labor.[7] Third, domestic workers authored new terms for social movements through this policy victory. Their ILO activism became a new model of using traditional institutions to mobilize civil society for change. By bringing together unions and NGOs, domestic workers garnered substantial influence within the ILO, as the largest coordinated movement of "actual workers" to co-shape global policy.

The IDWN also earned extraordinary global attention and public relations accolades because of the reach of this victory and the speed of its policy accomplishments. At a celebration dinner at the close of the 2011 meetings, Marty Chen, feminist policy expert, director of WIEGO, and founding visionary behind the formation of the IDWN, reminded domestic workers of the profound movement they had launched in such an incredibly short time.

> I want to say that I know of no other social movement in the world that went from ground level to cruising altitude in *three* years! You went from forming a network to moving a convention, in *three* years! There is no other movement in the world. So really you have to all take real pride in what has happened.

The victory gave the IDWN a great deal of positive PR, while instilling new forms of hope among a wider network of allies invested in the capacities of social revolutions. Dan Gallin recollected, "It was like the collapse of the Soviet Union. I knew it was coming but I never expected so soon and so fast and so total," he said with a laugh.[8] With the Convention 189 win, then, domestic workers worldwide earned policy protections, symbolic recognition of dignity, and ownership of a model social movement.

With the convention, what had once seemed impossible became concrete. According to one domestic worker activist, "This fight is fair; we finally have an international law."[9] Beyond putting the most comprehensive standards in place, Convention 189 set an "international benchmark for years to come." This recognition and attainment of rights broke new ground in the UN policy world, as evident in both the process and the outcome. Alongside the policymaking was a human rights triumph, invigorating hopes in the power of social movements and the potential for even those most marginalized to mobilize. Convention 189 thus became a blueprint for transnational organizing and the possibility of creating social change from the ground up.

This occasion produced nostalgic rhetoric about the summit histories of social struggles. Betsey McGee, an employer from New York who had aligned herself with domestic workers, placed the domestic workers' victory alongside other historic movements for justice and equality.

> I expect that there is going to be a great shift across the world, like there's been a great shift across the world in how we think about women, and about gay people, and about some other issues of the last 20, 30, 40 years. There's going to be a great shift in how people think about domestic workers and how they think about the employers of people who work in their home. And that shift will be in the direction of understanding the rights and responsibilities much more completely than is the case today.

Her observation reflects a pervasive spirit of optimism among the many who took part in this landmark policy. At the onset of the negotiations, when asked about the possibility of global recognition and change for domestic workers, Juan Somavía assured all of the delegates, "I am absolutely certain. Why, because we were told that apartheid would never end. Women would never have roles, et cetera. It is possible, but it means a very important part of making it possible is in your hands." As he spoke directly to domestic workers in 2010, Somavía attributed his belief in social change to the power of social movements.

> First of all, congratulations not only for the work that you have done as a network, but that all over the world, different ways of organizing domestic workers have taken place. I think that what has happened in terms of global consciousness on the issue is the result of organization, as always. You never have social progress unless you have an organized vision, and people saying, "Look we have to move in this direction."

With the Convention 189 victory, domestic worker rights joined those social revolutions once considered impossible. US delegate Robert Shepard compared it to other defining social justice movements. "I mean, make the analogy to the civil rights movement, make the comparison to where gay rights was 10 or 15 years ago, but it came a long way very quickly, and other similar causes; AIDS was hidden for a long time."

The activists at the ILO represented many domestic workers around the world, many of whom did not live to see this opening for rights. As one IDWN leader expressed when the convention vote approached, "This is for my grandmother, my mother, for my kids, and for all generations, for everything we've gone through. This is recognition for everything we've gone through.[10] Hester Stephens called for a moment of remembrance, as she celebrated this extraordinary victory.

> To have a convention for domestic workers, it is such a history, and it will be a history worldwide, that we pick the fruit from the tree, that we plant over the years. And we were all, some of the workers, still suffering in the backyard of the employers. And today, I would like to take the opportunity to keep in our hearts and our minds, those domestic workers who lost their lives on the premises of the employers, and even their children that remain behind.

Fataou Raimi, the one male member of the IDWN, extended gratitude to "everyone who has contributed to this victory, those visible and nonvisible," as he reflected upon his own journey of activism, and those workers he represented.

I was very happy yesterday when this convention passed, because in my
country a lot of people have worked under very difficult conditions. Many
have died . . . So I am thinking about all who have never been able to see
this. With this victory it is the end of a struggle and the commencement
of a new struggle.

This new struggle, in Raimi's eyes, would honor those who had suffered
without global protections, those for whom the convention had come
too late. In these narratives, domestic workers saw themselves as part of
a larger struggle, and accountable to those denied justice.

"Yes We Did!": Measuring the Movement

Convention 189 marks a moment to measure a movement.[11] The inclusion of such detailed protections in this first international law is certainly
worthy of tremendous recognition, as rights "on paper" documented the
long-standing recognition of this sector. Beyond this legal recognition in
the largest global house of labor governance, however, Convention 189 gave
purpose to a movement. Its accomplishments stretched far beyond Geneva,
as domestic workers built upon their victory, now focusing on ratification
efforts within states. Convention 189's real measure post-2011 takes form in
the effort toward *realizing* the protections laid out in the policy.

The three-year organizing work of domestic workers also gave a mo-
rale boost to women historically left outside organized labor structures.
With the support of their sisters worldwide, and the confidence instilled
by their experiences at the ILO and the substantive credibility the policy
victory had given them, activists went forward with strength and strong
organizational ties. Shirley Pryce shared her sentiments at the closing
circle of the IDWN, shortly after the policy win. "I just feel loved, and as
part of this family, you don't want anything else. That was being together
here, you know." She continued, with emotion, "It is sad to go," while
also stating confidently, "Going home, I feel rich."[12] When asked for her
takeaway on the policy victory, leading Hong Kong advocate Ip Pui Yu
exclaimed, "Domestic Workers are organizable!" Now she would bring
that message home to the tens of thousands of domestic workers labor-
ing in the glossy metropolis of Hong Kong. With the global convention
now in her pocket and the support of a transnational coalition behind

her, "Little Fish" set out to teach domestic workers in her home state about the labor protections they were due and immediately push her government for ratification.

The transition from the ILO to the "real work" of implementation reflects a pivotal turn in this global movement's trajectory. As Sam Gurney, policy officer to the ILO Governing Body, contended,

> Domestic workers have set the agenda, inside, behind us in the UN building, because, an ILO convention, it can do some things, it is a template, it is something to build on, but to win real rights, to prove that domestic workers are workers, that takes domestic workers to organize, to be in unions, to work with NGOs, to fight for their rights.[13]

As this narrative reflects, the real measure of domestic workers' victory and organizing capacity would be seen in the changes that emerge from this symbolic victory "on paper." Chris Bonner, the lead organizing strategist and long-standing domestic work expert at WIEGO, marked this transitional moment as an incentive for organizing. The ILO convention, she stated, is "as much about process as it is about the outcome. Now we can move to building organizations versus lobbying for rights. That work is nearly over."[14] Indeed, domestic workers had built a movement through Convention 189. Thereafter, they carried with them formidable power, inspiration, and an onus of responsibility to draw upon the strengths of their collective effort to ensure the rights of domestic workers everywhere.

From Network to Federation

Step one: changing the terms of organization. The rights victory fortified an orchestrated effort to move domestic workers more closely into the established structures of the labor movement. The looser network formation served as an effective means of initially drawing together the established domestic worker organizations throughout the world. Yet in order to carry forward with a movement and government ratification, domestic worker leaders and their supporters saw a model of trade union organization as the next critical step. On October 23, 2013, 18 months after Convention 189 passed, the International Domestic

Workers Federation (IDWF) became the first global union of domestic workers and the only international labor federation run by women for work dominated by women.[15] In honor of one of the leading countries to support domestic worker rights, they chose Montevideo, Uruguay, as this first global union's launching site.[16]

Here, after investing decades in his "great dream" to see domestic workers gain rights in the ILO and form their own union, Dan Gallin spoke of the significance of the union's formation and the vision for its future:

> One thing . . . is clear: your future is with the labor movement.
>
> You will contribute to shape it, perhaps more than you now realize. You have created the first international trade union federation in history that will be run entirely by women. The gender issue is now also a class issue, but it is in fact much older and more fundamental, because it goes back to the dawn of human society.
>
> We still live in a patriarchal society and we will not reach our goal—a society fit for all human beings to live in—until we have shaken off this burden. You have taken a huge step in that direction. You have also created a federation of workers who until recently were not even perceived as workers. You have demonstrated that there is no such thing as "unorganizable" workers.[17]

To inaugurate their efforts, Uruguayan president José Mujica attended the final meeting and offered the closing speech. After extending "a warm hug from my small country" and "a shout to poor people in the world," Mujica recognized the "service workers and domestic workers, you can find them by the thousands, and they have started to have rights as any other worker does."[18] A head of state who stands in line for the cinema and joins his country's compatriots at local cafés, Mujica, in his recognition of domestic workers, expressed his ideological commitment to the workers of the world. He acknowledged that "those who work with their hands find it very difficult to be recognized," as he celebrated domestic workers with an inspirational speech encouraging their continued struggle.

> We only live once, and it is almost a miracle that we are alive. It is a miracle that we are alive. It is worth to give our lives content. And it is

Figure 7.3. Dan Gallin at the IDWF founding in Montevideo.

worth to fight for a little bit of happiness. Also fight for people and for the children of poor people. And I would say that this is almost an obligation, don't forget this. Don't feel ashamed of being poor because you live from your own hands. And you share with Uruguay thanks to the people of your class and the various communities of the world. This is a country with many [faces], with many classes, but profoundly we are a country where nobody is more than any body. This is why we welcome you with open arms and thank you for this meeting, for this congress.

This tribute from a national president to the global domestic workers' movement and the attainment of Convention 189 was evidence that domestic worker mobilization was now "on the map."

In the course of the union's founding congress, delegates adopted a constitution and elected officers, of all whom took leading roles in Geneva: Hong Kong's Elizabeth Tang as general secretary, South Africa's Myrtle Witbooi as president, Peru's Ernestina Ochoa as vice president, and regional representatives, including Jamaica's Shirley Pryce for the Caribbean and the United States' Juana Flores for North America.[19] With new leadership in place, and continued support from the WIEGO/ IUF foundational team, this newly formed union set out to envision its goals in a global context where rights had been attained, and realities demanded even more coordination of their efforts. Their focus emphasized growth and investment in the union and civil-society partnerships, such as the ITUC and the ILO, that emerged from the core connections made in Geneva. From all of the policy promises, the newly formed federation identified priorities that would push forward implementation through a strategic effort focus on two ends of the applied continuum—elimination of abuse (namely in child labor and agencies) and the protection of basic labor rights. With these immediate goals, the IDWF also set plans to develop its educational and research capacity, with a focus on homecare industries and migrant domestic work, two burgeoning trends worldwide.[20]

The expansion of domestic worker organizing to the federation scale raised new levels of consideration about how this global effort would draw lines around membership and representation. All of the members of the IDWN remained active to form the new federation. Yet, the ILO exposure generated greater levels of interest and a much wider investment in the full representation of domestic workers worldwide. The organization maintained its democratic commitment to language accessibility, where all participants would be assured interpretation in each meeting. Yet with the wider involvement of new organizations, this ideological commitment required extensive economic and staff resources, at times drawing lines around the politics of participation, such as in the case of Brazil where Portuguese interpretation did not always materialize. The new federation's opening in South America also drew more attention in the region, with the Uruguayan delegation ceasing the public relations opportunity, even though they did not join the federation.[21] These political maneuvers around domestic worker organization thus emphasize the importance of the global stage it assumed through Convention 189, as well as the politics of domestic worker organizing that surfaced as the organization developed its transnational presence.

The formative work of the IDWN required consideration of these foundational questions of inclusion, standpoint, and representation. Who would be "in" the global organization? And to what extent could this organization speak as a global voice "for" domestic workers worldwide. These questions became more pressing as the federation chose its future leadership and set a vision to build the global movement far beyond its origins as a formative network organized around one policy goal. Like other unions, funding realities grew in scope, as the organization contemplated its longer-term livelihood. While a celebrated moment in the labor and women's movement, this fledgling union continued to rely on funding and core support from its foundational IUF and WIEGO organizations. Much like the national struggles, domestic workers' international organizational resource bases will always face limitations, given the nature of the labor sector's low wages. Thus, the IDWF's potential growth would continually be assessed next to the pragmatic realities of the costs of organizing and physically gathering such a wide network of representative domestic worker organizations. As the movement continues to grow, this balance between wide reach and most efficient use of resources holds central weight. With their bona fide emergence as a global union, however, the IDWF could access wider resource bases among other unions and NGOs. Its established success, policy victory and increased credibility made this newly formed global union both credible and attractive to donors and allies who wished to invest in the longer-term growth of the only global union led by women. In the long run, the IDWF's longevity will require the assurance of both this expansive representation of domestic workers worldwide and reliance upon ally and partner NGO relationships to realize its vision.

Ratification Reaches

The most direct use of Convention 189 came from the IDWF's focus on ratification as its first concrete agenda. Only with state protection of domestic worker rights can the dictates of Convention 189 be realized. With ratification, the state is accountable to the ILO, like any other treaty.[22] Unless nations sign on to this convention, however, domestic workers' access to its protections become extremely remote and virtually impossible to access. To bring these rights from the global to the national, the IDWF worked with key organizations on a ratification campaign as its first priority. The ITUC took the frontline role in setting the stage for ratification, with the "12 x 12" goal of reaching 12 countries just one year after the 2011 ratification. This campaign paired the IDWF with existing union and NGO efforts, while providing a concrete means to link the international law with state efforts. As domestic workers repeatedly contended, "only with ratification will real change begin."[23] This collective purpose kept the IDWF in connection with the key organizations and transnational networks that emerged from the ILO process. The ongoing mobilization of domestic workers, human rights organizations, women's organizations, scholars, policymakers, and global trade unions provided a space to continue the momentum of this global activist networks' collective work in Geneva. With the convention passed, organizations could also develop campaigns that brought it to life in ways relevant to a range of national contexts. Movements like the "Caring Across Generations" theme of the National Domestic Workers Alliance in the United States and the global "My Fair Home" campaign held governments and employers accountable to the promises they made in support of Convention 189, while allowing each national organization to adapt universal standards to the particular needs of their countries.

This ratification process served as a central indicator of states' seriousness in this 'making rights real' project. The first to ratify, Uruguay set the stage for national commitments, with an exposé of its lauded legislation, including a process of home inspections to overcome the compliance and enforcement challenges, and one of the strongest national legislative packages in line with Convention 189. This initial effort to give Convention 189 "teeth" resulted in 22 country ratifications by 2016. With these national models in place, key advocate countries could enact their own commitments and gain support in their contribution to the assurance of Convention 189's strength as a widely ratified document. Many of the strongest state advocates on the ILO floor, however, did not follow suit with ratification efforts. The US faces the pervasive limitation of the National Labor Relations Act, which has excluded domestic workers from key protections since 1935. Without the massive undertaking of an amendment to this formative legal framework, the strong US voice in support of Convention 189 is rendered silent at the implementation level. Robert Shepard recognized this limitation, even as he spoke so vehemently in favor of rights on behalf of the US government on the negotiation floor. When asked what it would take to get the US to ratify, he spelled out the reach of the historical redress.

I mean first you would have to change the NLRA, which has not essentially been changed since 1935, well there have been minor changes since the 30s, but it is what an 80-year-old law? The Fair Labor Standards Act may be a little easier because that covers domestics, but there are a lot of exemptions. So you are talking about two of the major labor laws that would need amendment, so it would be kind of hard.[24]

Such obstacles echo the ongoing need for global and national pressure from domestic worker organizations as one of the most influential voices for change. Ideally, with the ILO convention in place, domestic workers can influence "from the ground" in ways that bring much stronger political persuasion, even in a nation like the United States, where the barriers to ratification are so strictly embedded. From this Convention, however, the National Domestic Workers Alliance's capacity to adapt its efforts to focus on state-level change gains strength through a moral and ideological backing adopted at the international level. While the US has not yet made any plans for ratification, the prominence of the ILO process certainly strengthened domestic workers' agency in ways that allowed their collective influence to gain meaningful ground in state campaigns. Whether or not states ratify, for activists within countries, the convention serves as a transnational ideological benchmark for rights. Furthermore, domestic workers' knowledge of this international law gives them that much more strength, as they lobby for the rights most relevant to the range of national contexts and household labor circumstances that prevail.[25]

Domestic workers in the IDWF held greater political and social capital when they could return to their countries with the knowledge of ratification and an aligned set of demands for implementation. After the convention win, IDWF president Myrtle Witbooi went "on the road," with and average of 10 annual international visits to six continents, promoting the convention, advocating for domestic workers rights broadly, and holding states accountable to ratification. In Washington, DC, when she won the Global Fairness Award, Witbooi used this international stage to call "those with all the world's resources" to support Convention 189. She spoke of the great ironies that continue to define this work, even though the international policies in place promised a more democratic set of relations in this private household work setting. As she held her elegant glass trophy, Witbooi exclaimed, "The struggle is far from over."[26] In order to bring decent work home to the millions of domestic workers around the world, she pronounced "this Federation must be a voice for the voiceless." In this sense, Witbooi's reference to transnational organizing kept the movement alive. Beyond the victory in Geneva, the public stages IDWF leaders commanded strengthened international movements and built transnational domestic worker platforms well beyond global policy. As these efforts reflect, the IDWF's public relations campaign focused on assuring relevance and meaning for Convention 189 in the "real world."

Policy and Practice: The Limits of the ILO

It's not enough to have rights; one has to have a conscience.
We need to be organized to defend them.
—Marcelina Bautista

The IDWF's identity continues to follow from its participation in the ILO and the reach of Convention 189. Yet knowledge of the ILO and its policies is not widespread in most societies. Robert Shepard, lead US government delegate at the ILO, chuckled at the irony of his expansive investment in this international policymaking process in relation to the general population's knowledge of the ILO, as well as the limitations of any convention's direct implementation in the United States, given the barriers to ratification.

> I would hope, personally, that these [recommendations] go somewhere, but to most people, these are pretty obscure organizations, even though here everybody speaks as if they are representing all the workers of the world![27]

In the ILO, the United States gained substantive attention because the National Domestic Workers Alliance had just won the first Bill of Rights at the state level. Yet going home, as Shepard repeatedly contended, efforts to put Convention 189 into practice would serve as a real test of the relevance of relying on rights through the ILO's global governance, where international standards may even threaten state sovereignty. The real work, according to Shepard, is after the ILO.

> So, you know, when people ask about the next step, it is kind of hard because some organization that nobody has heard of has passed this, and we have either great success or great failure but you get on the plane and you see the real world. And I think what is really interesting is whether or not anything will flow out of this organization and seep into the real world.[28]

For domestic workers, this gap between the negotiations in Geneva and the work they would face upon return drew deep trenches along lines of power and privilege. "You go back to your offices and we must go back to clean the houses,"[29] one IDWN leader proclaimed. Thus, as the IDWF formed and turned its work to the longer-term rights campaign, the global movement of domestic workers shifted from the honeymoon stage of chanting, cheering, and media attention on this rights adoption in the ILO to the enduring demands of accessing these protections in practice in their national contexts. To shift governments' awareness and improve the collective livelihoods of domestic workers would require massive national campaigns, mobilization of resources, and coordination with state officials—an undertaking that would stretch far beyond the finite first three years of this global movement's establishment.

One central implementation fissure: the vast majority of domestic workers around the world don't know about the ILO or its newly assured protections of their human rights. Eunice Dhladhla, who saw domestic workers organize throughout South Africa during apartheid, holds a lead position within the national union. Soon after the attainment of Convention 189, Eunice shared her uncertainty about "what we won in Geneva." As she conveyed in an interview a year after Convention 189 passed:

> Although in Jo-burg, I cannot tell you what is ILO. Maybe we don't have many ideas about ILO, but what we know is just the government of the country signed that document of domestic workers. At this moment, we don't know anything about ILO. But we know this thing is coming to help domestic workers for the whole world, not only South Africa, you know.[30]

For workers in unions and organizations throughout the world, their knowledge of the ILO often comes through the messaging they experience in organizational meetings and the time their leaders may spend with the international network. While national domestic worker activists recognize that their organization shared an involvement with a global movement, and reaped some rewards from this, they also saw their leaders travel often and balance the work of national and global engagement. Thus, while the ILO put so many rights in place, to workers in national unions, its expectations shift the leadership and organizational processes in ways that provide new incentives, while also demanding leaders' time and the restructuring of established agendas. Furthermore, the majority of domestic workers are not unionized, without access to the organizations that carry out the immediate translation of the ILO policy. To them, the ILO is as remote as Wall Street. While its determinants shape their everyday lives, its scale and inaccessibility make the ILO so remote that its capacity to make a difference on the ground remains a far reach for the majority of domestic workers. These dynamics shape the relationship between global and national levels of rights claims, as a central assessment of this policy's potential in practice.

Sociologist Shireen Ally critiques this ILO infusion in domestic worker organizations as another level of governance paternalism, this time through an international institution.[31] As she points out, in many case the ILO sets the agenda for organizational meetings, enticing members to join in conversations through the "hot food" upgrade their resources provide, in exchange for the assurance that these local meetings have addressed the ILO's priority areas, such as migration and occupational safety. Although the actual convention deals with migration in very limited terms, the post-Convention 189 emphasis places high expectations on domestic worker organizations to bring migrants into their priority areas. After its adoption and success, the convention morphed into a channel for larger UN and NGO foci on migration, since so many domestic workers fall into this category. Yet the inclusion of migrants is not often a priority, nor is it a tangible reality for many local unions. With the ILO's expectations to implement these priorities, local domestic worker unions, with limited resources and leadership structures, began organizing study groups for migrants, delivering recruitment plans to the ILO, and providing researchers with content on the integration of migrants within the larger scope of projects. One national union leader proclaimed, "We are not interested in migrants because they are not going to help our membership."[32] Yet, to access the ILO resources and assure compliance with its priorities, the organization had to develop elaborate plans that turned attention to this global issue, rather than the particular needs of their own organization and local circumstances.

For the ILO, the responsibility to monitor the instrument assures the legitimacy of its work. After such wide public attention to the adoption of Convention 189, the ILO remained accountable to its implementation. Martin Oelz, the legal specialist who crafted Convention 189, described the ILO's role in overseeing implementation after the policy's adoption.

> So countries are asking us, 'Ok, the convention asks for compliance and enforcement, but how are we going to do it?' So we need to bring those together that really can hammer this out right . . . We need to inject some fresh thinking. Because otherwise they're cooking in their old soup, and we need some fresh. So we're trying to create these opportunities for policy development and knowledge consolidation at the same time.[33]

As Oelz described, this would involve a focus on labor inspectors, national compliance structures and direct work with national labor departments and domestic workers' organizations. These roles are critical to the implementation of the convention, and any hope that its practice would match its rhetorical hype. Oelz shared his ongoing sense of responsibility for the instrument, even when his legal expertise moved to the next projects within the ILO.

> . . . we are the bookkeepers. We collect information on progress, on ratification, on national law and policies, and so we're trying to be sort of the catalysts in this, because we feel some responsibility for this instrument.

Yet the resources devoted to overseeing implementation pale in comparison to the grand global attention domestic work received during the formation of the policy. After the convention passed, the organization afforded resources for only four staff members to oversee all aspects of the policy's monitoring, training outreach, and compliance.

Furthermore, those who served as such central figures in crafting the policy within the ILO got promoted, retired, or moved on to other responsibilities demanded of the organization. Thus, sustainability efforts remain compromised, while domestic worker organizations pick up the slack of assuring compliance.

The ILO remains extremely limited in its capacity to make "decent work" a reality across such a wide range of contexts. The attention this organization gave to domestic work placed wide expectations on the potential for international governance to shift daily household labor practices. Yet, policy is only the starting gate for the kind of change that would reach the majority of domestic workers, whose lives are shaped by everyday circumstances where decency, dignity and democracy remain far from home. Thus, policy's role in the domestic workers' movement marks more of the galvanizing public relations moment that anchored a movement, rather than the actual transformation of power relations. The long-term work to redress systemic injustices, as expressed in this vital human relationship of care, will be the ultimate measure of this policy's impact.

The ILO's "decent work for domestic workers" campaign made another critical marker on this social movement. By placing domestic work within the priorities of this macro-level of international governance, this sector became an instrument to express the overarching values of this institution. Through household labor, the ILO could legitimate its language on decency and fair globalization, as domestic workers encapsulated the ultimate stretch of policy protections. By including this sector under its umbrella, the ILO boldly amplified its own profile and outreach efforts. With domestic workers under its policy purview, the ILO could be seen as a compassionate vehicle of global governance, with the profound capacity to set an international moral agenda to outlaw contemporary slavery, condemn human rights abuses and mediate migration. This policy work set the ILO up as the fair hand of globalization—delivering a new deal to the frailest workers in the context of the global economy's inevitable dependence on the "care and repair"[34] labor of women. Furthermore, by passing Convention 189, Juan Somavía could punctuate the end of his leadership era, with a legacy underscored by the organization's capacity to reach the world's most precarious workers in the policies that emerged during his legacy. Under

Convention 189's discussions, the social constructions of domestic work shifted from former notions of servitude to a newly packaged notion of "decent work" that integrally connected to the values of human dignity and the moral underpinnings of this global labor institution.

Social movement scholar Manisha Desai contended that the ILO engagement with domestic work deradicalized a movement.[35] Rather than demanding state investments in care labor as a vital component of the public good, the ILO process accepted the outsourcing of this labor to migrants and those most marginalized sectors of the global economy. By calling it "decent work," the ILO mainstreamed domestic work, and even integrated it within the entire UN system, with UN Women standing behind this policy victory. Furthermore, as long as this form of work is seen as a legitimate source of commodity import, men remain freed from expectations to share in responsibility for household labor. Women continue to provide this service—whether it is outsourced or integrated within the family unit—and feminism returns to its origins of thought and praxis. At the end of the 2011 negotiations, Barbro Budin, gender specialist within the IUF, shared her "dream" with her IDWN colleagues. To shift the circumstances of domestic labor, she envisioned a radical revolution of care.

> My dream is that no single woman will ever have to leave her country and her children to go and take care of children in another country; and that she can work in her own country as a quality public service professional instead, taking care of and being able to be with her children, and that in each country we have a strong and united union for domestic workers, and that all those strong unions strengthen the international trade union movement.

This socialized vision of care work protects the wellbeing and livelihoods of the caretakers and their families, in a global climate where states assure their own capacity to meet the needs of social reproduction. While Budin held strong support for the convention, and devoted a large portion of her professional life to it, she also placed its victory within a larger trajectory where the ultimate vision of "dignity for all" would expand far beyond a global policy as the penultimate expression of human rights and applied change. As Budin's reflection illustrates, the ILO is not in a position to fix this gendered, racialized, class/caste-based institution alone. Rather, it serves as a guiding post within a larger need for an integrated scheme that will assure human dignity through the participation of states, employers, domestic worker organizations, and invested civil society networks. In order to see an authentic realization of "decent work," this symbolic site of extensive oppression and expansive opportunity for change will require that the moral compass of Convention 189 be taken up by all of these invested publics.

Staking a Movement

The ILO policy on domestic work is best measured as the origins of a global movement. Its footprint is widest as a galvanizing moment to bring shared purpose to the first organization of domestic workers worldwide. This symbolic occasion holds a series of extraordinary serendipities: the first project of a newly formed transnational organization takes place at the level of the UN, within the largest international labor body of governance; key advocates within and outside of the ILO system prioritized this investment as their cumulative life work; and the original pillars of support in the IUF and WIEGO ushered this first network through the Convention 189 victory to establish the first global union led by women workers. As Eileen Boris contends, the public relations that emerged from this process did more to serve a movement than the actual global policy, given the multiple limitations to its implementation.[36] From this global campaign, Carmen Cruz, Costa Rica's lead domestic worker activist, contended, "We're no longer invisible. Now we're visible, and our rights are being recognized." By placing domestic workers "on the map" through the ILO, the movement gained five concrete outcomes : (1) building bridges; (2) establishing relationships with governments; (3) documenting domestic work; (4) bringing workers to the table; and (5) changing mindsets. In the end, these accomplishments allowed the movement to take expression far beyond its origins in the ILO.

Bridge Builders

The movement built around domestic work fostered formative relationships across divides. By housing rights within the ILO, domestic workers not only earned global recognition, they gained a place at the top of the agendas of many of the world's leading human rights and labor organizations. For the first time, NGOs and unions aligned around domestic work, making it an issue of mutual gender and labor justice. As one of the leading domestic worker activists proclaimed:

> It has been a hard battle since last year, and really difficult, but I think the ILO convention has united the world, not just the governments, not just the employers, but the NGOs, all sectors came together. It is already the right time to really recognize domestic workers as workers.[37]

With the aid of the IUF and WIEGO, domestic workers' reach went far beyond national organizations. The ILO victory and the loyal backing of these organizations further amplified the political capital domestic workers earned through the relationships at the core of the Convention 189 undertaking. Michelle Bachelet, then director general of UN Women, participated in the closing day of the deliberations to legitimate the victory, solidify support on the wider public ground, and promise the ongoing commitment of the UN agency.

> In closing I want to reiterate that UN Women will work closely with the ILO, with other UN agencies, governments, and all relevant stakeholders to support the implementation of labour and social protections for domestic workers. This is not only the right thing to do. But it is a matter of social justice and dignity, a matter of human rights. This is a long-awaited recognition for the extraordinary work done by 52.6 million women and men domestic workers worldwide. They simply deserve it.[38]

In essence, domestic workers brought organizations together in new forms. Just as the ILO galvanized a movement, this particular policy created linkages that would fortify wider parties' investments in a range of causes, as domestic workers became ambassadors for human rights, the elimination of slavery, migrant protections, informal workers' justice, and the global women's struggle. With the wide attention gained from their participation in the ILO, domestic workers carried forward a much more far-reaching "people's movement."

New Relationships with Governments

By meeting in the house of international governance, domestic workers took home new relations to the state in ways that increased their exposure and positively advanced their rights campaign. Because of the public attention they received within the ILO, domestic workers gained political and social capital that allowed them to lobby their governments in more persuasive ways. With the knowledge of global rights in their hands, IDWN leaders also carried the strength of these moral standards back to their countries, where their influence held the most weight. Ida le Blanc described her feelings just before the convention vote:

> I am here with my minister of labor and the president of the trade Union Congress in Trinidad and Tobago who all voted yes. And I am feeling, I cannot explain the feeling that I have here today. And I feel this positive will go through out this meeting here today, and we will win! We have no other choice but to win. Freedom is now and we are coming out of slavery. Yes. We are free at last!

Le Blanc carried this feeling home, where she not only continued to work directly with her government to increase national protections for domestic workers, she became an ambassador for UN Women, as a model of "grassroots" global women's activism, working across the ILO, her own government, and women "on the ground." Shirley Pryce's work with the ILO strengthened her "open door" relationship with her national government, along with the prime minister's office. Her high public profile during the ILO negotiations translated into easy accessibility to top government officials. She recollected, "I can make a phone call, 'I need to speak with the minister.' And the secretary will say, 'Hold on Shirley.'" As she looked to the future of domestic worker rights, she asserted:

> You have to work with the trade union, you have to work with the government, and you have to work with the NGOs. That is the key, in any country. You must work with those groups to move forward.

The relationships established in the ILO, and the points of connection forged around the policy itself, made domestic workers' access to each of these stakeholders that much easier, while assuring their increased capital across relations.

Documenting the Reality

In building a case for domestic worker rights, invested organizations and the ILO itself generated a large collection of data on domestic work and its related conditions. While prior studies had documented conditions in particular countries, a transnational collection of evidence on the global domestic-work industry only emerged after domestic work was placed on the ILO agenda. These data proved enormously influential in generating interest and resource commitments from governments, funders, and allies. In the launching of the Domestic Workers Research Network, at the 2011 meetings in Geneva, Frank Hoffer, one of the lead officials within the ILO's labor division and a key proponent of Convention 189, placed the policy process in context, as a larger victory for labor and justice struggles.

> The ILO is a very particular animal . . . It is not particularly clear because it is tripartite. But it is very helpful for people in countries to say, "Look the world has agreed on something, that you have to do in our own country." And I think that you have achieved that together. The world has agreed on something. And to make that heard is important, and research is important because we live in a time where everybody says, OK we don't need values, we need evidence. We all know that the research is value based at the end of the day, but give us the evidence, and I think we will all push that the values comes through.

Following Convention 189, international research networks emerged with a particular focus on domestic work, while state and international funders have invested heavily in this cause—a result of it being embraced by NGOs as a "sexy topic" within the ILO negotiations. Achievement of the international convention elevated domestic workers' status and gave them a pivotal place in the larger research, NGO, union, and government spheres. These investments enabled the domestic workers' movement to form the first global union of domestic workers, allowing its influence to reach even employers' organizations.

As the topic moved from the "cause of the day" to simply "the right thing to do" for those "who have a heart," paid household labor was mainstreamed, provoking the larger global community's investment in domestic workers' emergent rights.

Workers at the Table

Convention 189 set a policymaking precedent that in the end may be even more influential than the policy outcome. First and foremost, domestic workers got to the ILO table in Geneva's international forum. Unlike any other policy process, this inclusion of "actual workers," and not just any workers but those perceived as "the most vulnerable," shifted policymaking perceptions and practices. Domestic workers claimed their place in the ILO—a maneuver that placed them "on the map" of global institutions. By showing up in large numbers and in an organized fashion, domestic workers solidified their foothold in the corridors of institutional power. As Sharan Burrow, general secretary of the ITUC, proclaimed, "We know there is a link between the number of organized workers and these achievements."[39] Halimah Yacob celebrated the prominence of workers' investments in the final ILO document, as she spoke to her delegation at the closing of the 2011 meetings.

> I am sure you all have all of your prints all over the document. So you can go and campaign all over the world and say that this is *all of our work.* Each and every one of us. We all put our prints on the domestic workers' convention and recommendations, and we can all be proud of instruments that are very strong, and really very good for the domestic workers all around the world . . . So I think brothers and sisters, the honor goes to you. And I hope that we will be able, *together*, we will be able to improve the lot of working people, especially the domestic workers.

When Myrtle Witbooi exclaimed, "This is something the ILO has never seen before" at the 2010 opening meetings, she was acknowledging the strength and extent of a global movement. Indeed, the ILO had never seen this level of worker involvement before in the crafting of rights, protections, and practices.

Changing Mind-Sets

Finally, domestic workers gradually changed mind-sets as their plight reached the ILO. Certainly rights "on paper" do not guarantee everyday practices of dignity and respect. Yet the domestic worker movement marks a beginning in the changing of attitudes and perceptions. As Robert Shepard asserted, "I don't think people are going to follow the issue because the ILO did it, but they will follow it when it sort of just makes its way into the culture, or gets elevated."[40] Indeed, the domestic workers' movement raised the profile of domestic workers across state, civil society, and employer divides. Martin Oelz put the policy in perspective, claiming that its impact is in the campaign's capacity to frame domestic work as something "of concern" to "me and you."

> I think it is something that can do some good. It's not going to be the miracle solution to all the issues, but it will have quite an impact, you know, changing mind-set and giving people a platform. "This is addressed to me and you and it concerns me."[41]

Domestic workers have carried this platform into everyday social relations in ways that make it nearly "impossible to ignore" their demands. By showing how vital their contributions are to providing not just household labor but *love* to families, children, and elders, domestic workers' ability to change mind-sets has grown substantively. Monica Ntuli shared how her awareness of the law allowed her to shift relations with employers, among those who work with her in the South African domestic workers union. As she spoke about employers' shifts in their treatment of domestic workers, she referenced the law as a vital tool:

> They must take us like human beings, not like a slave. That's what I can say. And when it can come to employees, domestic workers, we must use the law. The law is not a monster; it's the way, which came in between employer and employee to build a relationship. Actually it's not a monster, just to build a relationship.[42]

As more and more laws come into practice through the ratification of Convention 189, domestic workers like Monica will be able to use these policy achievements as a platform to shift the actual relations of their daily experiences. In many cases, this foundation of protections only emerged through state ratification of the international convention.

Last Word

I think there is a moral obligation that gets fulfilled with the realization of domestic worker rights. As if the world is falling apart, but in this venue, if we can get it, we will realize something greater, morally.
—Chris Bonner, WIEGO

The real measure of the movement will be in the changes domestic workers experience in their everyday lives. As a leading advocate of the National Domestic Workers Alliance proclaimed, "Nothing is won until people's lives are changed."[43] Similarly, Louise McDonough, of the Australian government, asserted, "The convention is not just a piece of paper, but a reality."[44] When domestic workers reached the ILO, they had already laid the foundations of a movement. The workspace is where its ultimate impact will be tested. Convention 189 is a blueprint for the creation of new circumstances ensuring "decent work" and dignity and respect for workers.

Again and again, domestic workers, policymakers, governments, and even employers saw the symbolic victory of domestic workers reaching the ILO. Juan Somavía claimed this "hook" as heralding protections for the masses of domestic workers in the global economy:

I certainly feel that what you are engaged in is that. You are engaged in assuring that for the millions of workers out there, they will have an instrument. We know that instrument and reality differ, but you will have a hook, a flag.

In his immediate reflections just moments after the Convention 189 vote, Paul Mackay, leader of the employers' group, named this victory as the beginning of a new season for domestic workers, even with the obstacles that would inevitably follow:

I think we just saw a ringing endorsement of the importance of the issue of domestic work. Some governments might not be able to ratify this later, but that is actually less important right now than the issue being recognized on the global stage. And I think what you will see, and the pleasure that you saw here, is a recognition of that fact. There is a lot of work to be done, some countries will have difficulties, hours of work, things like that can cause problems for some, but at least it is on the agenda now, and I think that what you will see is people working towards solutions in their own countries. Some will be faster than others, but it doesn't really matter. It has started. And I think that is the point.[45]

Mackay, like so many at the center of this first undertaking in domestic workers' global organization, identified the symbolic power of the convention. As Carmen Cruz of the Costa Rican domestic worker movement proclaimed, "With this document we will begin to repay a debt due to domestic workers."[46]

So many assessments of this victory pointed to tangible changes it brought about as the true measure of its success. As Ip Pui Yu asserted: "We have got a little bit of liberation, but I am sure that in our lives, with all the sisters, we will get liberated, somewhere, sometime."[47] Similarly, one prominent leader contended:

The success will be that time in the future when domestic workers themselves say, this was the start. These documents were the start of a change in our lives. That is what success will look like. Not these documents, we have just started the job.[48]

Having achieved a victory, domestic workers repeatedly told their sisters, "We have to keep the fire burning."[49] Kenyan domestic worker activist Evelyn Mulo, one of the youngest members of the IDWN and one of the first voting delegates, stated, "My dream, is in 10 years to come, my fellow domestic workers will be enjoying the fruits of the convention with the recommendations which have met their terms and conditions to be improved."[50] As many of her comrade domestic workers recognized, the test of success would hinge on their continued capacities to carry on with the "just fight." As Sister Escaline Miranda of India proclaimed:

We know that if we put only a small seed, that a tree will give after five years, six years. It all depends on us, how we push to our government, nationally. If every country pushes, one day it will become paradise.

Perhaps one of the greatest accomplishments in this global domestic workers' movement is the convention's capacity to make "paradise" even imaginable. While to many the ILO's idealistic language exists at a far remove from the global circumstances of domestic work, the "dream rhetoric" domestic workers employed throughout the negotiations was consistent with their commitment to social justice.

Indeed, going forward, the realization of this international policy depends on three intertwined dimensions of social justice: (1) respect for workers; (2) the establishment of social and labor rights; and (3) the responsibility of employers, governments, and international institutions to enforce these rights. Setting standards through national legislation and international policy is just one avenue to aligning household labor relations with larger human rights ideologies of social equality and justice.

Ultimately, the ILO standards on domestic work are important because they set an ideal—a benchmark in the construction of a more egalitarian global community. In the case of the general working conditions of domestic workers, such standards are considered to represent a "moral compass" for the treatment of those most at risk within societies. Without consequent action, however, these standards are meaningless. Continued pressure from social-activist movements, the assurance of systems of enforcement and accountability, and the larger reconfiguration of transnational capitalism are also necessary components of actualizing social policies in ways that directly impact domestic workers. While Convention 189 promises substantive changes on paper, the test of its ideals will unfold in the long-term process of implementation at the level of the private household. As Louise McDonough, representative of Australia, contended in her final 2011 closing statement, "There is no doubt that the measure of our success is in terms of the impact the convention will have in the real world."[51]

The domestic workers' global rights movement realized the largest and most tangible recognition of the value of paid household labor. While the struggle to bring policy into practice will continue, for the first time domestic work gained formal legitimacy and tangible global standards, meriting recognition as one of the most vibrant human rights campaigns of the 21st century. As Convention 189 encourages more "peace in the home," it holds the potential to legitimately shift relations of power, leading to more just and equitable workspaces and communities. As Ai-jen Poo reflected at the closing of Convention 189,

> our work is not done; we have a long road ahead. As a reminder and an inspiration, I want to share some words spoken by a worker from the Guatemalan domestic workers union after the adoption of the draft convention: "We have broken the silence. We have yet to break our chains." As we mark our progress, we take our place in a growing global effort to transform the world of work and bring dignity to the work that makes all other work possible.[52]

Finally, with this global movement, domestic workers set a collective path to claim their dignity overdue.

NOTES

CHAPTER 1. "LOOK DEEP IN YOUR HEARTS"

1 Public speech at the General Assembly of Women in Informal Employment: Globalizing and Organizing, Yogyakarta, Indonesia, November 11, 2014.

2 Public lecture at Old Dominion University, Norfolk, VA, November 24, 2014.

3 Full names indicate that profiled individuals have given consent for their identities to be shared in this book. They are not pseudonyms.

4 South Africa's apartheid system employed four racial-identification categories: black/African, mixed-race "colored," Indian, and white. "Black women" as used here refers to both black and colored domestic workers.

5 Household labor has long been a subject of feminist inquiry. Critiques of gender inequality address both paid and unpaid reproductive labor, both of which are feminized, devalued, and rooted in the patriarchal division of private and public labor. While the domestic work industry stems directly from essentialized notions of women's unpaid cooking, cleaning, and personal-care labor, this book deals with paid household labor as a global commodity and the quest for rights for workers in this sector.

6 Schwenken and Heimeshoff, *Domestic Workers Count*; Oliveira, *Domestic Workers Across the World*.

7 International Labour Organization, *Domestic Workers Across the World*, 19.

8 International Labour Organization, *ILO Global Estimates on Migrant Workers*, 5.

9 Francisco, "Transnational Family as Resource for Transnational Migrant Activism." For analysis of domestic workers in the Philippines, see also Parreñas, *Servants of Globalization*; Constable, *Maid to Order in Hong Kong*; Chin, *In Service and Servitude*; Pei-Chia, "Maid or Madam?"; Chang and Ling, "Globalization and Its Intimate Other"; and Cheng, "Contextual Politics of Difference in Transnational Care."

10 Fiona Williams, personal conversation, recollections from poetry dialogues between Fiona Williams and domestic workers in the United Kingdom, University of Toronto, October 16, 2015.

11 Doctors in many parts of the world face serious ethical dilemmas, as they decide whether to provide universal care for all or report undocumented immigrants who seek public services.

12 Pemba Lama (Nepal member of Parliament) in discussion with the author, May 2016.

13 Varia, *Maid to Order*.

14 Gabrielle Marcelletti Rocha de Olievera, "The Effects of Mexican Maternal Migration on Children's Education and Social Opportunities: A Study of Both Sides of the Border" (PhD diss., Columbia University, 2016).

15 Migrant Forum Asia, *Reform of the Kafala (Sponsorship) System*.

16 While these sectors challenge any notion of accurate accounting, given a range of illicit networks and practices, domestic work and sex work compete as the largest sources of human trafficking for women, according to the most recent reports of international agencies and antitrafficking organizations. Both domestic worker and antitrafficking activists repeatedly call for an end to "modern slavery." For direct analyses of domestic work and slavery, see, for example, Rollins, *Between Women*; Jones, *Labor of Love, Labor of Sorrow*; Davis, *Women, Race and Class*; Dill, *Across the Boundaries of Race and Class*; Hoerder, Van Nederveen Meerkerk, and Neunsinger, eds. *Towards a Global History of Domestic and Caregiving Workers*; and Sabrina Marchetti, *Black Girls: Migrant Domestic Workers and Colonial Legacies* (Leiden, Netherlands: Brill, 2014). For in-depth analyses of the relationship between domestic work and sex work in the narrative of US policymaking, see Denise Brennan's ethnography of human trafficking survivors and activists, *Life Interrupted*.

17 For an overview of employment agencies, see, for example, Varia, "Sanctioned Abuses."

18 Du Toit, "Domestic Workers' Convention: A Breakthrough."

19 As shared in the author's original 2001 research. See Fish, *Domestic Democracy*.

20 Hand in Hand: The Domestic Employers Network and Jews for Racial and Economic Justice are two examples of strong domestic worker rights advocacy groups.

21 This expression has become a popular motto for domestic worker rights, as evident in the 2014 conference "Justice in the Home: Domestic Work Past, Present, and Future" (Barnard Center for Research on Women, New York City, October 16–17).

22 Fieldnotes, ILC, 2011.

23 A lengthy body of literature has developed around the historical and global conditions of care work. While not exhaustive, the list that follows provides a substantive foundation of key sources in the field. For domestic work, migration, and global care chains, see Romero, *Maid in the USA*; Heyzer, Lycklama à Nijeholt, and Weerakoon, eds., *The Trade in Domestic Workers*; Bakan and Stasiulis, *Not One in the Family*; Chang, *Disposable Domestics*; Anderson, *Doing the Dirty Work?*; Gamburd, *The Kitchen Spoon's Handle*; Boris and Parreñas, eds., *Intimate Labors*; Hondagneu-Sotelo, *Doméstica*; Cox, *The Servant Problem*; Zimmerman, Litt, and Bose, *Global Dimensions of Gender and Carework*; Fudge, "Global Care Chains"; Lutz, *The New Maids*; Glenn, *Forced to Care*; Pratt, *Families Apart*; Williams, "Converging Variations in Migrant Care Work"; Palenga-Möllenbeck, "Care Chains in Eastern and Central Europe"; Romero, Preston, and Giles, eds., *When*

Care Work Goes Global; Parreñas, *Servants of Globalization*; Cranford, "Toward Particularism with Security." For historical analyses of domestic work, see May, *Unprotected Labor*; and Nadasen, "Power, Intimacy, and Contestation." For postcolonial domestic work relations, see Ray, "Masculinity, Femininity, and Servitude"; Banerjee, *Men, Women, and Domestics*; Fauve-Chamoux, *Domestic Service and the Formation of European Identity*; Haskins, *One Bright Spot*; Haladara, *A Life Less Ordinary*; Steedman, *Master and Servant*; Gutiérrez Rodríguez, *Migration, Domestic Work and Affect*; Ally, "Domestics, 'Dirty Work' and the Effects of Domination"; Haskins, *Matrons and Maids*; Marchetti, *Black Girls*; Ally, "Slavery, Servility, Service"; Banerjee, "Baby Halder's *A Life Less Ordinary*"; Haskins and Lowrie, eds., *Colonization and Domestic Service*; and Neunsinger, "From Servitude to Domestic Service." For specific national and regional contexts, see Cock, *Maids & Madams*; Ally, *From Servants to Workers*; Fish, *Domestic Democracy*; Salzinger, "A Maid by Any Other Name"; Bunster and Chaney, *Sellers & Servants*; Chaney and Castro, eds., *Muchachas No More*; Gill, *Precarious Dependencies*; Constable, *Maid to Order in Hong Kong*; Elizabeth Frantz, "Of Maids and Madams: Sri Lankan Domestic Workers and Their Employers in Jordan," *Critical Asian Studies* 40, no. 4 (2008): 609–38; B. W. Higman, *Domestic Service in Australia* (Melbourne: Melbourne University Press, 2002); Kathleen M. Adams and Sara Dickey, *Home and Hegemony: Domestic Service and Identity Politics in South and Southeast Asia* (Ann Arbor: University of Michigan Press, 2000); Silvey, "Transnational Domestication"; and Hordge-Freeman and Harrington, "Ties That Bind." For home and care labor and policy, see Boris and Klein, eds. *Caring for America*; Michel and Mahon, *Child Care Policy at the Crossroads*; and Peng, "Lone Mothers in Japan and South Korea." For domestic workers' organizing around rights and policy change, see Karides, "Linking Local Efforts with Global Struggle"; Milkman, *Organizing Immigrants*; Yeoh and Annadhurai, "Civil Society Action and the Creation of 'Transformative' Spaces"; Thomson, "Workers Not Maids"; Hobden, *Winning Fair Labor Standards for Domestic Workers*; Günther, "Struggling for Recognition"; Milkman and Ott, eds., *New Labor in New York*; Tracy, Sieber, and Moir, *Invisible No More*; Boris and Nadasen, "Domestic Workers Organize!"; Anderson, "Mobilizing Migrants, Making Citizens"; and Chun, "Organizing Across Racial Divides."

24 Keynote address at the Colonization and Domestic Service Symposium, Research Institute for Social Inclusion and Wellbeing, University of Newcastle, Newcastle, Australia, July 16, 2012.

25 Brown, *Raising Brooklyn*.

26 Some international domestic worker organizing took place around the UN conferences on women organized by Clotil Walcott. The Amsterdam gathering marks the largest, longest-standing international gathering of domestic workers to date. For a detailed account of this first meeting, see IRENE and IUF, *Respect and Rights*.

27 For analyses of the informal economy and regulations, see Cobble and Vosko, "Historical Perspectives on Representing Nonstandard Workers"; Kabeer, Mil-

ward, and Sudarshan, *Organizing Women Workers in the Informal Economy*; and Lund and Nicholson, eds., *Chains of Production*.

28 International Domestic Workers Network, *Platform of Demands*.

29 International Labor Conferences are the annual meetings of the ILO, where new policies are proposed and discussed among the tripartite government, employer, and worker bodies over a two-year period.

30 Former ILO policy discussions saw the participation of workers and sector allies, including the Home Work Convention 177 discussions of 1996 and the Maritime Labor Convention of 2006. Yet no other international convention has seen the scale of worker participation that characterized the domestic work negotiations.

31 Sofia Trevino worked directly with the IDWN through her professional association with Women in Informal Employment: Globalizing and Organizing (WIEGO). She is quoted in the documentary film that tells the story of this policy movement: See Crockett, Fish, and Ormiston, *C189: Conventional Wisdom*.

32 Fieldnotes, ILC, 2011.

33 I thank Rae Blumberg for this analysis, as articulated during our personal conversations at the 2015 Sociology of Development Conference at Brown University, Providence, RI, March 14, 2015. For a larger perspective on the domestic work story in the context of global development crises, see Blumberg and Cohn, *Development in Crisis*.

34 ILO conventions are binding treaties that require all countries that ratify them to change their national laws in accordance with the international standard-setting instrument. Recommendations are nonbinding instruments intended to provide guidelines for governments and social partners on the implementation of national labor and social policies. Conventions and recommendations for the same topics are often adopted simultaneously.

35 Ehrenreicht and Hochschild, *Global Woman*.

36 International Trade Union Confederation, *Union View: Domestic Work*.

37 Dan Gallin (former IUF general secretary) in discussion with the author, June 2010. For Gallin's ideological perspectives on global labor, domestic workers, and unionization, see, for example, Gallin, *Trade Unions and NGOs*; and Gallin and Pat Horn, *Organizing Informal Women Workers*.

38 ILO officials, and domestic workers themselves, repeatedly used this phrase to depict workers' heavily marginalized social status. While measures of poverty take many forms, and domestic workers are among the lowest paid and most precarious workers in the informal economy, this expression is generally used here to convey the sector's isolation from traditionally regulated forms of labor.

39 Throughout the discussions, domestic workers repeatedly used this expression to position their work as equal to other forms of work. See chapter 4 for an analysis of this standpoint.

40 This insight is drawn from a personal conversation with Ai-jen Poo at the 2011 ILC meetings in Geneva.

41 Marty Chen, founder of WIEGO, originally made this statement at the 2010 ILC meetings for domestic worker representatives.

42 Student discussion with the Women's Studies Department at Old Dominion University, Norfolk, VA, March 22, 2016.

43 Public speech at the ILC, 2010.

44 Drawn from the Fourth Conference of the Sociology of Development Section in reference to earlier work. See Solari, "Resource Drain vs. Constitutive Circularity."

45 This expression is used by feminist international relations scholars who emphasize service labor within the larger context of global restructuring. See, for example, Ling, *Postcolonial International Relations*.

46 This quote is drawn from Witbooi's original statement to the South African government in their deliberations on the first Unemployment Insurance Fund policy in March 2001. Witbooi and other domestic worker leaders have developed this direct tactic of holding decision makers accountable to their personal employment practices in both national and international policy dialogues. See Fish, *Domestic Democracy*.

47 Cock, *Maids and Madams*.

48 I extend gratitude to David C. Earnest for this insight, personal communication, January 2015.

49 Naples and Desai, eds., *Women's Activism and Globalization*, 8.

50 For the full poem, see "Domestic Workers Speak Out Through Song and Poetry," *IDWN ILO Blog*, June 7, 2011, idwnilo.wordpress.com.domestic worker.

51 This language was frequently used by domestic workers in their global campaign rhetoric.

52 Solnit, *Hope in the Dark*, 14.

53 King, "Sermon at Temple Israel of Hollywood."

54 Fieldnotes, ILC, 2011.

55 I independently compiled and coded these data thematically, according to source, context, and content, to synthesize the multiple voices that contributed to this large-scale global story. A qualitative computer software program facilitated the data analysis.

56 *C189: Conventional Wisdom* can be viewed on the website of the International Domestic Workers Federation, http://archive.idwfed.org.

57 Closing speech at the International Domestic Workers Federation Congress, October 2013, Montevideo, Uruguay.

58 For examples of collective scholar-activist publications that reflect these commitments, see Nadasen, *Household Workers Unite*; Goldberg, "Giving Back in Solidarity"; Goldberg, "Our Day Has Finally Come"; Romero, *The Maid's Daughter*; Goldsmith, *Collective Bargaining and Domestic Workers in Uruguay*; and Maich, "Marginalized Struggles for Legal Reform."

59 I extend profound gratitude to Bette J. Dickerson for her formative teachings on scholar-activism, and to Mary Romero for her most generous mentoring of my

research from its earliest stages. They are pivotal life mentors who work to ensure that social research is grounded in a commitment to social justice.

CHAPTER 2. "DIGNITY OVERDUE"

1 Trethewey, *Domestic Work.*
2 This excerpt is translated from the original Spanish CONLACTRAHO song that is based upon this poem.
3 Poems from Aida Moreno's unpublished collection have been translated from their original Spanish for this publication. I am deeply grateful to Sofia Trevino for her translations of both my interviews with Spanish-speaking members of IDWN and key documents for this research.
4 Chaney and Garcia Castro, eds., *Muchachas No More,* and Bunster and Chaney, *Sellers & Servants.*
5 See Rodgers et al., *The ILO and the Quest for Social Justice,* and Lubin and Winslow, *Social Justice for Women.*
6 Unlike with other UN conventions, the ILO requires states to adhere to all the terms of the ratified instrument. States cannot "pick and choose" standards by way of exclusionary clauses. Ratification of an ILO convention acknowledges adherence to each of its dimensions.
7 Fieldnotes, ILC, 2011.
8 Martin Oelz in discussion with the author, December 2012. For Oelz's reflections on the ILO process, see Oelz, Preiser, and Muller, *Effective Protection for Domestic Workers.*
9 Quotes attributed to domestic worker representatives and civil society organizations speaking during the ILC proceedings referenced in this book come from these officially sanctioned times in which the floor is open to these speakers.
10 Global Women's Strike, "For Clotil Walcott, Beloved Comrade."
11 Public speech at the ILC, 2010.
12 Ibid.
13 For analyses of domestic work in Brazil, see, for example, Hordge-Freeman and Harrington, "Ties That Bind."
14 Fieldnotes, Brazil government statement, ILC, 2011.
15 Fish, *Domestic Democracy.*
16 WIEGO also provided research support for this convention, as the relationship between Marty Chen and Ela Bhatt testifies.
17 The IDWN repeatedly referenced this phrase in its call for protections.
18 For a more detailed historical account of these meetings, see IRENE and IUF, *Respect and Rights.*
19 Dan Gallin (former IUF general secretary), in discussion with the author, June 2010.
20 Boris and Fish, "'Slaves No More.'"
21 Luc Demaret, interview by Natacha David, International Trade Union Confederation, June 4, 2010.

22 Moghadam, Franzway, and Fonow, eds., *Making Globalization Work for Women.*

23 ILO website, www.ilo.org.

24 Ibid.

25 Fieldnotes, ILC, 2010.

26 For analysis of the Home Work Convention and women workers' advocacy, see Boris and Prügl, eds., *Homeworkers in Global Perspective*; Prügl, *The Global Construction of Gender*; Delaney, Tate, and Burchielli, "Homeworkers Organizing for Recognition and Rights"; and Boris, "Reorganizing the Home Workplace."

27 For in-depth analyses of the changes in the global economy and its impact on workers, see Weil, *The Fissured Workplace.*

28 International Trade Union Confederation, *Union View: Domestic Work.*

29 International Labour Organization Bureau for Workers' Activities, *Decent Work for Domestic Workers.*

30 International Trade Union Confederation, "Briefing Note for Worker Delegates" (internal document, Geneva, 2010).

31 Luc Demaret, interview by Natacha David, International Trade Union Confederation, June 4, 2010.

32 The 2012 NDWA Care Congress employed the term "anchoring movement" frequently. Here, it referenced domestic work as an anchor for a larger labor movement, beyond the women's movement. Within the ILO, the domestic worker rights campaign had the capacity to tap into immigration, child labor, trafficking, and gender rights concerns.

33 The phrase "No such thing as 'unorganizable workers'" comes from Gallin, *Solidarity.*

34 Ida le Blanc, "Report Back on Decent Work for Domestic Workers at the International Labour Conference (ILC) 2010" (internal document, National Union of Domestic Workers of Trinidad and Tobago, 2010).

35 Dan Gallin in discussion with the author, June 2010.

36 Ibid.

37 Meeting between the IDWN and Juan Somavía at the 2010 ILC.

38 For a sample of Chen's research on the informal economy, see Chen, "Recognizing Domestic Workers, Regulating Domestic Work."

39 "Martha (Marty) Chen," staff profile on WIEGO website, http://wiego.org.

40 Chen, "From India to Conn College—and Back."

41 This excerpt is drawn from information provided on the organization's website. For more information on the WIEGO philosophy and its focus projects, see www.wiego.org.

42 Dan Gallin (former IUF general secretary) in discussion with the author, December 2012.

43 Cited from an interview conducted with Isabel Garcia Gill for *Le Temps*, June 2011.

44 Nadasen, *Household Workers Unite.*

45 Myrtle Witbooi has used this expression while speaking before a range of audiences, including university students, policymakers, and NGO colleagues, as observed by the author over 15 years of attending her public presentations.

46 Fieldnotes, ILC, 2011.

47 Workshop statement at the 2014 activist-academic conference, "Justice in the Home: Domestic Work Past, Present, and Future," Barnard Center for Research on Women, New York City, October 16–17, 2014.

48 Mather, *Yes We Did!*

49 Fieldnotes, domestic worker policy meetings, Washington, DC, 2015.

50 As frequently articulated by Ai-jen Poo.

51 McAdam, McCarthy, and Zald, eds., *Comparative Perspectives on Social Movements*.

52 Schwenken, "The Emergence of an 'Impossible Movement,'" 208.

53 See Reese, Petit, and Meyer, "Sudden Mobilization"; and Rose, *Coalitions Across the Class Divide*.

54 Statement of Nisha Varia of Human Rights Watch at the 2010 ILC.

55 Poo, "Who Cares? Preparing for the Elder Boom." See also Poo's *The Age of Dignity*.

56 The term "anchoring movement" emerged in the 2012 National Domestic Worker Alliance General Assembly, Washington, DC.

57 Excerpt from Florencia P. Cabatingan, executive board member of the Trade Union Congress of the Philippines (TUCP-ITUC), address to the workers' group of the Committee on Domestic Work, Fieldnotes, ILC, 2010.

58 Fraser, "Social Exclusion, Global Poverty, and Scales of (in)Justice."

59 María Luisa Escorel de Moraes (government of Brazil) in discussion with Mary Goldsmith, June 2011.

60 I am grateful to Chris Butler for this conceptualization of "in-betweenedness" as a framework for social movements.

61 Schwenken, "The Emergence of an 'Impossible' Movement," 207.

62 Roth and Horan, "What Are Social Movements and What Is Gendered About Women's Participation?"

63 For in-depth analyses of the institution of domestic labor and its embedded race, class, gender, and geographic divides, see, for example: Rollins, *Between Women*; Dill, *Across the Boundaries*; Romero, *The Maid's Daughter*; Romero, *Maid in the USA*; Parreñas, *Servants of Globalization*; Chang, *Disposable Domestics*; Hondagneu-Sotelo, *Doméstica*; and Gill, *Precarious Dependencies*.

64 Fieldnotes, ILC, 2011.

65 Ally, *From Servants to Workers*.

66 International Labour Organization, *Report IV(1): Decent Work for Domestic Workers*.

67 Sassen, *Globalization and Its Discontents*.

68 Chang and Ling, "Globalization and Its Intimate Other."

69 A rich body of literature exists on the relationship between policy and women's transnational movements. See, for example, Staudt, *Policy, Politics, and*

Gender; Maxine Molyneux, "Analysing Women's Movements"; Moghadam, *Globalizing Women*; Franzway and Fonow, *Making Feminist Politics*; Thayer, *Making Transnational Feminism*; Brenner, "Transnational Feminism"; Karides et al., *The United States Social Forum*; Brenner, "21st Century Socialist-Feminism."

70 For an analytic discussion of essentialized African girlhood in development discourse, see Switzer, "Disruptive Discourses."

71 I am grateful to Mary Margaret Fonow for this insight, as conveyed during our discussions at Arizona State University, March 2013.

72 Gay Young (professor of sociology) in discussion with the author, August 2015; See Young, *Gendering Globalization on the Ground*.

CHAPTER 3. GETTING "ON THE MAP"

1 UNESCO International Commission for the Study of Communication Problems, *Many Voices, One World*.

2 ILO, "Juan Somavía," International Labour Organization, www.ilo.org.

3 Ibid.

4 For a wider background on gender and notions of "decent work" in the ILO, see Boris, "The Employment and Conditions of Domestic Workers,"; Boris, "Difference's Other"; and Vosko, "'Decent Work.'"

5 Halimah Yacob, Opening Statement, ILC, 2010.

6 Fieldnotes, ILC, 2010.

7 Ibid.

8 Ibid.

9 Fieldnotes, Press Statement, ILC, 2011.

10 Fieldnotes, IDWN meeting with Juan Somavía, ILC, 2010.

11 Ibid.

12 Fieldnotes, Press Statement, ILC, 2011.

13 The 2012 NDWA Care Congress in Washington, DC, spoke of a "compassion deficit" in its efforts to build a campaign on "Caring Across Generations."

14 Fieldnotes, ILC, 2010.

15 Ibid.

16 Ibid.

17 Related expressions of "those who toil" came up repeatedly in the 2010 and 2011 ILC conversations by Halimah Yacob and some related domestic worker representatives.

18 Martin Oelz (ILO legal adviser) in discussion with the author, December 2012.

19 The ILO passed Convention 169, Indigenous and Tribal Peoples Convention, in 1989. Interestingly, many of the key players in Convention 189, including Luc Demaret, Manuela Tomei, and Claire Hobden worked on indigenous rights prior to their focus on domestic work.

20 Martin Oelz (ILO legal adviser) in discussion with the author, December 2012.

21 Ibid.

22 Louise McDonough (Australian government delegate) in discussion with the author, June 2011.

23 Statement by Virgil Seifield, South African delegate, on behalf of the African group, ILC, 2011.

24 While civil society organizations represent mainly workers' groups, employer NGOs also participate in the tripartite system.

25 Ai-jen Poo, email message to NDWA colleagues, friends, and family, June 13, 2011.

26 As stated by Halimah Yacob throughout the ILC negotiations, 2010 and 2011.

27 US Government Opening Statement to the Committee on Domestic Workers, ILC, 2011.

28 International Labour Organization, *Decent Work for Domestic Workers*.

29 International Labour Organization, *Report IV(2): Decent Work for Domestic Workers*.

30 Dan Gallin (former IUF general secretary) in discussion with the author, June 2010.

31 Barbro Budin, email message to WIEGO affiliate team, June 17, 2010.

32 Fieldnotes, ILC, 2010.

33 Ibid.

34 Ibid.

35 Ibid.

36 Ibid.

37 Fieldnotes, ILC, 2011.

38 Statement made by NDWA leader Narbada Chhetri to Halimah Yacob at the closing meetings of the workers' group of the Committee on Domestic Workers, ILC, 2011.

39 Closing meetings of the workers' group of the Committee on Domestic Workers, ILC, 2011.

40 International Organisation of Employers, "About IOE," 2016, www.ioe-emp.org.

41 Fieldnotes, ILC, 2010.

42 Ibid.

43 Ibid.

44 Ibid.

45 Fieldnotes, ILC, 2011.

46 Domestic worker representatives used the term "reasonable employer" throughout the negotiations to identify sympathetic employers in the field. Spokespersons repeatedly acknowledged the bifurcation of employers as "good" and "bad."

47 Fieldnotes, ILC, 2011.

48 Ai-jen Poo, leader of the National Domestic Workers Alliance, drew upon this national campaign statement during her reflections on the 2011 ILC.

49 Fieldnotes, ILC, 2011.

50 US Government Opening Statement, Committee on Domestic Workers, ILC, 2011.

51 Ibid.

52 As "Provisional Record 12 of the Fourth item on the agenda: Decent work for domestic workers" states: The results were as follows:
    For the amendment: Bahrain, Bangladesh, India, Indonesia, Islamic Republic of Iran, Kuwait, Malaysia, New Zealand, Oman, Panama, Qatar, Saudi Arabia, Singapore, United Arab Emirates. The members of the Employers group also voted for the amendment. Against the amendment: Argentina, Australia, Austria, Barbados, Belgium, Botswana, Brazil, Burkina Faso, Chad, Chile, China, Czech Republic, Denmark, Dominican Republic, Ecuador, El Salvador, Finland, France, Gabon, Germany, Ghana, Greece, Honduras, Hungary, Italy, Kenya, Lebanon, Lesotho, Maldives, Mali, Mexico, Mozambique, Namibia, Netherlands, Nigeria, Norway, Peru, Philippines, Portugal, Romania, Russian Federation, Senegal, Slovakia, Slovenia, South Africa, Spain, Sri Lanka, Suriname, Swaziland, Sweden, Switzerland, Syrian Arab Republic, United Republic of Tanzania, Thailand, Turkey, United Kingdom, United States, Uruguay, Vanuatu, Bolivarian Republic of Venezuela, Zimbabwe. The members of the Workers' Group voted against the amendment. The Government members of the following countries abstained from the vote: Congo, Estonia, Israel and Japan.

53 Statement made at the WIEGO media training workshop for members of the IDWN, June 16, 2011.

54 Fieldnotes, IDWN meeting with Juan Somavía, ILC, 2010.

55 Witbooi, "The White Apron."

56 Statement to the 2011 workers' group of the Committee on Domestic Workers.

57 Manuela Tomei (ILO director, ILO Conditions of Work and Employment) in discussion with the author, June 2010.

58 Fieldnotes, ILC, 2010.

59 Ibid.

60 WIEGO informal-economy meeting at the ILC, June 3, 2011.

61 Ibid.

62 Shirley Pryce (president, Jamaica Household Workers Union) in discussion with the author, June 2011.

63 Garcia-Gill, "Domestic Workers Out of the Shadows."

64 For one example of West's guiding ideology, see West, "A Love Supreme."

65 Maysoon Qara (National Jordanian Women's Commission) in discussion with the author, June 2011.

66 Fieldnotes, ILC, 2010.

67 Ibid.

68 Escaline Miranda (National Domestic Workers Movement, India) in discussion with the author, June 2011.

69 Fieldnotes, ILC, 2010.

70 María Luisa Escorel de Moraes (government of Brazil) in discussion with Mary Goldsmith, June 2011.

71 Fieldnotes, ILC, 2011.

72 Fieldnotes, ILC, 2010.

73 Ibid.

74 International Labour Organization, "Provisional Record 19, 99th Session, Geneva, 2010" (organizational report, Geneva, 2010), 36.

75 Interview with Dan Gallin, June 2015.

76 Statement by Halimah Yacob, ILC Fieldnotes, 2010.

77 Statement by the government of Paraguay, ILC Fieldnotes, 2010.

78 Domestic workers used this statement throughout both sessions, as a strategic tool to ellicit an emotional response in negotiation participants.

79 Fieldnotes, ILC, 2010.

80 Public statement at the 2011 ILC Domestic Workers Committee Meetings.

81 Luc Demaret (ILO Bureau for Workers Activities) in discussion with the author, June 2010.

82 Natacha David, "Spotlight Interview with Luc Demaret," International Labour Organization, www.ilo.org.

83 Ibid.

84 Statement by Myrtle Witbooi, ILC Fieldnotes, 2011.

85 International Labour Organization, Report IV(1): Decent Work for Domestic Workers.

86 Opening speech by Manuela Tomei at the 2010 Domestic Workers Committee, ILC Fieldnotes, 2010.

87 Ibid.

88 For more on the advocacy of femocrats in achieving a domestic worker convention, see chapter 6.

89 Fieldnotes, ILC, 2010.

90 Pryce, "My Journey to Geneva," 9.

91 Fieldnotes, ILC, 2010.

92 Pryce, "My Journey to Geneva," 9.

93 Fieldnotes, ILC, 2011.

94 Robert B. Shepard (US government delegate) in discussion with the author, June 2011.

95 Fieldnotes, ILC, 2010.

96 Fieldnotes, ILC, 2011.

97 Manuela Tomei (ILO director, ILO Conditions of Work and Employment) in discussion with the author, June 2010.

98 Fieldnotes, ILC, 2010.

99 International Domestic Workers Network, "About the Proposed New International Convention for Domestic Workers' Rights" (organizational document, Geneva, 2011), 1.

100 Fieldnotes, ILC, 2010.

101 This concept is adapted from Cynthia Enloe's theoretical notion that "gender makes the world go ground." See Enloe, Bananas, Beaches and Bases.

CHAPTER 4. "FIRST TO WORK; LAST TO SLEEP"

1 Statement by Juan Somavía to the opening 2010 Domestic Workers Committee, Fieldnotes, ILC, 2010.

2 Becker, *Campaigning for Justice.*

3 DuBois, *The Philadelphia Negro*, 136.

4 Fieldnotes, ILC, 2010, 2011.

5 Interview with the author, June 8, 2011.

6 Fataou Raimi (Syndicat des Employés d'hôtel de Maison [SYNEHM], Benin) in discussion with the author, June 2011.

7 María Luisa Escorel de Moraes (government of Brazil) in discussion with Mary Goldsmith, June 2011.

8 Fieldnotes, ILC, 2011.

9 The full terms can be found in International Labour Organization, *Report IV(2): Decent Work for Domestic Workers.*

10 Fieldnotes, ILC, 2011.

11 Statement by Kamran Rahman, Fieldnotes, ILC, 2010.

12 Fieldnotes, ILC, 2011.

13 Workers' Delegates, Domestic Workers Committee, "Decent Work for Domestic Workers Briefing Note for Workers' Delegates" (organizational report, Geneva, 2010).

14 Fieldnotes, ILC, 2010.

15 Luc Demaret (remarks, meeting of NGO advocates and affiliates to the ILC, Geneva, June 6, 2010).

16 Robert B. Shepard (US government delegate) in discussion with the author, June 2011.

17 Fieldnotes, ILC, 2011.

18 Ibid.

19 Statement by Ida le Blanc, ILC Fieldnotes, 2011.

20 Statement by child domestic workers, Fieldnotes, ILC 2011.

21 Fieldnotes, ILC, 2011.

22 Fieldnotes, ILC, 2010.

23 Fieldnotes, ILC, 2011.

24 Ibid.

25 Fieldnotes, ILC, 2010.

26 Ibid.

27 Ibid.

28 Ibid.

29 International Labour Organization, *Report IV(1): Decent Work for Domestic Workers.*

30 Ibid.

31 Ibid.

32 Fieldnotes, ILC, 2010.

33 Ibid.

34 Ibid.

35 The ILC discussions used these working figures in the negotiations, with recognition that accurate estimates had not yet been attained. For the most contemporary assessment of domestic work and migration, see International Labour Organization, *ILO Global Estimates on Migrant Workers*.

36 Ibid.

37 Luc Demaret, interview by Natacha David, International Trade Union Confederation, June 4, 2010.

38 Fieldnotes, ILC, 2010.

39 For a discussion of migrant domestic workers and global cities, see Sassen, *Globalization and Its Discontents*.

40 Hester Stephens (general secretary, South African Domestic Service and Allied Workers Union) in discussion with the author, June 2013.

41 Fieldnotes, ILC, 2010.

42 Ibid.

43 Ibid.

44 Statement at an NGO domestic worker demonstration, Geneva, 2011.

45 Marie Elena Valenzuela, meeting statement at the International Labour Organization Global Action Programme on Migrant Domestic Workers and Their Families Advisory Board Meeting, February 4, 2014.

46 Sring Atin, interview by Celia Mather, WIEGO, June 8, 2010.

47 Ip Pui Yu, "To the Plenary of the International Labour Conference" (speech, ILC, Geneva, June 9, 2011).

48 Ibid.

49 Fieldnotes, ILC, 2010.

50 Ibid.

51 Statement by Kamran Rahman, Fieldnotes, ILC, 2010.

52 Fieldnotes, ILC, 2010.

53 Ibid.

54 See Smith, "Regulating Paid Household Work," and Smith, "Work Like Any Other, Work Like No Other."

55 For a fuller discussion of colonial practices and domestic labor, see Haskins and Lowrie, *Colonization and Domestic Service*.

56 Fieldnotes, ILC, 2010.

57 Ibid.

58 Ida le Blanc, "Speech at Plenary of International Labour Conference" (ILC, Geneva, June 8, 2011).

59 Ibid.

60 Fieldnotes, ILC, 2011.

61 Ibid.

62 Ibid.

63 Ibid.

64 Ida le Blanc, "Speech at Plenary of International Labour Conference" (ILC, Geneva, June 8, 2011).

65 Fieldnotes, ILC, 2011.

66 Alfers, "Occupational Health and Safety and Domestic Work."

67 Fieldnotes, ILC, 2011.

68 Ibid.

69 Fieldnotes, ILC, 2010.

70 Ibid.

71 Aida Moreno (founding member of CONLACTRAHO) in discussion with the author, June 2010.

72 Fieldnotes, NDWA Care Congress, 2012.

73 Maria Lorenzo de Sanchez (Uruguayan Housewives' League) in discussion with Mary Goldsmith, June 2011.

74 Fieldnotes, ILC, 2010.

75 Eunice Mdhalala (SADSAWU national office holder) in discussion with the author, December 2012.

76 Shirley Pryce (president, Jamaica Household Workers Union) in discussion with the author, June 2011.

77 Ida le Blanc, "Speech at Plenary of International Labour Conference" (ILC, Geneva, June 8, 2011).

78 Fieldnotes, ILC, 2011.

79 Ibid.

80 María Luisa Escorel de Moraes (government of Brazil) in discussion with Mary Goldsmith, June 2011.

81 Fieldnotes, ILC, 2011.

CHAPTER 5. "MY MOTHER WAS A KITCHEN GIRL"

1 This story is adapted from an account shared by domestic worker activists in India. I did not interview Sunita directly. Rather, I pieced her story together through associations with domestic workers in her local and national context.

2 Clifton, *Blessing the Boats.*

3 Fieldnotes, ILC, 2010.

4 Ibid.

5 Statement by Juan Somavía to the opening 2010 Domestic Workers Committee, Fieldnotes, ILC, 2010.

6 Fieldnotes, ILC, 2010.

7 International Domestic Workers Network, "About the Proposed New International Convention for Domestic Workers' Rights" (organizational document, Geneva, 2011), 1.

8 Fish, *Domestic Democracy.*

9 Crockett, Fish, and Ormiston, *C189: Conventional Wisdom.*

10 Fieldnotes, ILC, 2011.

11 H.E.M. Christian Guillermet-Fernandez (deputy permanent representative of the Republic of Costa Rica to the United Nations Office in Geneva, statement at the panel discussion on young child domestic workers, with Anti-Slavery International and the UN Voluntary Trust Fund on Contemporary Forms of Slavery in cooperation with Children Unite, the Permanent Missions of Costa Rica and Uruguay to the United Nations, Geneva, June 1, 2011).

12 Keck and Sikkink, *Activists Beyond Borders.*

13 Guillermina Castellanos, statement on behalf of the IUF, Fieldnotes, ILC, 2011.

14 Barbro Budin (IUF) in discussion with the author, June 2011.

15 For more on the Anti-Sweatshop campaign see Brooks, "The Ideal Sweatshop?"

16 For an examination of the use of affect in social movements, see Massumi, *Parables for the Virtual.*

17 Fieldnotes, ILC, 2010.

18 Ibid.

19 Ally discusses South Africa's use of "vulnerability" as a guiding paradigm that reinforced structures of power in the postapartheid rights-centered democracy. See Ally, *From Servants to Workers*, 8.

20 International Labour Organization, *Report IV(1): Decent Work for Domestic Workers.*

21 Ally, *From Servants to Workers*, 88.

22 Mohanty, "Under Western Eyes."

23 Monica Phumzile Ntuli (SADSAWU national office holder) in discussion with the author, December 2012.

24 As articulated by the South African national trade union COSATU; see Fish, *Domestic Democracy.*

25 For a thorough analysis of domestic worker organization in North America, see Boris and Nadasen, "Domestic Workers Organize!"

26 International Domestic Workers Network, *Platform of Demands.*

27 Aida Moreno, (founding member of CONLACTRAHO) in discussion with the author, June 2010.

28 Schwenken, "The Emergence of an 'Impossible Movement,'" 224.

29 Dan Gallin (former IUF general secretary) in discussion with the author, June 2012.

30 For analyses of global human rights, see, for example, Sen, "The Global Status of Human Rights"; Piper, "Temporary Economic Migration and Rights Activism"; and Minow, "Interpreting Rights."

31 Here, as a persuasive strategy, domestic workers use the language of human rights taken from larger United Nations documents. Fieldnotes, ILC, 2010, 2011.

32 WIEGO, "Domestic Workers," WIEGO, www.wiegoinbrief.org.

33 Vicky Kanyoka, "To the ILC Plenary" (speech, ILC, Geneva, June 10, 2010).

34 Marcelina Bauista (CONLACTRAHO) in discussion with Sofia Trevino, June 2011.

35 Fieldnotes, ILC, 2011.

36 Elizabeth Prügl, "Comments on History and Paid and Unpaid Labor" (discussion remarks, NGO forum accompanying the 2010 ILC, Geneva, June 9, 2010).

37 Fieldnotes, ILC, 2010.

38 For an example of this connection between women's paid reproductive labor and a developing country context, see Cock, *Maids and Madams.*

39 Domestic workers tend to give the term "feminism" a mixed review, given its origins in Western discourse among more privileged women. The link to wider women's movements through the ILO convention process drew closer associations between domestic workers and a women's movement, even though the term "feminist" did not often emerge in the IDWN discourse.

40 See, for example, Rollins, *Between Women*; Thornton Dill, *Across the Boundaries of Race and Class*; Romero, *Maid in the USA*; and Cock, *Maids and Madams.*

41 Fieldnotes, ILC, 2010.

42 This excerpt is drawn from the statements of domestic workers and governments within the Domestic Workers Committee during the first ILC discussions, June 1, 2010. The statement sets the stage for domestic workers' repeated challenges to unions for their histories of gender exclusions and their pervasive unwillingness to recognize household workers in national labor struggles.

43 Fieldnotes, ILC, 2010.

44 Public statement at the Domestic Workers Committee Discussions of the 2011 ILC.

45 Domestic worker representatives repeated this statement throughout the 2010 and 2011 ILC public discussions and surrounding events.

46 WIEGO training experts emphasized this point, as they prepared domestic workers to deal with the media, just before the 2011 vote on Convention 189.

47 Parreñas, *Servants of Globalization*; Boris and Parreñas, *Intimate Labors.*

48 Barbro Budin (IUF) in discussion with the author, December 2012.

49 Fieldnotes, ILC, 2010.

50 Eileen Boris posits the notion of domestic workers as hybrid workers because of this dual plight for recognition as workers and consideration as a special category. For further discussion of this concept, see Boris and Klein, *Caring for America.*

51 For the most contemporary analyses of the care economy, see, for example, Boris and Parreñas, *Intimate Labors*, and Poo, *The Age of Dignity.*

52 The NDWA launched these campaigns at the 2012 Care Congress, Washington, DC.

53 Fieldnotes, NDWA Care Congress, 2012.

54 Fieldnotes, ILC, 2010.

55 Poo, *The Age of Dignity.*

56 Vicky Kanyoka, "Speech to the Tripartite Committee on Domestic Work" (ILC, Geneva, June 3, 2010).

57 Vicky Kanyoka, "To the ILC Plenary" (speech, ILC, Geneva, June 10, 2010).

58 International Labour Organization, "Provisional Record 19, 99th Session, Geneva, 2010" (organizational report, Geneva, 2010), 36.

59 Statement to the media, 2011 ILC.

60 ILC Fieldnotes, 2010.

61 Ibid.

62 ILC Fieldnotes, 2011.

63 Hester Stephens (SADSAWU) in discussion with the author, May 2014.

64 ILC Fieldnotes, 2010.

65 Ibid.

66 Vicky Kanyoka, "To the ILC Plenary" (speech, ILC, Geneva, June 10, 2010).

67 Anonymous ILO delegate, personal communication to author, December 2012.

68 ILC Fieldnotes, 2011.

69 Spivak, "Can the Subaltern Speak?"

70 This reference is drawn from a conversation with photographer Eric Miller and artist Mel Miller, Cape Town, South Africa, May 2014.

71 See Rollins, *Between Women.*

72 This quote is drawn from my original research with domestic workers in Cape Town, South Africa, from 2000 to 2001.

CHAPTER 6. "PUT YOURSELF IN HER SHOES"

1 Freire, *Pedagogy of the Oppressed.*

2 Elizabeth Tang, interview with author, August 26, 2016.

3 ILC Fieldnotes, 2011.

4 Maysoon Qara (National Jordanian Women's Commission) in discussion with the author, June 2011.

5 Myrtle Witooi, "Closing Plenary Speech" (ILC, Geneva, June 16, 2010).

6 ILC Fieldnotes, 2011.

7 Ibid.

8 Jill Shenker (NDWA) in discussion with the author, June 2011.

9 This expression is commonly used by domestic workers in South Africa, who were relegated to living accommodations in the backyards of their employers under apartheid.

10 For an analysis of NGOs' use of tragedy to sell causes, see Hua, *Trafficking Women's Human Rights*, and Brennan, *Life Interrupted.*

11 A *duk* is a traditional domestic workers' head covering worn in South Africa.

12 Mohanty, "Under Western Eyes."

13 Statement by Myrtle Witbooi, ILC Fieldnotes, 2010.

14 ILC fieldnotes, 2011.

15 For a visual reference to this image, see Boris and Fish, "'Slaves No More.'"

16 Statement by Nisha Varia, ILC Fieldnotes, 2010.

17 I am grateful to Lindal Buchanan for her consultation on this analytic insight.

18 Child domestic workers spoke through the side forums organized around the ILC negotiations, much like the UN Women conferences; however, they were not present in the formal discussions. While NGOs organized many events surrounding the ILC, unlike the UN Women's conferences, they also attended the ILO ses-

sions as observers. This case of child domestic workers is distinct because of their age and particular social location.

19 Here, child domestic workers are referring to the emphasis on exploitation of marginalized populations, such as migrants and women in Article 4. This article is particularly relevant because of its specific reference to the Convention on the Rights of the Child and the International Convention on the Protection of the Rights of All Migrant Workers and Members of Their Families.

20 ILC Fieldnotes, 2011.

21 Robert B. Shepard (US government delegate) in discussion with the author, June 2011.

22 Ibid.

23 Ibid.

24 Statement by the Namibian government, ILC Fieldnotes, 2011.

25 Louise McDonough, "Australian Government Closing Statement Domestic Workers Committee" (speech, ILC, Geneva, June 15, 2011).

26 For further discussion of the role of Human Rights Watch, see Becker, *Campaigning for Justice*, 49.

27 Ibid.

28 Dan Gallin (former IUF general secretary) in discussion with the author, December 2012.

29 Ibid.

30 Fieldnotes, ILC, 2010.

31 Pryce, "My Journey to Geneva," 15.

32 Fish, *Domestic Democracy*.

33 This interview is drawn from Sofia Trevino's conversations with Marcelina Bauista for WIEGO, June 2011.

34 In some cases, the underrepresentation of domestic workers revealed pervasive gender politics, whereas in other cases the formal registration of national trade union delegates may have precluded formal registration.

35 Fieldnotes, ILC, 2010.

36 Fieldnotes, ILC, 2011.

37 Dan Gallin (former IUF general secretary) in discussion with the author, June 2011.

38 Louise McDonough, "Australian Government Closing Statement Domestic Workers Committee" (speech, ILC, Geneva, June 15, 2011).

39 María Luisa Escorel de Moraes (government of Brazil) in discussion with Mary Goldsmith, June 2011.

40 For more detailed references to this concept of "one in the family," see, for example, Romero, *The Maid's Daughter*; Bakan, *Not One in the Family*; and Rollins, *Between Women*.

41 Fieldnotes, ILC, 2010.

42 Statement at the public negotiations, Fieldnotes, ILC, 2010.

43 This popular antiapartheid slogan held symbolic meaning during the country's liberation movement.

44 Opening statement at the public negotiations, Fieldnotes, 2010.

45 Statement at the public negotiations, Fieldnotes, ILC, 2010.

46 Darcy du Toit (Social Law Project, University of the Western Cape) in discussion with the author, December 2012.

47 Myrtle Witbooi (SADSAWU) in discussion with the author, May 2014.

48 Statement at the public negotiations, Fieldnotes, ILC, 2011.

49 Ibid.

50 Louise McDonough, "Australian Government Closing Statement Domestic Workers Committee" (speech, ILC, Geneva, June 15, 2011).

51 For a discussion of femocrats, see, for example, Gouws, "The Rise of the Femocrat?," and Britton, *Women in the South African Parliament*.

52 Fieldnotes, ILC, 2011.

53 Statement by Ernestina Ochoa, Fieldnotes, ILC, 2011.

54 Fieldnotes, ILC, 2011.

55 See, for example, Boris, "Difference's Other"; Bessis, "International Organizations and Gender"; and Lubin and Winslow, *Social Justice for Women*.

56 María Luisa Escorel de Moraes (government of Brazil) in discussion with Mary Goldsmith, June 2011.

57 Both Nisha Varia and Robert B. Shepard concurred that in the case of the United States, the Obama administration's focus on social protections, such as health care, and international diplomacy, substantially influenced the government's position on domestic work. Under a different political leadership, Shepard contended, the US government's position would have likely been more restrained regarding support for Convention 189.

CHAPTER 7. "A LITTLE BIT OF LIBERATION"

1 This vote also included the accompanying set of recommendations.

2 Swaziland was the only government that did not vote in favor of the convention. Some experts suggest that this may have been an error, given the country's general support for the convention throughout the process. With the abstentions, the convention passed with an 83 percent majority.

3 Fieldnotes, ILC, 2011.

4 Ibid.

5 Pryce, "My Journey to Geneva," 1.

6 The IDWN imported this campaign slogan from national human rights movements and used this phrase throughout both years.

7 I am thankful to Eileen Boris for this analytic insight, expressed in the early stages of this book.

8 Dan Gallin (former IUF general secretary) in discussion with the author, June 2011.

9 Leddy Mozombite Linares (Peruvian domestic worker activist) in conversation with Sofia Trevino, June 2011.

10 Ernestina Ochoa (IDWN) in conversation with Sofia Trevino, June 2011.

11 IDWN leaders chanted "Yes we did!" outside the doors of the Palais des Nations, after the vote to adopt Convention 189. Scholars of domestic work have begun to analyze Convention 189's larger meaning for domestic work, rights, and legal frameworks, the ILO, and women's movements. See Schwenken et al., "Conversations, an ILO Convention for Domestic Workers"; Tomei, "Decent Work for Domestic Workers"; Blackett, "Promoting Domestic Workers' Human Dignity"; Blackett, "Introduction: Regulating Decent Work"; Albin and Mantoubalou, "The ILO Convention on Domestic Workers"; Goldsmith, "Los Espacios Internacionales"; Kawar, "Making the Machine Work"; Mahon and Michel, "Not in Focus"; Pape, "ILO Convention C189" ; Fish, "A Contemporary Perspective"; Fish and Turner, "The Global Domestic"; and Boris and Fish, "Decent Work for Domestics." Some scholars are analyzing the diffusion of rights. See Poblete, "The Diffusion of International Labor Standards."

12 Fieldnotes, ILC, 2011.

13 Sam Gurney, "Statements on Global Mobilization of Domestic Workers" (demonstration speech, domestic worker/NGO demonstration at the Broken Chair monument at UN Headquarters, June 10, 2010).

14 Fieldnotes, ILC, 2011.

15 International Domestic Workers Federation, "Domestic Workers of the World Unite."

16 Mather, *"Yes, We Did It!"*

17 Gallin, *Solidarity.*

18 Fieldnotes, IDWF Founding Congress, 2013.

19 International Domestic Workers Federation, "IDWN Congress: Building Domestic Workers' Organizations," 2013, www.idwfed.org, accessed May 6, 2014.

20 IDWN, Founding Congress, "Item 6: IDWN 5 Years Action Plan," 1–3 (author's copy); Boris and Fish, "Slaves No More."

21 Uruguay's hosting of the IDWF founding reflects the complexities of domestic worker organization. While the country's location symbolized its prominent place as the first to ratify Convention 189, the national domestic workers' unions had not joined the IDWN at the time of the congress. In many instances, local and regional politics played central roles in determining organizations' willingness and capacity to join the IDWF. At the same time, organizations' decisions and stances surrounding global affiliation sometimes enunciated existing divisions and relative alliances among national and regional domestic worker organizations.

22 Governments are required periodically to report on their compliance with and progress in implementing conventions, a process overseen by the Committee of Experts on the Application of Conventions and Recommendations and the Conference Committee on the Application of Standards.

23 WIEGO meeting on domestic worker organizing strategies, Fieldnotes, ILC, 2011.

24 Robert B. Shepard (US government delegate) in discussion with the author, June 2011.

25 Boris and Undén, "From the Local to the Global."

26 Myrtle Witbooi received this award alongside Nobel Peace Prize winner Houcine Abassi and Stanford law professor emeritus Paul Brest. Her speech can be viewed at www.fairnessaward.org.

27 Robert B. Shepard (US government delegate) in discussion with the author, June 2011.

28 Ibid.

29 Fieldnotes, ILC, 2010.

30 Eunice Dhladhla (SADSAWU national office holder) in discussion with the author, December 2012.

31 Shireen Ally (University of Witwatersrand) in discussion with the author, September 14, 2013.

32 Fieldnotes, ILC, 2011.

33 Martin Oelz (ILO legal adviser) in discussion with the author, December 2012.

34 I thank Elizabeth Losh for this expression, as shared in her keynote address at the 2016 Works in Progress feminist conference at Virginia Wesleyan University.

35 Manisha Desai shared this perspective during a panel conversation at the Sociologists for Women in Society meetings in Washington, DC, February 19, 2015. For a larger analytic framework on gender and globalization, see Desai, *Gender and the Politics of Possibilities*.

36 See Boris and Fish, "'Slaves No More,'" 441.

37 Marissa Begonia (Justice for Domestic Workers, UK) in conversation with Sofia Trevino, June 2011.

38 Address to the ILO Domestic Work Committee, June 13, 2011.

39 Fieldnotes, ILC, 2011.

40 Robert B. Shepard (US government delegate) in discussion with the author, June 2011.

41 Martin Oelz (ILO legal adviser) in discussion with the author, December 2012.

42 Monica Phumzile Ntuli (SADSAWU national office holder) in discussion with the author, December 2012.

43 Fieldnotes, NDWA Care Congress, 2012.

44 Fieldnotes, ILC, 2011.

45 Paul MacKay (employer vice chairperson) in discussion with the author, June 16, 2011.

46 Ibid.

47 Ibid.

48 Paul Mackay (employer vice chairperson) in discussion with the author, June 16, 2011.

49 Fieldnotes, ILC, 2011.

50 Fieldnotes, IDWN Workshop, ILC, 2011.

51 Louise McDonough, "Australian Government Closing Statement Domestic Workers Committee" (speech, ILC, Geneva, June 15, 2011).

52 Ai-jen Poo, personal reflection on the ILO process, June 13, 2011.

REFERENCES

Albin, Einat, and Virginia Mantoubalou. "The ILO Convention on Domestic Workers: From the Shadows to the Light." *Industrial Law Journal* 41, no. 1 (2012): 67–78.

Alfers, Laura. "Occupational Health and Safety and Domestic Work: A Synthesis of Research Findings from Brazil and Tanzania." Cambridge, MA: WIEGO, 2011.

Ally, Shireen. "Domestics, 'Dirty Work' and the Effects of Domination." *South African Review of Sociology* 42, no. 2 (2011): 1–7.

———. *From Servants to Workers: South African Domestic Workers and the Democratic State.* Ithaca, NY: Cornell University Press, 2010.

———. "Slavery, Servility, Service: The Cape of Good Hope, the Natal Colony, and the Witwatersrand, 1652–1914." In Hoerder, Van Nederveen Meerkerk, and Neunsinger, *Towards a Global History of Domestic and Caregiving Workers,* 254–70.

Anderson, Bridget. *Doing the Dirty Work?: The Global Politics of Domestic Labour.* London: Zed Books, 2000.

———. "Mobilizing Migrants, Making Citizens: Migrant Domestic Workers as Political Agents." *Ethnic and Racial Studies* 33, no. 1 (2010): 60–74.

Bakan, Abigail, and Daiva Stasiulis. *Not One in the Family: Foreign Domestic Workers in Canada.* Toronto, ON: University of Toronto Press, 1997.

Banerjee, Swapna M. "Baby Halder's *A Life Less Ordinary*: A Transition from India's Colonial Past?" In Haskins and Lowrie, *Colonization and Domestic Service,* 239–55.

———. *Men, Women, and Domestics: Articulating Middle-Class Identity in Colonial Bengal.* New York: Oxford University Press, 2004.

Becker, Jo. *Campaigning for Justice: Human Rights Advocacy in Practice.* Stanford, CA: Stanford University Press, 2013.

Bessis, Sophie. "International Organizations and Gender: New Paradigms and Old Habits." *Signs: Journal of Women in Culture & Society* 29, no. 2 (2004): 633–47.

Blackett, Adelle. "Introduction: Regulating Decent Work for Domestic Workers." *Canadian Journal of Women & the Law* 23, no. 1 (2011): 1–46.

———. "Promoting Domestic Workers' Human Dignity Through Specific Regulation." In Fauve-Chamoux, *Domestic Service and the Formation of European Identity,* 247–76.

Blumberg, Rae Lesser, and Samuel Cohn. *Development in Crisis: Threats to Human Well-Being in the Global South and Global North.* New York: Routledge, 2016.

Boris, Eileen. "Difference's Other: The ILO and 'Women in Developing Countries.'" In Jensen and Lichtenstein, *The ILO from Geneva to the Pacific Rim,* 134–58.

———. "The Employment and Conditions of Domestic Workers in Private Households: An ILO Survey." *International Labour Review* 102, no. 4 (1970): 391–401.

———. "Reorganizing the Home Workplace: Making Workers Through Global Labor Standards." In *Global Women's Work: Perspectives on Gender and Work in the Global Economy*, edited by Beth English, Mary Frederickson, and Olga Sanmiguel-Valderrama. Forthcoming.

Boris, Eileen, and Jennifer Fish. "Decent Work for Domestics: Feminist Organizing, Worker Empowerment, and the ILO." In Hoerder, Van Nederveen Meerkerk, and Neunsinger, *Towards a Global History of Domestic and Caregiving Workers*, 530–52.

———. "'Slaves No More': Making Global Labor Standards for Domestic Workers." *Feminist Studies* 40, no. 2 (2014): 411–43.

Boris, Eileen, and Jennifer Klein, eds. *Caring for America: Home Health Workers in the Shadow of the Welfare State*. Oxford: Oxford University Press, 2012.

Boris, Eileen, and Premilla Nadasen. "Domestic Workers Organize!" *WorkingUSA:The Journal of Labor and Society* 11, no. 4 (2008): 413–37.

Boris, Eileen, and Elisabeth Prügl, eds. *Homeworkers in Global Perspective: Invisible No More*. New York: Routledge, 1996.

Boris, Eileen, and Rhacel Salazar Parreñas, eds. *Intimate Labors: Cultures, Technologies and the Politics of Care*. Stanford, CA: Stanford University Press, 2010.

Boris, Eileen, and Megan Undén. "From the Local to the Global: Circuits of Domestic Worker Organizing." In *Gender, Migration and the Work of Care: A Multi-Scalar Approach to the Pacific Rim Book Workshop*. Toronto, ON: University of Toronto, 2015.

Brennan, Denise. *Life Interrupted: Trafficking into Forced Labor in the United States*. Durham, NC: Duke University Press, 2014.

Brenner, Johanna. "Transnational Feminism and the Struggle for Global Justice." In *World Social Forum: Challenging Empires*, edited by Jai Sen and Peter Waterman, 25–34. Montreal: Black Rose Books, 2007.

———. "21st Century Socialist-Feminism." *Socialist Studies* 10, no. 1 (2014): 31–49.

Britton, Hannah. *Women in the South African Parliament: From Resistance to Governance*. Champaign: University of Illinois Press, 2005.

Brooks, Ethel. "The Ideal Sweatshop?: Gender and Transnational Protest." *International Labor and Working-Class History* 61 (2002): 91–111.

Brown, Tamara Mose. *Raising Brooklyn: Nannies, Childcare, and Caribbeans Creating Community*. New York: New York University Press, 2011.

Bunster, Ximena, and Elsa Chaney. *Sellers & Servants: Working Women in Lima, Peru*. Granby, MA: Bergin & Garvey, 1989.

Chaney, Elsa M., and Mary Garcia Castro, eds. *Muchachas No More: Household Workers in Latin America and the Caribbean*. Philadelphia: Temple University Press, 1989.

Chang, Grace. *Disposable Domestics: Immigrant Women Workers in the Global Economy*. Cambridge, MA: South End Press, 2000.

Chang, Kimberly, and L.H.M. Ling. "Globalization and Its Intimate Other: Filipina Domestic Workers in Hong Kong." In *Gender and Global Restructuring: Sightings, Sites and Resistances*, edited by Marianne Marchand and Anne Sisson Runyan. London: Routledge, 2002.

Chen, Martha Alter. "From India to Conn College—and Back: The Personal Journey of a Missionary Daughter." Paper presented at the Connecticut College Colloquium, New London, CT, 2013.

———. "Recognizing Domestic Workers, Regulating Domestic Work: Conceptual, Measurement, and Regulatory Challenges." *Canadian Journal of Women & the Law* 23, no. 1 (2011): 167–84.

Cheng, Shu-Ju Ada. "Contextual Politics of Difference in Transnational Care: The Rhetoric of Filipina Domestics' Employers in Taiwan." *Feminist Review*, no. 77 (2004): 46–64.

Chin, Christine. *In Service and Servitude: Foreign Female Domestic Workers and the Malaysian "Modernity" Project.* New York: Columbia University Press, 1998.

Chun, Jennifer Jihye. "Organizing Across Racial Divides: Union Challenges to Precarious Work in Vancouver's Health Care Sector." *Progress in Development Studies* 16, no. 2 (2016): 1–16.

Clifton, Lucille. *Blessing the Boats: New and Selected Poems 1988-2000.* Rochester, NY: BOA Editions.

Cobble, Dorothy Sue, and Leah F. Vosko. "Historical Perspectives on Representing Nonstandard Workers." In *Nonstandard Work: The Nature and Challenges of Changing Employment Arrangements*, edited by Francoise Carré et al., 291–311. Ithica, NY: Cornell University Press.

Cock, Jacklyn. *Maids & Madams: Domestic Workers Under Apartheid.* 2nd ed. London: Women's Press Limited, 1989.

Constable, Nicole. *Maid to Order in Hong Kong: Stories of Filipina Workers.* Ithaca, NY: Cornell University Press, 1997.

Cox, Rosie. *The Servant Problem: Domestic Employment in a Global Economy.* London: I. B. Tauris, 2006.

Cranford, Cynthia. "Toward Particularism with Security: Immigration, Race and the Organization of Personal Support Services in Los Angeles." In *When Care Work Goes Global: Locating the Social Relations of Domestic Work*, edited by Mary Romero, Valerie Preston, and Wenona Giles, 203–26. Surrey, UK Ashgate, 2014.

Crockett, Rachel, Jennifer N. Fish, and Robin Ormiston. *C189: Conventional Wisdom.* Norfolk, VA: Sisi Sojourner Productions, 2012. DVD.

Davis, Angela Y. *Women, Race and Class.* New York: Random House, 1981.

Delaney, Annie, Jane Tate, and Rosaria Burchielli. "Homeworkers Organizing for Recognition and Rights: Can International Standards Assist Them?" In Jensen and Lichtenstein, *The ILO from Geneva to the Pacific Rim*, 159–79.

Desai, Manisha. *Gender and the Politics of Possibilities: Rethinking Globalization.* Lanham, MD: Rowman & Littlefield, 2008.

Dill, Bonnie Thornton. *Across the Boundaries of Race and Class: An Exploration of Work and Family Among Black Female Domestic Servants.* Studies in African American History and Culture. New York: Garland, 1994.

DuBois, W. E. B. *The Philadelphia Negro: A Social Study*. Philadelphia: University of Pennsylvania Press, 1899.

Du Toit, Darcy. "Domestic Workers' Convention: A Breakthrough in Human Rights, Editorial." *Law, Democracy & Development* 15 (2011): 4–7.

Ehrenreich, Barbara, and Arlie Russell Hochschild. *Global Woman: Nannies, Maids, and Sex Workers in the New Economy*. 1st ed. New York: Metropolitan Books, 2003.

Enloe, Cynthia. *Bananas, Beaches and Bases: Making Feminist Sense of International Politics*. Berkeley: University of California Press, 1990.

Fauve-Chamoux, Antoinette, ed. *Domestic Service and the Formation of European Identity: Understanding the Globalization of Domestic Work, 16th–21st Centuries*. New York: Peter Lang, 2004.

Fish, Jennifer N. "A Contemporary Perspective: 'Picking the Fruit from the Tree': From Colonial Legacy to Global Protections in Transnational Domestic Worker Activism." In Haskins and Lowrie, *Colonization and Domestic Service*, 328–47.

———. *Domestic Democracy: At Home in South Africa*. New York: Routledge, 2006.

Fish, Jennifer N., and Jennifer Turner. "The Global Domestic: Mapping Decent Work in International Dialogues." In Jensen and Lichtenstein, *The ILO from Geneva to the Pacific Rim*, 180–205.

Fonow, Mary Margaret. "The Role of the ILO in Building and Sustaining Women's Transnational Labor Activism." In meeting document for "West Meets East: The International Labor Organization from Geneva to the Pacific Rim," 1–21. University of California, Santa Barbara, February 3–5, 2011. Available at ILO.org.

Francisco, Valerie. "Transnational Family as Resource for Transnational Migrant Activism." Lecture presented at "Global Workers' Rights: Patterns of Exclusion, Possibilities for Change" *international symposium*. Center for Global Workers' Rights, Penn State University, March 21, 2013.

Franzway, Suzanne, and Mary Margaret Fonow. *Making Feminist Politics: Transnational Alliances Between Women and Labor*. Urbana: University of Illinois Press, 2011.

Fraser, Nancy. "Social Exclusion, Global Poverty, and Scales of (in)Justice: Rethinking Law and Poverty in a Globalizing World." *Stellenbosch Law Review* 22, no. 3 (2011): 452–62.

Freire, Paulo. *Pedagogy of the Oppressed*. New York: Herder & Herder, 1970.

Fudge, Judy. "Global Care Chains, Employment Agencies, and the Conundrum of Jurisdiction: Decent Work for Domestic Workers in Canada." *Canadian Journal of Women and the Law* 23 (2011): 235–64.

Gallin, Dan. *Solidarity: Selected Essays*. Berlin: LabourStart, 2014.

———. *Trade Unions and NGOs: A Necessary Partnership for Social Development*. Geneva: United Nations Research Institute for Social Development, 2000.

Gallin, Dan, and Pat Horn. *Organizing Informal Women Workers*. Geneva: Global Labor Institute, 2005.

Gamburd, Michele Ruth. *The Kitchen Spoon's Handle: Transnationalism and Sri Lanka's Migrant Housemaids*. Ithaca, NY: Cornell University Press, 2000.

Garcia-Gill, Isabel. "Domestic Workers out of the Shadows." *Global Journal*, August 2011.

Gill, Lesley. *Precarious Dependencies: Gender, Class, and Domestic Service in Bolivia.* New York: Columbia University Press, 1994.

Glenn, Evelyn Nakano. *Forced to Care: Coercion and Caregiving in America.* Cambridge, MA: Harvard University Press, 2012.

Global Women's Strike. "For Clotil Walcott, Beloved Comrade," November 20, 2007, www.globalwomenstrike.net.

Goldberg, Harmony. "Giving Back in Solidarity." *Journal of Research Practice* 10, no. 2 (2014).

———. "Our Day Has Finally Come: Domestic Worker Organizing in New York City." City University of New York Graduate Center, 2014.

Goldsmith, Mary. "Los Espacios Internacionales De La Participación Política De Las Trabajadoras Remuneradas Del Hogar." (Spanish.) *International Spaces for the Political Participation of Paid Female Household Workers*, no. 45 (2013): 233–46.

Goldsmith, Mary R. *Collective Bargaining and Domestic Workers in Uruguay.* Cambridge, MA: WIEGO, 2013.

Gouws, Amanda. "The Rise of the Femocrat?" *Agenda* 12, no. 30 (1996): 31–43.

Günther, Sylvia. *Struggling for Recognition: The Unionization of (un-)Documented Migrant Domestic Workers in the Netherlands.* Amsterdam: Universiteit van Amsterdam, 2011.

Gutiérrez Rodríguez, Encarnación. *Migration, Domestic Work and Affect: A Decolonial Approach on Value and the Feminization of Labor.* Routledge Research in Gender and Society. New York: Routledge, 2010.

Haladara, Bebi. *A Life Less Ordinary: A Memoir.* Translated by Urvashi Butalia. Repr. New York: Harper Collins, 2007.

Haskins, Victoria K. *Matrons and Maids: Regulating Indian Domestic Service in Tucson, 1914—1934.* Tucson: University of Arizona Press, 2012.

———. *One Bright Spot.* London: Palgrave Macmillan, 2005.

Haskins, Victoria, and Claire Lowrie, eds. *Colonization and Domestic Service: Historical and Contemporary Perspectives.* New York: Routledge, 2015.

Heyzer, Noeleen, Geertje Lycklama a Nijeholt, and Nedra Weerakoon, eds. *The Trade in Domestic Workers: Causes, Mechanisms and Consequences of International Migration.* London: Zed Books, 1994.

Hobden, Claire E. *Winning Fair Labor Standards for Domestic Workers: Lessons Learned from the Campaign for a Domestic Worker Bill of Rights in New York State.* Edited by Pierre Laliberte. Geneva: International Labor Organization, 2010.

Hoerder, Dirk K., Elise van Nederveen Meerkerk, and Silke Neunsinger, eds. *Towards a Global History of Domestic and Caregiving Workers: Histories of Domestic Work as Global Labor History.* Leiden, Netherlands: Brill, 2015.

Hondagneu-Sotelo, Pierrette. *Doméstica: Immigrant Workers Cleaning and Caring in the Shadows of Affluence.* Berkeley: University of California Press, 2001.

Hordge-Freeman, Elizabeth, and Jaira J. Harrington. "Ties That Bind: Localizing the Occupational Motivations That Drive Non-Union Affiliated Domestic Workers in Salvador, Brazil." In Hoerder, Van Nederveen Meerkerk, and Neunsinger, *Towards a Global History of Domestic and Caregiving Workers*, 137–57.

Hua, Juliette. *Trafficking Women's Human Rights*. Minneapolis: University of Minnesota Press, 2011.

Human Rights Watch. *Swept Under the Rug: Abuses Against Domestic Workers Around the World*. New York: Human Rights Watch, 2006.

International Domestic Workers Network. "About the Proposed New International Convention for Domestic Workers' Rights." Briefing. Geneva, June 14, 2011.

———. *Platform of Demands*. Geneva: WIEGO, 2010.

International Domestic Workers Network, International Trade Union Confederation, and Human Rights Watch. *Claiming Rights: Domestic Workers' Movements and Global Advances for Labor Reform*. New York: Human Rights Watch, 2013.

International Labour Organization. *Decent Work for Domestic Workers*. Geneva: International Labour Organization, 2007.

———. *Domestic Workers Across the World: Global and Regional Statistics and the Extent of Legal Protection*. Geneva: International Labour Organization, 2013.

———. *ILO Global Estimates on Migrant Workers: Results and Methodology, Special Focus on Migrant Domestic Workers*. Geneva: International Labour Organization, 2015.

———. *Report IV(1): Decent Work for Domestic Workers*. Geneva: International Labour Organization, 2010.

———. *Report IV(2): Decent Work for Domestic Workers*. Geneva: International Labour Organization, 2010.

International Trade Union Confederation. *Union View: Domestic Work—Mobilising for an International Convention*. Brussels: ITUC, 2010.

IRENE and IUF. *Respect and Rights: Protection for Domestic/Household Workers*. Tilburg, Netherlands: IRENE, 2007.

Jensen, Jill M., and Nelson Lichtenstein, eds. *The ILO from Geneva to the Pacific Rim: West Meets East*. International Labor Organization Series, 1–11. New York: Palgrave Macmillan, 2016.

Jones, Jacqueline. *Labor of Love, Labor of Sorrow: Black Women, Work, and the Family from Slavery to the Present*. New York: Random House, 1985.

Kabeer, Naila, Kirsty Milward, and Ratna M. Sudarshan. *Organizing Women Workers in the Informal Economy: Beyond the Weapons of the Weak*. Feminisms and Development. London: Zed Books, 2013.

Karides, Marina. "Linking Local Efforts with Global Struggle: Trinidad's National Union of Domestic Employees." In *Women's Activism and Globalization: Linking Local Struggles and Transnational Politics*, edited by Nancy Naples and Manisha Desai, 156–71. New York: Routledge, 2002.

Karides, Marina, et al. *The United States Social Forum: Perspectives of a Movement*. Chicago: Changemaker, 2010.

Kawar, Leila. "Making the Machine Work: Technocratic Engineering of Rights for Domestic Workers at the International Labour Organization." *Indiana Journal of Global Legal Studies*, no. 2 (2014): 483–511.

Keck, Margaret E., and Kathryn Sikkink. *Activists Beyond Borders: Advocacy Networks in International Politics*. Ithaca, NY: Cornell University Press, 1998.

King, Martin Luther, Jr. "Sermon at Temple Israel of Hollywood." American Rhetoric Online Speech Bank, www.americanrhetoric.com.

Lan, Pei-Chia, and Leslie Salzinger. "Global Cinderellas: Migrant Domestics and Newly Rich Employers in Taiwan." *Gender & Society* 22, no. 1 (2008): 129–32.

Ling, L.H.M. *Postcolonial International Relations: Conquest and Desire Between Asia and the West*. London: Palgrave, 2002.

Lubin, Carol Riegelman, and Anne Winslow. *Social Justice for Women: The International Labor Organization and Women*. Durham, NC: Duke University Press, 1990.

Lund, Francie, and Jillian Nicholson, eds. *Chains of Production, Ladders of Protection: Social Protection for Workers in the Informal Economy*. Durban: School of Development Studies, University of Natal, 2003.

Lutz, Helma. *The New Maids: Transnational Women and the Care Economy*. London: Zed Books, 2011.

Mahon, Rianne, and Sonya Michel. "Not in Focus: Migrant Caregivers as Seen by the ILO and the OECD." In *Gender, Migration and the Work of Care: A Multi-Scalar Approach to the Pacific Rim Book Workshop*. Toronto, ON: University of Toronto Centre for Social Policy, 2015.

Maich, Katherine. "Marginalized Struggles for Legal Reform: Cross-Country Consequences of Domestic Worker Organizing." *Social Development Issues* 36, no. 3 (2014): 73–91.

Marchetti, Sabrina. *Black Girls: Migrant Domestic Workers and Colonial Legacies*. Studies in Global Migration History. Leiden, Netherlands: Brill, 2014.

Massumi, Brian. *Parables of the Virtual: Movement, Affect, Sensation*. Durham, NC: Duke University Press, 2002. doi:10.2307/1354446.

Mather, Celia. *Yes We Did!: How the World's Domestic Workers Won Their International Rights and Recognition*. Cambridge, MA: WIEGO Secretariat, 2013.

May, Vanessa. *Unprotected Labor: Household Workers, Politics, and Middle-Class Reform in New York, 1870–1941*. Chapel Hill: University of North Carolina Press, 2011.

McAdam, Doug, John D. McCarthy, and Mayer N. Zald, eds. *Comparative Perspectives on Social Movements: Political Opportunities, Mobilizing Structures, and Cultural Framings*. Cambridge Studies in Comparative Politics. Cambridge: Cambridge University Press, 1996.

Michel, Sonya, and Rianne Mahon. *Child Care Policy at the Crossroads: Gender and Welfare State Restructuring*. New York: Routledge, 2002.

Migrant Forum in Asia. *Reform of the Kafala (Sponsorship) System*. Quezon City: Migrant Forum in Asia.

Milkman, Ruth. *Organizing Immigrants: The Challenge for Unions in Contemporary California*. Ithaca, NY: Cornell University Press, 2000.

Milkman, Ruth, and Ed Ott, eds. *New Labor in New York: Precarious Workers and the Future of the Labor Movement*. Ithaca, NY: Cornell University Press, 2014.

Minow, Martha. "Interpreting Rights: An Essay for Robert Cover." *Yale Law Journal* 96, no. 8 (1987): 1860–1915.

Moghadam, Valentine. *Globalizing Women: Transnational Feminist Networks*. Themes in Global Social Change. Baltimore: John Hopkins University Press, 2005.

Moghadam, Valentine M., Suzanne Franzway, and Mary Margaret Fonow. *Making Globalization Work for Women: The Role of Social Rights and Trade Union Leadership*. Suny Series. Albany: State University of New York Press, 2011.

Mohanty, Chandra Talpade. "Under Western Eyes: Feminist Scholarship and the Colonial Discourses." In Mohanty, Russo, and Torres, *Third World Women and the Politics of Feminism*, 51–80.

Mohanty, Chandra Talpade, Ann Russo, and Lourdes Torres, eds. *Third World Women and the Politics of Feminism*. Bloomington: Indiana University Press, 1991.

Molyneux, Maxine. "Analysing Women's Movements." *Development and Change* 29 (1998): 219–45.

Nadasen, Premilla. *Household Workers Unite: The Untold Story of African American Women Who Built a Movement*. Boston: Beacon Press, 2015.

———. "Power, Intimacy, and Contestation: Dorothy Bolden and Domestic Worker Organizing in Atlanta in the 1960s." In Boris and Parreñas, *Intimate Labors*, 204–16.

Naples, Nancy, and Manisha Desai, eds. *Women's Activism and Globalization: Linking Local Struggles and Transnational Politics*. New York: Routledge, 2002.

Neunsinger, Silke. "From Servitude to Domestic Service: The Role of International Bodies, States and Elites for Changing Conditions in Domestic Work Between the 19th and 20th Centuries: An Introduction." In Hoerder, Van Nederveen Meerkerk, and Neunsinger, *Towards a Global History of Domestic and Caregiving Workers*, 389–99.

Oelz, Martin, Rachel Preiser, and Angelika Muller. *Effective Protection for Domestic Workers: A Guide to Designing Labour Laws*. Geneva: International Labour Organization, 2012.

Oliveira, Gabrielle Marcelletti Rocha de. "Transnational Care Constellations: Mexican Immigrant Mothers and Their Children in Mexico and in New York City." PhD diss., Columbia University, 2015.

Palenga-Möllenbeck, Ewa. "Care Chains in Eastern and Central Europe: Male and Female Domestic Work at the Intersections of Gender, Class, and Ethnicity." *Journal of Immigrant & Refugee Studies* 11, no. 4 (October–December 2013): 364–83.

Pape, Karin. "ILO Convention C189—A Good Start for the Protection of Domestic Workers: An Insider's View." *Progress in Development Studies* 16, no. 2 (2016): 189–202.

Parreñas, Rhacel Salazar. *Servants of Globalization: Women, Migration and Domestic Work*. Stanford, CA: Stanford University Press, 2001.

Pei-Chia, Lan. "Maid or Madam?: Filipina Migrant Workers and the Continuity of Domestic Labor." *Gender & Society* 17, no. 2 (2003): 187–208.

Peng, Ito. "Lone Mothers in Japan and South Korea: Active Labour Market and Social Policy Reforms Since the 1990s." *Journal of Political Science and Sociology* 8 (2007): 69–86.

Piper, Nicola. "Temporary Economic Migration and Rights Activism: An Organizational Perspective." *Ethnic and Racial Studies* 33, no. 1 (2010): 108–25.

Poblete, Laura. "The Diffusion of International Labor Standards: Domestic Work Regulation in Argentina, South Africa & the Philippines." In *The Fourth Conference of the Sociology of Development Section*. Brown University, Providence, RI, 2015.

Poo, Ai-jen. *The Age of Dignity: Preparing for the Elder Boom in a Changing America*. New York: New Press, 2015.

———. "Who Cares? Preparing for the Elder Boom in a Changing America." Paper presented at the Old Dominion University President's Lecture Series, Norfolk, VA, March 22, 2016.

Pratt, Geraldine. *Families Apart: Migrating Mothers and the Conflicts of Labor and Love*. Minneapolis: University of Minnesota Press, 2012.

Prügl, Elisabeth. *The Global Construction of Gender: Home-Based Work in the Political Economy of the 20th Century*. New York: Columbia University Press, 1999.

Pryce, Shirley. "My Journey to Geneva: Advocacy to Adopt Convention 189: Decent Work for Domestic Workers." Center for Global Workers' Rights, Penn State University, 2015.

Ray, Raka. "Masculinity, Femininity and Servitude: Domestic Workers in Calcutta in the Late Twentieth Century." *Feminist Studies* 26, no. 3 (Fall 2000): 691–718.

Reese, Ellen, Christine Petit, and David S. Meyer, "Sudden Mobilization: Movement Crossovers, Threats, and the Surprising Rise of the US Antiwar Movement." In *Strategic Alliances: Coalition Building and Social Movements*, edited by N. Van Dyke and H. J. McCammon, 266–291. Minneapolis: University of Minnesota Press, 2010.

Rodgers, Gerry, et al. *The International Labour Organization and the Quest for Social Justice, 1919–2009*. Ithaca, NY: Cornell University Press 2009.

Rollins, Judith. *Between Women: Domestics and Their Employers*. Philadelphia: Temple University Press, 1985.

Romero, Mary. *The Maid's Daughter: Living Inside and Outside the American Dream*. New York: New York University Press, 2011.

———. *Maid in the USA* New York: Routledge, 1992.

Romero, Mary, Valerie Preston, and Wenona Giles, eds. *When Care Work Goes Global: Locating the Social Relations of Domestic Work*. Surrey, UK: Ashgate, 2014.

Rose, Fred. *Coalitions Across the Class Divide: Lessons from the Labor, Peace, and Environmental Movements*. Ithaca, NY: Cornell University Press, 2000.

Roth, Benita, and Marian Horan. "What Are Social Movements and What Is Gendered About Women's Participation in Social Movements? A Sociological Perspective." Women and Social Movements in the United States, 1600–2000, womhist.alexanderstreet.com.

Salzinger, Leslie. "A Maid by Any Other Name: The Transformation of 'Dirty Work' by Central American Immigrants." In *Ethnography Unbound: Power and Resistance in the Modern Metropolis*, edited by Michael Burawoy, 139–60. Berkeley: University of California Press, 1991.

Sassen, Saskia. *Globalization and Its Discontents.* New York: New Press, 1998.

Schwenken, Helen. "The Emergence of an 'Impossible' Movement: Domestic Workers Organize Globally." In *Transnational Struggles for Recognition: New Perspectives on Civil Society Since the 20th Century*, edited by Dieter Gosewinkel and Deiter Rucht, 205–28. New York: Berghahn, 2013.

Schwenken, Helen, and Lisa-Marie Heimeshoff. *Domestic Workers Count: Global Data on an Often Invisible Sector.* Kassel, Germany: Kassel University Press, 2011.

Schwenken, Helen, et al. "Conversations, an ILO Convention for Domestic Workers: Contextualizing the Debate." *International Feminist Journal of Politics* 13, no. 3 (2011): 437–61.

Sen, Amartya. "The Global Status of Human Rights." *American University International Law Review* 27, no. 1 (2012): 1–15.

Silvey, Rachel. "Transnational Domestication: State Power and Indonesian Migrant Women in Saudi Arabia." *Political Geography* 23, no. 3 (2004): 245–64.

Smith, Peggie R. "Regulating Paid Household Work: Class, Gender, Race and Agendas of Reform." *American University Law Review* 48 (1998): 851–923.

———. "Work Like Any Other, Work Like No Other: Establishing Decent Work for Domestic Workers." *Employee Rights and Employment Policy Journal* 15, no. 1 (2012): 159–200.

Solari, Cinzia. "Resource Drain vs. Constitutive Circularity: Comparing the Gendered Effects of Post-Soviet Migration Patterns in Ukraine." *Anthropology of East Europe Review* 28, no. 1 (2010): 215–38.

Solnit, Rebecca. *Hope in the Dark: Untold Histories, Wild Possibilities.* New York: Nation Books, 2004.

Spivak, Gayatri Chakravorty. "Can the Subaltern Speak?" In *Marxism and the Interpretation of Culture*, edited by Cary Nelson and Lawrence Grossberg, 271–316. Champaign: University of Illinios Press, 1988.

Staudt, Kathleen. *Policy, Politics, and Gender: Women Gaining Ground.* West Hartford, CT: Kumarian, 1998.

Steedman, Carolyn. *Master and Servant: Love and Labour in the English Industrial Age.* Cambridge Social and Cultural Histories. Cambridge: Cambridge University Press, 2007.

Switzer, Heather. "Disruptive Discourses: Kenyan Maasai Schoolgirls Make Themselves." *Girlhood Studies* 3, no. 1 (2010): 137–55.

Thayer, Millie. *Making Transnational Feminism: Rural Women, NGO Activists, and Northern Donors in Brazil.* Perspectives on Gender. New York: Routledge, 2010.

Thomson, Marilyn. "Workers Not Maids: Organising Household Workers in Mexico." *Gender and Development* 17, no. 2 (2009): 281–93.

Tomei, Manuela. "Decent Work for Domestic Workers: Reflections on Recent Approaches to Tackle Informality." *Canadian Journal of Women and the Law* 23, no. 1 (2011): 185–212.

Tracy, Natalicia, Tim Sieber, and Susan Moir. *Invisible No More: Domestic Workers Organizing in Massachusetts and Beyond.* Boston: Brazilian Immigrant Center, Labor Resource Center at the University of Massachusetts, 2014.

Trethewey, Natasha D. *Domestic Work: Poems.* Saint Paul, MN: Graywolf Press, 2000.

UNESCO International Commission for the Study of Communication Problems. *Many Voices, One World: Communication and Society Today and Tomorrow.* Paris: UNESCO, 1980.

Varia, Nisha. *Maid to Order: Ending Abuses Against Migrant Domestic Workers in Singapore.* New York: Human Rights Watch, 2005.

———. "Sanctioned Abuses: The Case of Migrant Domestic Workers." In *Human Rights Brief*, 17–20, 2007.

Vosko, Leah F. "'Decent Work': The Shifting Role of the ILO and the Struggle for Global Social Justice." *Global Social Policy* 2, no. 1 (2002): 19–46.

Weil, David. *The Fissured Workplace: Why Work Became Bad for So Many and What Can Be Done to Improve It.* Cambridge, MA: Harvard University Press, 2014.

West, Cornel. "'A Love Supreme.'" *Occupied Wall Street Journal* 5 (2011), http://occupiedmedia.us.

Williams, J. F. "Converging Variations in Migrant Care Work in Europe." *Journal of European Social Policy* 20, no. 4 (2012): 363–76.

Witbooi, Mrytle. "The White Apron." In *Labour Pains for the Nation: Eight Women Workers Tell Their Stories*, edited by Shirley Gunn and Rachel Visser. Cape Town: Human Rights Media Center, 2007.

Yeoh, Brenda S. A., and Kavitha Annadhurai. "Civil Society Action and the Creation of 'Transformative' Spaces for Migrant Domestic Workers in Singapore." *Women's Studies* 37, no. 5 (2008): 548–69.

Young, Gay. *Gendering Globalization on the Ground: The Limits of Feminized Work for Mexican Women's Empowerment.* New York: Routledge, 2015.

Yovel, Thiruvalluvar, and Bart Verstraeten. *Respect, Rights and Recognition: Domestic Work and the ILO Standard Setting Process 2010–2011.* Brussels: World Solidarity 2010.

Zimmerman, Mary K., Jacquelyn S. Litt, and Christine E. Bose. *Global Dimensions of Gender and Carework.* Stanford, CA: Stanford University Press, 2006.

INDEX

ABOUT THE AUTHOR

Jennifer N. Fish is a sociologist and Professor and Chair of Women's Studies at Old Dominion University. She has worked with domestic labor movements for over fifteen years, as a researcher, ally, and policy activist. Her publications include *Domestic Democracy: At Home in South Africa* and *Women's Activism in South Africa: Working Across Divides*.